No Glory Without a Story!
2nd Edition

A Shepherd's Journey Towards Winning Souls

Written by a Collection of Spiritual Leaders

Edited by
Dr. Mia Y. Merritt

Copyright © 2012

No Glory Without a Story!
A Shepherd's Journey Towards Winning Souls
a non-fiction book
Written by a collection of spiritual leaders/authors

All rights reserved. No part of this book
may be reproduced in any form without permission
in writing from the author(s) or publisher.

ISBN 13: 978-0-9835830-4-2 (paperback)
13: 978-0-9835830-5-9 (hardback)

Library of Congress Cataloging
in-Publication Data

First Printing 2011
Printed in the U.S.A.

Genre Category:
Spirituality, Christianity, personal development,
self-help, inspiration, motivation,
self-esteem/confidence building,
young adult

Edited by Dr. Mia Y. Merritt

Praise Reports for No Glory Without a Story!

Congratulations to all of the pastors on coauthoring this book, 'No Glory Without a Story'. The testimonies in this book are powerfully impactful and extremely vital for those in all aspects of leadership: public, private, and clergy. The chapters in this book give valuable insight on how to walk this journey of service with faith, strength, and assurance that God will never leave us alone. This book is a true blessing!

~ Shirley Gibson, Mayor
City of Miami Gardens

Reading this book was liberating for my soul! It helped me to remember how faithful God is and how He never leaves nor forsakes us. These powerful stories from the men that God is using to bless His people have enlightened me to a greater understanding that there is a blessing in the pressing. You too will be blessed as you take this spiritual journey of reading these powerful testimonies!

~Dr. Wilbert T. Holloway
Miami-Dade County Public School Member
District 1

While reading the book, 'No Glory Without a Story', I felt a deep sense of exhilaration and delight. The pastors in this book have opened their hearts, souls and spirits to the inner workings of God in the life of anyone who says "Yes" to the call of God. As the men of God in this book expressed the steps of their journeys into and through ministry, I was reminded of the fact that when God calls a person to ministry, the self has to undergo times of sacrifice and testing. In every revelation there is a cross. In every struggle there is a story. That "story" is the true stuff of effective service for God. I have been blessed by reading the journey of faith expressed by these stories.

~Bishop Billy Baskin
Senior Pastor/Teacher
New Way Fellowship Baptist Church

This book will inspire and encourage you as you read the testimonies of pastors who have been tested and tried. This book will remind you that there is something good that comes out of every test and trial. There is something in each chapter for whatever you may be going through and you will definitely be blessed by reading it! Read it and re-read it and then tell you friends about it...they will be glad you did!

~Willie Jolley, Best Selling Author of
"A Setback Is a Setup For a Comeback" &
"An Attitude of Excellence"

All who love God will be generously fed with food for the soul as written by men of God. This collection of truths must be read at one sitting or choose a chapter that will be fitting for your life daily. This collection of inspiration vignettes will have a positive effect every reader. Enjoy!

~Dorothy Bendross-Mindingall
Miami-Dade County Public School Board Member
District 2

This book is a must read for all. I was reminded that throughout history, God always had a point person to accomplish His divine purpose at pivotal points in time. The men of God in this book were open, honest and transparent with their lives, which increased my faith in the goodness of God who loves us in spite of our humanness. This book will give you hope and inspiration because through the pages, I've learned, if it's not fatal, it's not final!

~State Rep. Cynthia Stafford
Florida House-District 109

This book serves as a reminder that there is always something good that comes out of hard tests and trials. The testimonies shared by the pastors in this book will liberate the discouraged soul. It serves as spiritual inspiration and reveals the hand of God in every circumstance, showing that He will never leave you nor forsake you.

~State Rep. Barbara Watson
Florida House-District 103

This book is a must read for every Christian as well as other Pastors and ministers. I oversee 64 Churches and I am recommending this book to all of my Pastors.

~Rev. Samuel Aurelus
Mission Union Faternite Chetienne D' Haiti

My spirit, my heart, and my mind was tremendously blessed by reading "No Glory Without a Story!" If we are not careful, we can make the mistake of putting pastors on pedestals. We must remember that they too are human. May God bless them for their openness and honesty; and may God bless and enlighten you as you read their stories.

~Ann McNeill
President/CEO MCO Construction &
International Mastermind Association
Radio Talk Show Host WZAB 880am The Biz

"All things work together for good to them that love the Lord" is the scripture that I continued to resonate upon as I read 'No Glory Without a Story'. There is a spiritual lesson for EVERYBODY in each chapter of this powerful book! Reading it gave me the faith and strength to press on in spite of what I may go through! I thank God for this book. It will bless your soul and your life as it has mine!

~Piaget Hendrix
President/CEO South Florida Gospel Music Awards
State President, Florida Gospel Announcer's Guild

A pastor's life is not always understood nor appreciated. This book of frank and probing testimonials of some of our revered pastoral leaders will indisputably open your eyes to spiritual compassion and Christian love toward them. This must-read book will rightly prick one's spiritual consciousness profoundly! These riveting stories will enlighten, convict, and convince that parishioners have not remotely embraced nor considered the enormity of responsibilities and hardships of those called to Shepherd God's people. This book is a true blessing!

~Dr. R. Lorin Browne,
Licensed Christian
Marriage & Family Therapist

When I began reading this book, I could not put it down! This book is needed for every believer and especially those who have been called by God into the ministry! They must know what to expect after answering the call, but they must also know that God will be with them through every trial, test and struggle. There is no glory where there is no story. What an anointed book!

~Dr. Lydia Goodin
AM 1490 WMBM Radio
National Broadcast Hall of Fame Inductee

Dedication

This book is dedicated to those who have purposed in their heart to stand firm in their faith regardless of what challenges come their way. Making the decision to live for Christ can be equivalent to making the decision to start a fight with the enemy. Salvation is free but Christianity can be costly. There are sacrifices that must be made, behaviors and habits that must be given up and spiritual battles to fight; but through it all, God will be right there. Your faith will be tried and some of the trials and tests that come your way will make you cry out to God and say, "Why me Lord!" Why not you? He asks. Remember His servant Job? Just as gold is put in the fire to be purified, you too will be tried in the fire to be purified, purged, shaped, and molded into the person that God has predestined you to be. You are already victorious in the spirit realm. Your flesh just needs to catch up to where you are in the spirit. That can only be done by enduring tests and challenges in the natural. The enemy sees your victory in the spirit, which is why he tries to stop you from going there. Just hold on. God will never leave you nor forsake.

The stories in this book will show you how the Lord took powerful men of God through some of their toughest times, but they stood fast, held firm, persevered and received the blessings of being faithful. He will do the same for you!

~*Authors of No Glory Without a Story*
2nd Edition

About the Editor

Dr. Mia Y. Merritt was born and raised in Miami, Florida and attended school in the Miami-Dade County Public School System. She is an educator with over 17 years experience working with students as a teacher, Assistant Principal, and College Professor. She is a Certified Keynote Speaker, Teen/Youth Facilitator, Radio Talk Show Host, Prosperity Coach and Author.

Dr. Merritt is also the recipient of the 2011 African American Achiever's Award sponsored by JM Family Enterprises and has received many other awards, accolades, certifications and commendations. She holds a Bachelors Degree in Elementary Education, a Masters Degree in Exceptional Education, a Specialist Degree in Educational Leadership and a Doctorate Degree in Organizational Leadership with a concentration in Conflict Resolution.

Dr. Merritt is the published author of eight books on the subjects of spirituality, personal development, prosperity, self-empowerment, and adult education. Her books emphasize living in peace and harmony with oneself and others by serving, loving people, walking in integrity and putting God first. She is the President/CEO of M&M Motivating (www.miamerritt.com), which provides services in teen/youth training, corporate retreats, conference speaking, seminars and staff development.

Her Radio Talk Show is on 880AM, *The Biz* (WZAB) every Monday at 11:30am and Thursday at 11:00am and is also worldwide on the internet (www.880thebiz.com). It is called, *The Business of Money*. She and her co-host discuss ways that money can be made in various areas, industries and fields when people tap into and utilize the skills and gifts they possess within.

Introduction

The thing that hath been, it is that which shall be; and that which is done is that which shall be done: and there is no new thing under the sun.

Ecclesiastes 1:9

It is amazing how when we, as children of God go through the storms and tests of life, we seem to think that we are the only ones enduring such struggles. However, when we listen to the experiences of others, we realize that multitudes of people have endured and overcame similar, if not the same trials and tribulations that we have or are going through. Pastors are no different. They experience the same frustrations, discouragements, pain, tests and disappointments as everyone else. But unlike us as congregants, pastors must always appear strong, uplifted and preeminent to the people of God when they stand in that pulpit to speak. It seems as though pastors are not allowed to show weakness because they have an image to uphold as a strong, powerful leader for the sheep over which they shepherd. It is time for us to allow pastors to be human. We must understand that just as the pastor is constantly praying for the people of God, he needs to be prayed for as well. Just as he uplifts and imparts the living Word into the spirits of the weary, he needs to be uplifted and have a Word spoken into his spirit as well.

As you read the stories that these powerful men of God share, you will notice that there is a spiritual continuity that permeates throughout the book. Each of their stories compliments each other and substantiates the lesson that is being conveyed in the chapter before it. The most profound thing about this book, is the fact that prior to this book being printed, none of the pastors had read any of the other chapters and yet, they each support each other's message. This confirms the power of the Holy Spirit who imparts wisdom and gives the confirmation needed to bless our spirits. May your soul be blessed by reading these stories.

Table of Contents

Praise Reports iii

Dedication vi
Authors of No Glory Without a Story

About the Editor vii

Introduction viii
Dr. Mia Y. Merritt

CHAPTER 1: Pastor Johnny Barber II, TH. M..................... 1
The Wounded Healer

CHAPTER 2: Pastor Eric Jones.. 15
From Storms to Stepping Stones

CHAPTER 3: Pastor Wayne Lomax 31
Press Forward!

CHAPTER 4: Pastor Dwayne Richardson 45
The Cost of the Anointing

CHAPTER 5: Pastor Gaston E. Smith................................. 57
No Test, No Testimony!

CHAPTER 6: Pastor Isaiah Musgrove 69
Answering the Call

CHAPTER 7: Pastor Jimmie Brown, Ph.D 81
Walking in the Calling

CHAPTER 8: Pastor Kevin Williams, Ed.D 97
Thanks for the Push!

CHAPTER 9: Pastor Dennis M. Jackson, Ph.D................. 111
Becoming a Vessel of Honor

CHAPTER 10: Pastor Fred Cromity 125
The Heart of a Pastor

CHAPTER 11: Pastor Ranzer Thomas 139
Walking in Humility

CHAPTER 12: Pastor Richard Dunn 151
No Cross, No Crown!

CHAPTER 13: Pastor Ricardo Peters 163
From Altar Boy to Pastor: an Unlikely Progression

CHAPTER 14: Pastor Kenneth Duke 175
The Power of an Anointed Sermon

CHAPTER 15: Pastor Tracy McCloud, Div.D 185
Steadfast, Unmovable & Always Abounding

CHAPTER 16: Pastor Miles Fitzpatrick 201
Tested Faith

CHAPTER 17: Pastor Michael Anderson 213
Trusted With Trouble

CHAPTER 18 Pastor Reginald Daniels 227
Loving thy Neighbor as Thyself

CHAPTER 19: Bishop Fred Marshall 241
The Power of the Prophetic Ministry

CHAPTER 20: Pastor Robert Ward 255
This Sickness is not Unto Death

Epilogue 270

Church Directory 271

No Glory Without a Story!
2nd Edition

A Shepherd's Journey Towards Winning Souls

Written by a Collection of Spiritual Leaders

ABOUT THE AUTHOR

Pastor Johnny L. Barber, II is God's visionary for Mount Sinai Missionary Baptist Church, affectionately known as "The Mount," located in Miami, Florida. Serving as pastor since 2002, God has consistently blessed this union of church and pastor. The ministry has experienced growth in numbers, in spiritually, as well as financially. Pastor Barber was born in Miami, Florida, to Johnny L. Barber, Sr. and the late Mary R. Taylor. He is the husband to Kimberly I. Richardson-Barber. He has three lovely children, Morgan Fay Barber, Maegan Alice Barber, and Kiersten Savannah Barber. He is a graduate of Miami Central High School. Pastor Barber holds a Bachelor's degree in Information Technology from American InterContinental University, Plantation FL, as well as a Master's Degree in Theology from Barry University, Miami Shores, FL.

Pastor Barber has achieved many triumphs in his life along with awards. He presently is the Moderator of the Florida East Coast Missionary Baptist Association, Inc. He also has worked within the Florida East Coast Missionary Baptist Association as Assistant to the Moderator (the late Moderator Rev. Dr. Arthur Jackson, Jr.), Teacher/Tutor Southern Division Ministers and Deacon Union Youth Division, Second Vice President of the Florida East Coast Missionary Baptist Association's Congress of Christian Education, Corresponding Secretary for the Florida East Coast Missionary Baptist Church, and Coordinator of the Licentiate Workshop for the Southern Division Minister's and Deacon's Union. He has also served as President of the Southern Division Minister's and Deacon's Union for the Florida East Coast Missionary Baptist Association. Rev. Barber, as a brother of Kappa Alpha Psi Fraternity, Inc., has served as the Chaplain for the Miami Alumni Chapter. He has also served as the financial secretary for the Baptist Minister's Council of Miami Dade and Vicinity, along with several other local and state religious and community boards.

Chapter 1

The Wounded Healer

Written by Pastor Johnny Barber II, TH. M

"He saved others, but he can't save himself..."
Matthew 27:42

Out of the wounds of the wounded births healing! The relationship between the pastor and the parishioner is a very unique one. The parishioner and the expectations of their pastor create an environment that a pastor finds himself existing in and attempting to function out of. Unrealistically, there seems to be an expectation of perfection that is birthed from the reality that the human life is imperfect; so the human hope that perfection or some simile thereof has to exist somewhere is an inner secret search that is not admittedly ascribed to, nevertheless it is expected. This hidden subliminal ascription causes a belief and assumption that the parishioner has for and of their pastor. Hence, there is the expectation for the pastor to have a perfect life, perfect marriage, perfect language, perfect children, perfect behavior, as well as a lifestyle that has the "absence of." For instance it is expected that the pastor has the absence of pain, the absence of discouragement, and the absence of imperfection. Yet, this is an unrealistic reality that has become a truism for the parishioner. Despite its illusion, this expectation has far-reaching tentacles that have invaded the life of the preacher who, although aware of the unrealistic expectation of this truism has unknowingly embraced it. He now operates in this false reality perpetuating the error as he lives a life that contains contradictions due to the unreal expectancy. The true reality of it all however, is that sometimes real life is a life that has brokenness, a life that contains pain, a life that has heartache as well as a life that has divorce and broken relationships. The aforementioned is a more realistic picture of the humanity of the pastor. The fact of the matter is that he too experiences life as those over whom he pastors. The unrealistic world of perfection and the embracing of this world causes the preacher to hide and mask his imperfections. For varying reasons, this is done constantly and consistently. Consequently, it creates a festering wound from life as he shepherds the people while suffering with his own wounds and so it is, that *out of the wounds of the wounded comes healing.*

THE PERCEPTION
"In this world you shall have trouble. But cheer up! I have overcome the world."
John 16:33 (God's Word Translation)

Perception is the way of processing something; perception is also reality to the one doing the processing. It is baffling as to how and from where this imagery emerges, that the pastor is perfect and that the pastor does not have his share of trouble. It is the same word that finds application to the people that also gives application for the preacher. After all, it was Jesus who explained that in the world we shall have tribulation. This is a clear declaration that we will *all*, from the pulpit to the pew, encounter some trouble along the way. Yet, this has been disregarded when it comes to the pastor. This would certainly explain why there is public outcry when the minister stumbles and has a moment or season of weakness. For reasons unknown, the pastor has become god on earth to many. I want to dispel this erroneous perception that pervades the thoughts from the pulpit to the pew. Emphatically this is so far from the truth. The pastor is not God and the pastor is not "a god." God on earth was the incarnate Christ, Jesus. The pastor is merely a hireling, an under shepherd, a representative of God, but not God. God has chosen to use the vessel but the glory is not in the vessel; it is in God. This unfortunate perception of perfection, if it has its origin in the pew must have its clarity from the pulpit. Both pulpit and pew must abandon this notion of perfection and become thankful that God chooses to use the filthy rags that exist among us and in us. It is there where the glory and the magnificent power of God displays itself amazingly, choosing what would not be chosen for such an honorable purpose. The mere fact that HE uses us in spite of us is powerful in and of itself.

THE PASTOR'S OWN ISSUES

Life and the situations of life take its toll on every individual. It is in the shroud of secrecy that the pastor deals with his own personal issues. And usually because of the lateness of the day his issues go neglected. Therefore, year to year and day to day the pastor's issues remain just that, issues - unresolved issues. In fact, there exists an unknown inability to deal with his own internal struggles. The unintentional neglect of his issues while focusing on the issues and problems of others causes the pastor's issues to now have issues of their own. This neglect is largely due to the imagery and expectations that are thrust upon him to live a perfect life. Additionally, it is expected that the pastor is to be the one who has mastered biblical precepts. However, this is far from the truth as well; the fact is that preachers struggle just like everyone else striving to apply precepts and biblical principles into their own lives. We cry. We hurt. We stumble, and we do mess up. Simply put, we get wounded from the many complications, calamities, crowns and complexities that come with living as well as just that of being a minister. People get wounded from the trials, tribulations, hardships and difficulties of life and the preacher gets wounded as well. There are various wounds. Some are self-inflicted and others are inflicted from those both distant and near to us. Other wounds are those that come just because it's your time and season in life to experience them.

Many people often see the success of others and believe that the person had it easy getting to that level of success. This is a fallacy. People looking from the outside never get to the chance to go behind the veil to witness the private and personal struggles that the pastor/preacher/prophet/person had to go through. They know nothing about the battles that had to be fought, barriers that the person had to go around, obstacles they had to cross, discouragement, frustration and betrayal from others they experienced or the many days and nights of shed tears and wet pillows; not to mention the betrayal and disappointments that came from close friends and family members. The proper perception thus, should not be one of perfection but one of a real person living a real life and making real decisions, while at the same time trusting a real God to be the best that they can be.

DANGER IN MAINTAINING THE WRONG PERCEPTION

That perception of the pastor as one having a perfect lifestyle causes him to work to uphold this perception that the people have of him. I have personally dealt with this challenge and it proved to be a hurdle that I had to overcome while attempting to minister to the people of God effectively. A hurdle that presented itself is one where I looked at the people and at times would become upset within. This was because they wanted a perfect pastor, but they knew that they themselves were not perfect. What I found this did was cause me to wrestle with the following question: *Have I been genuine, in an effort to maintain the wrong perception?* I am not advocating the flaunting of flaws before each other because whether consciously or unconsciously operating in our flaws, it can easily be misconstrued as the glorifying of them. In my efforts to conceal my flaws and uphold the perception of perfection, I found that I would get dressed with smiles only to mask and confine the wounds that I was living with. I did not want to be viewed as the injured doctor professing the ability to help the sick but not able to help himself. These fabricated smiles that were on display often were put on to mask and disguise the pain that brewed on the inside. This had been a real struggle because I have often wondered if I am being genuine with the people I have encountered through ministry. Questions would arise within such as, *"Am I even being sinful as I uphold this image of being perfect."*

Needless to say, I had to seek spiritual release from this stronghold. One of the things that came about from this effort of upholding the perfect image was that it caused the public mask to often become a private mask. By this, I mean that I found myself at a place where there were unreal layers that prevented me from seeing the things that hindered me. It kept me from seeing the thorn that buffeted me. This was a potentially devastating blow to my walk. It was potentially devastating because it prevented me from going to God in prayer about my thorn. Again, this was done because I became so good at masking my thorn, masking my wound, masking my pain, my hurt, and the internal struggles that I had. It was expected for the pastor to be happy and in a good mood at all times. So I went about life working to be happy everyday while in reality there were things that were experienced in my life that constituted the emotion of sorrow. Unfortunately I could not be sorrowful; I had to uphold a "Godly" image. There were moments of experiences in my life that I requited a shoulder to lean on but I could not because I had to be the shoulder for everyone else to lean on. A close friend once said to me: *"You must think that you are superman."* But even superman had some weaknesses and needed help sometimes.

CLAY JARS

"So I went to the potter's house, and sure enough, the potter was there, working away at his wheel. Whenever the pot the potter was working on turned out badly, as sometimes happens

when you are working with clay, the potter would simply start over and use the same clay to make another pot."
Jeremiah 18:3-4 (Message Bible)

As a kid growing up, my mother, who has since made her transition from this earth, had a hobby that she loved of making ceramic figurines. On one occasion, I remember seeing her make a stallion. It was a beautiful piece of artwork upon completion. However, it did not start out as such. It wasn't beautiful at all in the beginning. When she started working on it, it was nothing more than wet unmolded clay. It was unattractive, messy to handle, and did not have any shape or form. In fact, I saw her reach into a pile of clay and place it on the table. She then proceeded to beat on the clay as she shaped and molded it. I watched as she continued to mold and beat on that clay attempting to smooth out the rough spots as well as to get the air bubbles out of it. My mother would examine the clay, and after a while of beating and molding it, she would place it into a cast. She then put it into the oven with the temperature turned up extremely high. After being in the oven for a period of time, she would then take it out and let it cool down. When the clay, which was still in the cast, cooled down, it was removed from the cast and she began to paint it. Back into the oven it went after being painted. This was done to bake the paint into the now hardened clay. Again, she removed it from the oven and painted it once again. This time when she painted the figurine, it was with a clear gloss coat to give it a nice shiny glow once it was complete. I thought to myself that this figurine would break under pressure exactly when she would finish. In contradiction to my eager assumption that it was finished, she placed the ceramic stallion back into the oven. This back and forth tedious process was done so as to create and bring about an inner beauty from that once messy clump of clay. Needless to say, it was a long process but in the end it was a necessary process in order to arrive at the completed beautiful artwork. My mother from the beginning knew the potential that the messy, wet, unmolded clay held from the moment she scooped it up and began to work on it. She knew the end from the beginning. She saw the stallion as she knew it would turn out to be. And so it is with God.

A SPIRITUAL PARALLEL

The wounded healer has great similarities to the clay. Just as the clay was chosen in the condition that it was in, God chose the wounded healer in the condition that they are in. God from the onset sees the potential of the wounded; He sees something in the preacher, in the parishioner, in the drug addict, in the prostitute, in everyone while they are yet in the condition they are in. He uses us just as we are and takes us through a refining process. Some of these processes are long and tedious as well as can be viewed as being unnecessary. Life, along with its situations and circumstances serves as that process. While we are experiencing the bumps and the bruises of losing along with the thrills and the triumphs of winning, God is using those experiences to bring about a beautiful work of art. It was the apostle Paul that stated in Romans 8:28 that, *"...we know that all things work together for good to those who love God, to those who are the called according to His purpose."* However, many only view the finished product, the glory (that clear coat, the gloss, and the shine), never seeing the process of getting there.

I vividly recall a day when my mother was at work and my brother and I were wrestling in the house. You know the old adage: *boys will be boys.* We could not see at the time that this rough wrestling in the house could only bring about trouble. Needless to say, while we were wrestling and horse playing, we broke the leg off of the beautiful ceramic stallion figurine that my mother had made. This is the same stallion figurine, which stood about two and a half feet high that my mother went through the long and tedious process of creating. Immediately, a moment of fear and apprehension came over us. If the wrestling in the house was not a scene of anarchy, surely the two of us frantically running around in utter bewilderment as to what we would do in this situation was. The consequences that would befall us crippled our cognitive and motor abilities. After about thirty minutes or so of mental and physical paralysis, we came up with a brilliant idea to glue the leg back onto the ceramic stallion. Thank God for crazy glue (we thought). We instantly became pottery and ceramic figurine repair surgeons. We repaired the stallion's leg to near perfection. We prayed that our mother would not discover our treacherously accidental deed and covert effort to cover our negligence. To this day, although mom is no longer with us, to our knowledge she never discovered the fracture. However, my brother and I knew of the stallion's brokenness and we could easily identify the place of the fracture. Yet to those who knew nothing of our indoor wrestling match and surgical procedure to repair and erase our error, the fracture in the ceramic stallion's leg was not visible. In the eye of every visitor to our home the ceramic stallion was a work of artistic beauty created by my mother's hands.

So too is it with the wounded healer. A work of artistic beauty created and blessed by God; yet fractured at the hands of wrestling with the experiences of life. The wounded healer being fractured has been glued together by God's crazy glue of grace and mercy. Before the eyes of those who are not witnesses or participants in the fracturing process, the pastor/prophet/teacher/parent, etc. is never viewed as having been wounded. However, it is when we are left alone, that the places of fracture are noticed by God as well as ourselves. It is therefore, only by God's grace and His mercy that though fractured, we are able to function. The wounded healer by all accounts should not be able to function under the weight of the parishioners' struggles as well as their own personal struggles and situations. Mere human ability cannot accomplish such a task. It is only by God's mercy and grace; empowered by God, thus the ability to function while fractured.

These ceramic pieces that my mother owned began as mounds of messy clay without purpose except in the eye of the potter, which reveals a great lesson: God does not haphazardly shape and mold us into something He wants us to be. He sees the shape that He has already placed in us from the day of our conception and chisels away everything that is not the shape in order to reveal to the world what was there all the time. He simply makes us more distinct, but the shape was there the whole time! Although going through the heated process to bring about beauty, the ceramic figurines are yet fragile and often get fractured. Just as my brother and I through rough play fractured that ceramic stallion in all of its beauty, it had been broken. So too do we who participate in the Kingdom work of God in all of our beauty, we are but clay jars that can be and have been broken. However, praise God that His grace and mercy can hold us together that we might function while fractured. As you look back at some of your accomplishments, you recognize that you should not have achieved those things, but that it was by His grace and mercy that you did. You should fall to your knees and give thank! It is only by His grace and mercy that you did not lose your mind nor break down. Herein is how the wounded healer is able to, despite being wounded, aid in bringing about healing to others.

A DIRTY VESSEL IN THE RIGHT HANDS CAN MAKE BEAUTIFUL MUSIC

I used to play in the Miami Central Senior High School Marching Band. Respectfully, I was raised in a poor family. We did not have money overflowing in excess. We barely had enough to keep the bare necessities covered (I thank God even now for the covering of the bare necessities). The high school was underfunded at the time and some of the students had to supply their own instruments. Needless to say, I fell into that category. My mother could not afford to purchase a brand new trombone from the music store, so we had to locate one that was being independently sold or one that had been pawned.

We found a horn that was within her financial ability, but it was dented and rusty. So there I was in the band with a trombone that was probably the worse looking instrument in the band. The slide on the horn had dents in it which made it difficult to slide with ease. This made the horn hard to play. However, despite its less-than-attractive appearance and the difficulty there was in playing it, this horn was able to produce a beautiful, loud, sweet robust sound. This amazed many of the band members - the fact that out of such an unsightly instrument came such a beautiful sound! My section leader would at times ask to use my horn because he wanted to make the same sound that I was able to produce from that old beaten up horn. In comparison to my horn, his horn was shiny and new, but for reasons unknown, it could not produce the sound that my old beaten down horn produced. Yet, there was something else that was amazing that occurred whenever my section leader played my horn - he could not produce the same sound as I did using the very same instrument! We concluded that it was not the instrument, but it was something about that old horn being played while in *Johnny's* hand. I see God now in all of this. God uses us just like I was playing that old horn and was able to produce beautiful music out of a less than beautiful horn. God makes miracles happen out of less than perfect people. With the same horn, my section leader could not produce the same sound as I was able to produce. This says that the hands that the horn was in made the difference. Just as with God, the hands that we (the old horn, wounded healer) are in makes the difference.

So we are all like that old horn of mine and God uses us to bring about beautiful music. It's not the horn (us), it is the hands that we are in that brings the best out of us. Herein, is the true lesson - that we must know that we are all nothing more than old, less than attractive horns, and difficult to play; yet God still uses us. The pastors as well as those in the pews are mere vessels that are in the right hands bringing about beautiful music.

HEALING OTHERS BRINGS ABOUT OUR OWN HEALING

"...the joy of the Lord will make you strong."
Nehemiah 8:10 (New Century Version)

There is a great desire to see the needs of self fulfilled. And so when the wounded healer discovers that he is wounded and he witnesses the joy that others have as a result of their wounds being healed, he desires the same joy from being healed. However, it is like after Jacob has had his encounter with wrestling with the angel that he leaves the wrestling encounter with a limp. There is never a record of Jacob ever having been healed of his limp. The silence of the bible concerning this matter leaves us to conclude that he lived the remainder of his days with this limp. Just as there is never a biblical record that after Paul had made a request to have a thorn from his flesh removed that it was ever removed. In 2nd Corinthians 12:8 Paul says that, *"Concerning this thing I pleaded with the Lord three times that it might depart from me."* God's response was not to remove it but He said, *"My grace is sufficient for you, for My strength is made perfect in weakness."* There then exists a possibility that the wounds of the wounded healer could never be healed and we must learn to live with what becomes our Jacob's limp or Pauline's thorn. Jacob's limp served as a reminder to him that he wrestled with an angel and was blessed as a result of it. Paul looked at his thorn differently and saw it as a gift that would keep him grounded and not rejoice in his flesh. In fact, his thorn helped him to see the grace of God more clearly in his life. For the wounded healer it is not that God is not able to heal the wounded healer, it could be that our wounds are there to remind us that we are blessed to be used of God as well as to keep us grounded that we would not be exalted by ourselves after being exalted by people. Therefore, I, just as others, must view our wounds differently. When the private wounds become publically displayed, we must view it as a grander stage for

God to prove Himself and perform so that all could see His wonderful works. There is a likelihood that the wounds of the wounded healer may remain with him and if he focuses on the unhealed wounds, sorrow could set in. Here is where we find a new source of joy. As the wounded healer helps to heal others, this begins to bring the wounded healer joy because he recognizes that these things bring joy to God and as God has joy, He gives the wounded healer strength. We hence learn to take joy in what brings God joy knowing that it will bring us strength. May the joy of the Lord continuously be your strength!

ABOUT THE AUTHOR

Pastor Eric H. Jones, Jr. is one who has a vision and heart compelled to do the will of God. As founder and senior pastor of Koinonia Worship Center and Village, his positive influence and leadership has evolved beyond the walls of the church. Koinonia operates seven days a week and has more than twenty-four ministries which include: Prison, Substance Abuse, Men, Women and Youth ministries. Rev. Jones is known locally and worldwide through weekly radio broadcasts on WHIM, WMBM, and International Trans World Radio.

Rev. Jones is a graduate of Attucks High School Class of 1965, Charron Williams Para-medical College; Southern Baptist Seminary Extension and is a Vietnam era Veteran. Before entering the ministry, Eric Jones worked in the area of pharmaceutical quality control as lab supervisor and general manager of Blood Banks.

In 2005, Eric H. Jones, Jr., was elected to serve Broward County's 31st city as the first Mayor of the City of West Park, Florida Commission for two years. He was again re-elected in 2007 to serve a four-year term and without opposition will serve as Mayor for the next term, 2012 - 2017.

Rev. Jones is married to Bloneva Jones and they two have three sons, Derrick Jones, Kaniel Jones, and Shevrin Jones. He is also the proud grandfather of Derrick Jr., Cyrus and Eric.

Koinonia Worship Center & Village
4900 W. Hallandale Beach Blvd.
Pembroke Park, FL 33023
Rev. Eric H. Jones, Senior Pastor

Chapter 2

From Storms to Stepping Stones
Written by Pastor Eric Jones

Now faith is the substance of things hoped for, the evidence of things not seen.
(Hebrews 11:1)

The things we are not closely familiar with or have the privilege of being behind the scenes in are often viewed in a flattering light. When you take a close look at and become familiar with the biblical characters in scripture, you see that they are authentic representations. They are not held up on some unreal pedestal. There is never any attempt on God's part to win our favor by portraying biblical characters as plastic saints with shiny halos who never did any wrong. Abraham lied, Noah got drunk, Moses lost his temper then committed murder, David was an adulterer and also committed murder, Mary Magdalene had seven demons, and I can go on and on. God paints His people just as they are. No matter how dignified or high their calling, they were fully human, just like you and I. Yet, we must keep in mind that God's Word, not our human strength or weakness, has priority over everything. However, many that are called are not prepared to accept this. This is the main reason why many ministers of the gospel feel frustrated and inadequate even though they read the Bible, pray, and witness for Christ. We can only experience victory in our lives when we become like Christ who experienced every human weakness in order to fulfill God's will. In Mark 8:33, Jesus rebuked Peter when he said, *"Get behind me Satan! You are not mindful of the things of God, but the things of men."* Peter, Jesus' disciple, had just proclaimed Jesus' true identity declaring, *"You are the Christ."* But when he heard the cost to be paid for the revelation of God's divine love and will for a sinful and broken world, he refused to believe it. He could not accept that Christ, who accepted every human weakness, would suffer those dreadful and horrible things at the hands of the elders, chief priests and scribes, then be killed and be raised the third day. He therefore took Jesus aside and began to rebuke Him. This same Peter, who a short time earlier had declared Jesus to be Lord, was now telling his Lord that He did not know what He was talking about. This sounds just like what we often do. Peter, a man like us, rebuking God and implying that he knew more than God did. To Peter, Jesus had to be wrong and he could not understand why Jesus was having difficulty understanding the obvious, that God would not allow Him to go through such suffering. Peter who had called Him Lord refused to trust and believe His words. He chose to rely instead on his own feelings and ignored what Christ was saying. He was mindful of the things of men rather than the things of God. What God wants is more important than what we feel. Acknowledging the Lordship of Christ is the beginning of a journey - an intimate relationship with Him. It is not following a set of laws, a set of beliefs, or relying on our thoughts and emotions - it is following Christ.

When the call of God came upon my life, I was aware of the storms that assailed those that He used as ministers and pastors. Now, it was my turn - What was I to choose? That was the question that I wrestled with at the start of the vision that the Lord gave me.

CHOICES

Have you ever been faced with choices? The dean of a university was at a faculty meeting when a professor from the antiquities department handed him an old brass lamp they had just acquired. The dean rubbed a smudge from it, and as he did, a genie appeared. *"I'm the genie from the lamp,"* he said, *"and I'm here on a special assignment, Dean. Your unselfish service has won you a reward. You have a choice - you can have either unthinkable wealth, infinite wisdom, or unsurpassed beauty."* Without hesitating, the dean selected wisdom. *"It is done!"* the genie said, and then he disappeared into a cloud of smoke and back into the lamp. All of the other members of the faculty stared at the dean with amazement. Finally one of them whispered, *"Now that you have infinite wisdom, Dean, say something."* The dean looked at them and said, *"I should have taken the money."* Life is full of interesting choices, isn't it? Even as you read this chapter you have already made several. Without thinking about it, you exercised one of the greatest God-given qualities you and I have as human beings - the ability to think for ourselves and make our own choices. However, none of us have any choice about being born, the family we have, or the era in which we live. The choosing begins with *how* we will use the circumstances we inherit.

In 1784, Ben Franklin wrote to his daughter expressing his disappointment at the poor choice the American government had made in selecting the eagle as our national symbol; Ben wanted the turkey (I'm so glad they didn't listen to him). Some choices carry greater consequences than others. A student nurse came into the hospital room to give her 79-year-old patient a shot. She asked him, *"Which hip do you want the shot?"* said he, *"Yours honey."* Choosing is important in the Christian life. Alaska's highway is well-known for its primitive roads, and the long, lonely stretches. A sign located at the beginning of one such stretch reads: CHOOSE YOUR RUT CAREFULLY...YOU'LL BE IN IT FOR THE NEXT 200 MILES! If you've ever read missionary biographies, they are full of stories of people who have given up a normal life, and in many cases extraordinary careers, in order to go to other parts of the world to tell people about Jesus. I guess most of us are familiar with the film 'Chariots of Fire'. It is about Eric Liddell, the runner who refused to compete on the Sabbath. As a result of his refusal to do so, he was unable to win the 100 meters Gold Medal in the Olympics. I wonder how many people realize that not only did he give up that medal, but a couple years later, he went off to China as a missionary, giving up his athletic ambitions altogether. And there are countless other examples of individuals who did similar things for the Kingdom. As I read these kinds of biographies I sometimes wonder what sort of processes these people went through before deciding to take such a huge step of faith. Did they decide instantaneously or did they think about it for a long time? For many I imagine the decision may have been very difficult. For most of us there are all sorts of stumbling blocks that spring to mind when God calls. What's more challenging is the fact that, God's call isn't always clear. Sometimes it is as clear as a bell, sometimes it comes in the form of a general call to Christian service.

In 1979, I had a hard choice in front of me. I was doing well in my career as a Laboratory Technologist, my family was comfortable, and I had, to a great degree, settled down for the long haul. My circumstances in life were good and getting better. *However*, life places us in numerous situations where we are faced with scores of tough decisions about family, job, relationships, and faith. We want to make sound decisions, and as believers, we want to make Christian decisions - choices that will be good for our welfare, the welfare of our family, and pleasing in God's sight. The question before me during this particular season of my life was, *"How can I make a sound Christian decision?"* I knew what I wanted. I wanted to please God.

C.S. Lewis, in 'Mere Christianity' wrote: *"...every time you make a choice, you are turning the central part of you, the part that chooses, into something a little different than it was before. And taking your life as a whole, with all your innumerable choices, you are slowly turning this central thing either into a heavenly creature or into a hellish creature..."* Through my struggle with choices, I learned a valuable lesson about choosing: When you choose Christ first, you begin to know Christ-like-ness firsthand. I often try to pattern my prayer after Jesus' prayer in Gethsemane, *"Lord, I want to be more like you when I make choices - NOT MY WILL, FATHER, YOURS!"* The reality is that when you begin to want Jesus, you will begin to want to *be* like Jesus, and decisions will be more like the ones Jesus would make. Jesus depended upon the Father. When Jesus prayed, He expected an answer, but it is important to note that HE ALWAYS LEFT THE *KIND* OF ANSWER IN THE FATHER'S HANDS. It is essential to make our requests known and even our wants....but it is so much smarter to leave the *way* God answers up to Him. He has been known to come up with better answers than what we usually come up with. All your plans for your family, ministry and relationships need room for the miracle-working power of God. Remember, if you are covering every angle, it is YOU that you are depending on, not God. This is a focus that requires a different kind of lens. Our decisions are not made in a vacuum. Everything we do affects other people. It is especially so as a leader in the body of Christ.

STEPPING OUT ON FAITH

Stepping out on God's command may appear to seem foolish to the natural eye and downright impossible at times, if not dangerous to our humanistic logic and reasoning, but a miracle may not be realized otherwise! In all of our efforts to grow and mature in Christ, it all starts with that first step of faith. Before God took the children of Israel into the Promised Land they needed to commit to Him with no turning back. God, in turn, provided a way to do the impossible. People sometimes do not realize how big a part faith plays in everyday life. It takes faith to eat in a restaurant. It takes faith to deposit money in a bank or in a mutual fund. It takes faith to sign a contract, drive on the highway, or get on an airplane or elevator. The journey of faith is not some kind of religious experience for the elite, it is the glue that helps hold people's lives together. But remember, faith is only as good as its object. If we trust people, we get only what people can do; if we trust money, we get only what money can do. If we trust ourselves, we get only what we can do, but if we trust God, we get what God can do - and He can do anything and everything! When God calls us and we step out for Him, He comes through. In life there is nothing more frightening than stepping out of your comfort zone into the unknown. This was my dilemma over thirty years ago when I responded to the call of God in my life. It was a time of fear and doubt, a time of wavering between should I or shouldn't I and the self-evaluating questions about readiness and the myriad of excuses about unconquered weaknesses in my life. Yet, in my heart of hearts I knew I had no choice. In writing this chapter, I reflect on the events that followed my choosing to accept the vision of God for my life. No one really feels competent to carry out the work of God in any area, much less the area of Pastoring a church. The Bible is replete with the replies of those who were called and the excuses that they made. The call of God, although extremely significant, is usually quite short. But God has a habit of packing an incredible amount of truth into a few words. The first thing I realized was that in order to obey the Divine Call, there had to be much sacrificing. Through experience, I have learned that failure to sacrifice is one of the greatest hindrances to Christian service. You can greatly limit your service or even miss God's calling altogether because you are unwilling to sacrifice much of anything for God. This sacrifice can involve position, possessions, family, friends, wealth, time, or comforts. The Call of God for me involved my pulling away from much that I had accomplished as a means of securing my family's economic well-being and having to rethink some relationships that I held dear. I discovered early that one must be prepared to take up the cross daily if they would follow where God leads. They must surrender to God their will, affections, body, and soul. They must not seek their own happiness as the supreme object, but be willing to renounce all, and lay down their life also, if required. To deny oneself is to avoid ease or indulgence; to take up the cross is to endure reproach or dishonor in the eyes of the world. The mark of the disciple, the characteristic which Jesus Himself looks for, is that we, like Him, deny ourselves, take up our crosses and follow Him. In the scripture, there are three words which express, with perfect insight, the darker and the more difficult experiences of a religious life. The three words are *burden, thorn, and cross.*

By the word "burden" both the Old Testament *and* the new means all the unavoidable care and strain of earthly life. The "thorn" always points to some singular trial. It describes some humbling infirmity, some devastating disability or weakness which makes us miserable, because it weakens us for our task. The "cross" symbolizes death to self. Every man must bear his own burden. Every man has his thorn in the flesh; however, the cross is not universal and the cross can be escaped. Many men and women never bear a cross at all. Many can refuse the cross if they so desire and many do refuse. The whole spiritual tragedy of many who are not Disciples of Christ will be found to lie here, that when the cross lay before them, they refused it. Each step of real advance in the divine life will involve a cross and an altar on which some cherished items of the self-life has been offered; or a tombstone where some treasured idol has been buried. There is a pre-salvific work that the Lord performs on all that He uses and I was no exception. As I look back over the path that I travelled, I realize that there was Divine Providence involved in all that I encountered.

To begin with, I became a sergeant in the Army at the age of 19. This was something that was out of the ordinary but a blessing for me. Many other unrealized miracles happened as God ushered me into a place for the work He had ordained for me. I realize that as a child of God, I had been given a purpose and a promise. I had a land awaiting me in which I had yet to inherit. It was already mine but for me to receive it I, like so many other visionaries of the Bible needed some instruction. The land I am talking about is not the blessed promised land of heaven but the promise of God building a group of people that would aid in enlarging His kingdom. I, like so many before me have done my share of wandering and had my times of discouragement, but as time slowly passed on, I found that it was time for me to move toward my Canaan, and then I had to CONQUER CANAAN.

THE WILDERNESS EXPERIENCE

Do you remember the times when you struggled with something or had been fighting a battle and it left you feeling like you had been run over by a mac truck? We feel like we are always spending our time trying to defeat a giant? If we are fortunate enough, we do not make it there often, but the reality is, we all make it there at some point and time in our lives. In some cases, we are up against a problem or distraction. In other cases, we are fighting sin that has taken a hold of us and as much as we want to defeat that giant in our lives, it rears its ugly head again and again. We have all been to the place where we have had to deal with giants; giants like worry, doubt, fear, anxiety, depression, or insecurity. Whatever the situation was, we have wandered through those dry valleys looking for answers and sometimes we came up empty. We may have felt a lot like David standing in the intimidating shadow of Goliath.

I recall that in the late 1960's there was a TV show called 'Land of the Giants'. Seven people from earth found their spaceship caught in a warp of some kind and ended up on a planet where everything was twelve times larger than on earth. Each week they battled giant cats, giant children and giant soldiers. It was a little strange, but raised an interesting question. *What would we do if everything and everyone were giants except for us?* The truth is that we do live in a land of giants. There are things that are bigger than us which seem to stand between us and being where God wants us to be. In the old Testament, God sent His people Israel to a place called

'The Promised Land'. It was a great place to live, but it also was inhabited by giants, which they would have to face and defeat before they could move in. We too live in a land of giants which we must face if we are to be where God wants us to be. A wilderness is whatever stands between you and the vision given to you by God. It can consist of personal failure, the opinions of others, rejection by peers, or just plain-ole' self-doubt. Consider this: Walt Disney was fired by a newspaper editor for lack of ideas. Walt Disney also went bankrupt several times before he built Disneyland. Leo Tolstoy, author of 'War and Peace' flunked out of college. He was described as both "unable" and "unwilling" to learn. Michael Jordan, perhaps the greatest basketball player of all time, did not make his high school basketball team his sophomore year. Beethoven's teacher called him hopeless as a composer. Winston Churchill failed the sixth grade. He did not become Prime Minister until he was 62. His greatest contributions came when he was a "senior citizen." Henry Ford failed and went broke five times before he finally succeeded.

    The ministry began in my living room as my wife and I agreed to a counseling session for a couple that was having marital problems. Little did I know that those sessions would become the point of reference that marked the beginning of Koinonia Worship Center. Within five months, there were over 40 people in my living room which prompted me to seek another location. That location was the Ramada Inn on Ansin Boulevard in Hallandale, Florida. That place served us well for about three months and a door opened in Miami-Dade County that allowed us to move into an old Jewish synagogue. After being there for one year, another church leased it from under us and we had to move. From there, we moved to the auditorium at an elementary school. There, we remained for one year and moved to the Police Benevolent Association Hall building in Hollywood, Florida for another three months. At this point, we had moved from my living room, to the Ramada Inn, to the Jewish Synagogue, to the elementary school, to the Police

Benevolent Association Hall, and now it was time to move again. However, there was a blessing in store before we made the next move. One of the members donated four lots to our Church to build a sanctuary. From that point, we could see an end to our wilderness wandering. Although we were moving again, it was different this time. We were moving with a plan. This move, we thought, was the beginning of the end of our moving. Thus, we located to the old fire house in Carver Ranches, Florida with renewed hope. There, we experienced tremendous growth for about three years, but characteristic of our wilderness travels, it was time to move again. From there we moved to the old Carver Ranches Elementary School auditorium. At this point we had moved a total of seven times and had not lost but gained members. Through all of this moving and growing, I had my own personal demons to deal with. I was an obedient shepherd, a submissive servant, uncompromising and forgiving, but there came a period where I went into a "spiritual slump" and made a series of drastic mistakes. This is a warning to those entering into the ministry of the danger of drifting. I went from a spiritual high to a spiritual low. Many ministers have the attitude that just because they answered the call and are in the will of God, that now God is supposed to give them everything pertaining to the vision without any effort, work, sacrifice, or discipline on their part. The fact is that it costs what it costs and the cost never goes on sale. Yes, God wants the ministry to prosper and be a blessing, but sometimes you are going to have to go through some things. Sometimes you have to struggle; sometimes you have to fight; sometimes you have to cry. However I discovered that there was something in the struggle that was necessary to my becoming what God had ordained for me to be. In the storm of my struggle was the material for stepping stones to the next level of the vision. God left giants in the promised land on purpose and when we study the story, we can see why:

- Because the Israelites needed to learn how to fight

- Because giants distinguished the difference between professors and possessors.

  It is one thing to confess the promises of God, but it's quite another to strap on your sword and go toe to toe with your giants to possess your promises.

- Giants expose the grasshoppers in the crowd (when giants show up, grasshoppers speak up).

  > *Grasshoppers usually blend into their environments but giants uncover them. Remember that grasshoppers don't eat grapes. You will never have promise-land faith with a grasshopper mentality.*

- You get to know yourself in the struggle. The real you shows up under pressure.

- You get to know your God. You realize that God is your only help.

- You become stronger; you put down roots and dig into the word and prayer.

- You become aware of the excesses and unnecessary things in your life.

- The struggle produces thanksgiving. For example, someone survives a tornado and their house, car, and all their possessions are is gone, but they are still thankful that they are yet alive and that the family is together.

- Struggles test your level of commitment.

The only way to truly gauge your level of commitment is through the struggle. We should understand that many times the struggle, the fight, the warfare, the praying, the waiting patiently, the enduring, is as important as the blessing and the reward. While we are looking at the reward, God is looking at the development that is taking place in you through the struggle. The caterpillar goes through a process of metamorphosis through which it changes from an earthbound crawly worm into a beautiful butterfly. But this process involves struggle. To cut the struggle short would be to rob the butterfly of its destiny. The baby chick in the egg goes through a process of growth inside the egg until it begins to outgrow the egg, but it must peck its way out. This struggle strengthens the baby chick and prepares it for life outside of the egg. To cut the struggle short would severely injure if not kill the chick. Through the struggle, it gains the strength it needs to survive and thrive in its new environment. I learned through my struggle that faith is forged in the furnace of adversity. I also learned through my struggles that God was bringing me to a place of greater influence and blessing to those that I was to lead. Yes, I may be still going through struggles but I am growing through my struggles. I am developing more spiritual muscles; I am developing greater compassion, extra patience, added endurance and long-suffering. I am developing the ability to put myself in the position where others are and to feel what they feel so I can speak a word in season to them. Yes, I may be struggling right now, but there is always something in the struggle I need in order to become all that God has ordained for me. I have learned how to use storms for molding stepping stones. Many of us say that we live by faith, that we have faith in God to do what He says He will do, but when it comes time to answer that call, to live that life that He calls us to live, we fail to completely trust Him. It is hard for us to depend on Him to take care of us - to trust that HE will provide all of our needs. We just do not believe that He will care about us enough that He will provide even the little things we need in our lives. Some pastors will even say that God expects us to take care of ourselves. But my Bible teaches that HE will provide for my needs if I trust Him with all my heart. Just as He provided for the needs of those He used before me, so will He provide what I need to carry out my service to Him.

And so I say to you: God expects us to react in faith not doubt. To be led by Him in whatever it is He has called us to do. Sometimes we say, *...but Lord I can't do that, or it's too hard. Is this really your will Lord? Why, that is crazy! There is no way I can do that.* So we ignore the call and refuse to do what the Lord is calling and equipping us to do. We are comfortable in our lives and we do not want to take any risk. *Is it worth risking,* we ask? It used to be that life was a matter of "this I will risk" but "that I won't." Risk was something that was weighed on a daily basis. It was a part of life. You picked one thing over another because you had weighed the risks involved and came to a conclusion that one risk was more palatable than another. For example, farmers traditionally have walked a risk-filled path in that daily they had to weigh whether this day or that day would be the better one to plow the field. Because the weather was something out of their control and all that they had was their "folk" prognostication and intuition for predicting rain or sun, farming had traditionally been a pretty risky business. Sometimes they decided correctly and other times they didn't. It was a matter of risk and faith and most farmers were attuned to that because that was the only choice that they had. That is, of course, until the advent of modern weather forecasting. Today, risk is far less of a factor in farming. The person we once knew as the weather-bitten and aggressive guy in the bib jeans who, without advice, arrived down at the mill each morning speculating on whether the skies would be dark by noon or not, is rapidly becoming an image of the past. Although we live in society that is no less "risky" than in the past, we live under a governing system that has made it its job to secure us from as much of that as possible. Seatbelts, helmets, social security, even weather forecasters tell us to board up our houses and stock up on necessary supplies just because the conditions are "right" for a hurricane. With all this "help" it seems we are rapidly becoming obsessed with living safely over living faithfully. Does God want us to take risks? Certainly not foolhardy ones! Yet, when He presents us with situations that require thoughtful deliberation and a faith-filled heart, He isn't expecting us to back down because there might be risk involved. God once told a soldier named Gideon to confront the risks and pull down the pagan altars in his land. Despite the risk that others would be offended, even moved to attack him, Gideon faithfully obeyed. When God puts us into pressure-filled situations, we always have a choice. We can pray for strength and take the risks He has put before us or we can weigh the risks and decide to walk away. If we walk away, we may never know the perfection God has reserved for us. Our next miracle may be only one choice and one risk away.

When you are fighting the storms that come your way, and you are tired and overwhelmed and feeling lost and alone, Jesus sees you. Why didn't Jesus come rescue the disciples immediately? Why did He let them struggle so long when they were obeying His command to row across the lake? Why did He let them face the storm? To grow stronger! Our spiritual muscles only grow stronger when they meet resistance. The same is true of our faith. As long as we don't give up, the storm makes us stronger. We don't need to know how long the storm will last, only that God is in control.

ABOUT THE AUTHOR

Pastor Wayne Lomax serves as the Senior Pastor and visionary leader of 'The Fountain of New Life' located in Pembroke Pines and Miami Gardens, FL. As the pastor and founder of The Fountain of Pembroke Pines, Pastor Lomax led in the unification of two local congregations into one dynamic church in two locations. Born in Pender County, North Carolina, Pastor Lomax attended the historic Lincoln University in Lincoln, Pennsylvania before receiving a degree in Chemistry from the University of North Carolina, Chapel Hill (1979). While dreaming of becoming a medical doctor, God called him to shepherd His people. Pastor Lomax enrolled at The Southern Baptist Theological Seminary in Louisville, Kentucky where he received a Master of Divinity Degree (1984). While attending seminary, Pastor Lomax served as pastor of the York Street Baptist Church in Louisville (1982-1984) before accepting the call to serve Dr. Mack King Carter at the Mount Olive Baptist Church (1985-1997).

Pastor Lomax has led The Fountain in serving others through multiple ministry streams. Following Jesus' example of serving others, Pastor Lomax's passion for international and domestic missions permeates the hearts of The Fountain's servants, resulting in mission presence in Nigeria, Honduras, Haiti, and throughout the United States. With more than thirty years of ministry experience, Pastor Lomax's thirst for Jesus has driven his faithfulness in serving others. In addition to his commitment to The Fountain, Pastor Lomax also serves as a member of Florida Memorial University's Board of Trustees and The P.R.E.S.S. Coalition. Pastor Lomax is also the founder and CEO of Youth Development Institute which provides free mentoring and tutoring to children in Hollywood and Miami Gardens.

Pastor Lomax and his beautiful wife Teresa, have three children, Christopher, Marcus and LeReine.

Chapter 3

Press Forward!
Written by Pastor Wayne Lomax

Behold, I have set the land before you: go in and possess the land which the Lord sware unto your fathers, Abraham, Isaac, and Jacob, to give unto them and to their seed after them.
(Deuteronomy 1:8)

It is amazing how we innocently, but ignorantly believe that stepping out on faith to do God's will be accompanied by a smoothly paved road. Not so! Between the calling and the actual possessing of the land, is a wilderness experience that may entail some wandering and what may seem like going around and around in circles. It takes great faith to believe that God will bring to pass what He has promised in your life.

The word faith is an integral part of the church lexicon. We speak of it at most of our gatherings and extol it as a supreme virtue. The words that we speak about faith are voluminous, yet in actuality we often demonstrate very little of it - especially in times of trials and testing. In the lives of many people, dreams are deferred or abandoned, not because of a lack of ability or opportunity, but because of a lack of faith. For some reason, it is very hard for the trained mind to believe that all things are truly possible through faith. This is because we have been conditioned to believe what we see and if we do not or cannot see it, we consider it impossible. This is the very opposite of faith. Faith is believing that what we pray for *does* exist even though we do not see it and there is no sign of it coming to pass. The bigger the dream, the greater the faith we must have. It takes very little faith to fetch a drink of water in Miami, Florida, but it takes a great deal of faith to find safe drinking water in Port au Prince, Haiti or Lagos, Nigeria. Relying totally on what is visibly certain is a grave error for the child of God. As children of faith, we must learn to look beyond what the natural eye can see and open our spiritual eyes to the *unseen* possibilities. I challenge you to dust off that mustard seed sized faith and learn to use it. God has a bigger plan for you and it will take a little faith to bring it to pass.

THE CALL TO START A MINISTRY

It was during a hot muggy night in Richmond, Virginia, during the National Baptist Congress of Christian Education in 1987, that I sensed a call in my spirit to start a ministry in what I understood to be western Broward County, Florida. In 1987, the population and development of Broward County was slowly pushing west from Fort Lauderdale and with the uninvited arrival of Hurricane Andrew in 1992, thousands of families left Miami-Dade County and began to purchase homes in Weston, Pembroke Pines, Cooper City, Southwest Ranches and Miramar, Florida. At that time, I was serving as the Assistant Pastor of the Mount Olive Baptist Church under the storied leadership of Dr. Mack King Carter. By many accounts, it was in every sense of the word a perfect place to serve; but I discovered that even paradise has its limitations. While all was well with the ministry, I could not quell the restlessness in my spirit that was prompted by the reemerging of the idea to "start a ministry in western Broward County." Therefore, in the fall of 1996, I, along with my wife, children and a few brave men and women whose lives had been broken or battered by a variety of personal storms, gathered together weekly in our living room to discuss the vision of forming a new church. There we studied the Bible, shared pain and joy and eventually gave birth to *The Fountain*. By March of 1997, I was no longer serving at *Mount Olive Baptist Church*. I was fully engaged and focused on building a church in a new community. We immediately embarked upon (what would end up being) a twelve-year journey to secure and purchase land for our growing ministry. I would frequently meet with a brother in the Lord who shared in our vision and we would call realtors, ride by parcels and pray for guidance. This process that I thought would be a relatively short one actually continued for more than a decade. The players varied as did the parcels but the vision remained the same: purchase property for *The Fountain*.

FAITH OR FEAR?

In 1998, I observed a "for sale" sign on a tract of land that we referred to as Flamingo and Sheridan. The tract reminded me of the "Promised Land". It was the perfect place for *The Fountain* as far as we could see. The land was twenty-two acres along a major thoroughfare which was known as "Church Row". Eighteen acres were parallel to Flamingo Road and in the back of it sat four acres of land with a monster house, pool, guest quarters, fruit trees and many more amenities for a gigantic cost of 2.5 million dollars! In 1998, that seemed extremely expensive, but in reality it was very reasonable. In my mind, this was the piece of land that would solve all of our land issues for years to come; but the problem with me was what I later diagnosed as a serious "lack of faith". We required too much information to act. Looking back, I know that we could have purchased that land very easily, but we did not have the faith to believe that we could do it. Hindsight is 20/20! The seemingly large price tag was all that we could see. The price tag was larger than the potential harvest of souls, the strengthening of families or our service to the poor. We suffered from a serious lack of faith in God. Therefore, the Father decided to take us on a rather interesting journey. He would take us through a wilderness experience until I was ready to walk by faith and not by sight.

Contrary to what many believe about the wilderness experience, it was not a place of great suffering for us. In fact, the wilderness was very comfortable, even productive. But in some ways, it was an unsustainable illusion. It was a place where we became comfortable with what we saw and what we had. We were comfortable beating the odds. We grew in obscurity. In 2002, we signed a lease to relocate from Walter C. Young Middle School to Chapel Trail Commerce Center. We invested three quarters of a million dollars to renovate and furnish 17,000 square feet (enough for a down payment on 22 acres, but we could not see it back then).

THE JOURNEY

Our monthly expenses tripled immediately! We hired painters, plumbers, carpet installers, etc. and we *built out* our worship site with lights, cameras, monitors and microphones. For seven consecutive years we made improvements and enhancements to a property that we would never own. One might even say that we were quite proud of that accomplishment. It was impressive to members and guests but it was also expensive. However, God did offset the costs with growth. We grew from one service to two and from 17,000 square feet to 24,000 square feet. The ministry developed, the staff expanded, and the search for a permanent place continued - but without success! The attempts were numerous. The *Home Depot Building*, the *Palladium*, a three acre tract over here and a nine acre tract over there - we looked at every possible parcel of land and vacant building in our geographic reach. We attempted to purchase the site that we were renting, but the owner offered to sell us the building but not the land under the building. Go figure! After reading through the contract and discovering that we would not own the land, we felt like Marvin Gaye in his classic hit "Inner City Blues"... **'Made me want to holler and throw up both my hands.'** However, we did neither. We pressed forward. We thought we were walking by faith when in reality we were walking in a lack of faith. If we are careful, one can easily equate activity with faith. *Faith is the substance of things hoped for; the evidence* *of things not seen.* (Hebrews 11:1) Faith is *believing* even when there is no empirical reason for that belief. Faith is continuing to pursue an unreachable goal when everyone who knows you and loves you would be proud if you settled for something less. Faith is declaring victory when by all standards of measuring, you are losing and the clock is ticking.

What sustained our lack of faith was the presence of obstacles. Every parcel had obstacles and we could not determine how to address the obstacles. The obstacles made each deal look unfavorable. Even if we could have done the deal, we would have used the obstacles as an excuse not to go forward with executing it. So it appeared as if we were pursuing land but we were only pursuing *the prospect* of purchasing land. The bottom line was that we were not ready for a commitment. We were not ready to personally sacrifice. We were not ready to trust God to address the obstacles. On the other hand, we were very comfortable riding on the cushion of large cash reserves, but we were not ready to deal with not having answers to very real and very important questions. Congregations and paying parishioners want to know the answer to every question they have. They expect the pastor to have all of the answers to all of their questions to make them feel at ease; while at the same time walking by faith. The truth is, we can only do one or the other. We can either know everything or we can walk by faith. Faith is the substance of things *hoped for*. Hope only exists where some of the very important questions remain unanswered. A freshman hopes to enroll in medical school. The grandmother hopes that her newborn grandson will be a godly man. The new business owner hopes for five franchises in the next five years. If one is to break through the threshold between effort and accomplishment, one will have to "press forward" with unanswered questions. Faith will have to bridge the chasm between what is known and what is unknown.

WRITE THE VISION

In the realm of major accomplishments, the lack of knowledge is pervasive. Do not allow a lack of knowledge to stymie your forward progress. We had many unanswered questions. How much does it cost? How much have we spent? How much will it cost to get permits? How many members will we lose because of the location of the property? Can we remove the toxins from the soil? How toxic are the toxins? Can we raise the money? Are the people tired of campaigns when we have not delivered on what we have asked for in the past nor have we adequately informed them on what has happened with each step? Who, what, when, where, why, how, how much, who do we tell, when do we tell it, how do we tell it? Do we announce it over the pulpit? Do we call a church meeting? Do we send a mail-out? Suppose people have questions that the mailer will not answer? Do we text it? Grandma does not text but she tithes. She has to know also. The leaders are requesting information. We have to do something. Then the unexpected happens. A leader approaches with a question from a member whose name is "They". *They want to know why... Brother "They" is asking me... or Sister "They" wants to know who gives authority for this and why is the board selected like that?* I will assure you that it is very difficult to walk by faith when the answers to our questions become more important than the command from the King. Faith does not cease to ask questions. Faith asks questions that will lead to the advancement of the church, the empowerment of the servants and the spread of the gospel of Jesus Christ! But even when we are faithless, God still answers prayer. In January of 2008, I posted a list of goals on my bathroom wall.

1. Train thirty new leaders
2. Grow the Sunday School to 250 students attending weekly
3. Receive 1.7 million dollars income in tithes and offerings

4. Purchase land for 'The Fountain'

I had to write the vision and make it plain (Habakkuk 2:2)! And then… a piece of property surfaced seven miles from the place we were renting. It was 22 acres, had a 16,000 square foot building on it, was three miles from the Florida Turnpike and faced the highly traveled US 27 highway. It was further south into Miami, Dade County but it was perhaps doable. The asking price was five million dollars, still not a bad price considering the times. It was 2008 and was the peak of the real estate market in South Florida. During that time, 1,200 square foot starter homes were selling for $200,000. Needless to say, we did the smart thing and did our due diligence on the property. Low and behold, the environmental report revealed that there were excessive levels of arsenic on the land. Holy Smoly! The sellers demanded another test and it produced the same results. At any rate it would cost at least one million dollars to remove the arsenic! We were ten months and hundreds of thousands of dollars down the road with a very hard decision to make. We decided to back out and not purchase. It was now January 2009. The 2008 financial goal was reached. We were seeing more than 250 students in the Sunday School classes and over fifty new leaders were trained that year, but as for the land, we fell short again. I looked at my goals yet again on the bathroom wall and prayed, *"Lord if you will give me an opportunity to acquire property this year, I will seize it."*

A TWO-SIDED BLESSING

This was the beginning of the most eye-opening journey with God. A realtor called me with a 31,000 square foot building in Miami Gardens, Florida. We were already renting property in a suburban community. Miami Gardens is an urban community. I was very reluctant but I agreed to see it. I took the board with me and we walked the premises. We measured the distance from western Broward to North Dade. We measured the emotional climate of our people. We were concerned about the *feelings* of the congregation. Without batting an eye, the board chair said, *"Pastor many of our people will reject a Dade County option. We came from Dade County and many are opposed to returning under any circumstances. But you will have to do what God says because this is God's business."*

After several months of negotiating, we knew we had to convey something to the congregation. Since the property was owned by another local congregation, we tried to be sensitive to the congregational issues on both sides of the table. We did not have a contract but the negotiations were getting serious. The asking price was 4.3 million dollars. There were no zoning issues to address. The seating capacity was adequate, but parking was limited. The drive for some would be very short and for others very long. The time came for us to share the opportunity with the members of the church. When I announced the location of the property, it was like we had announced the death of everyone's grandmother simultaneously! It was a cold silence in the sanctuary. You could feel it in the air and see it on many faces. This same reaction occurred at both services. We had a guest minister visiting us that day who also felt the cold reaction to the announcement. I was very much aware of the risks but I was also convinced that it was not the will of God that we continue to rent property. The deal began to deteriorate when we discovered that the property was in foreclosure. We decided to walk away until a counter offer came to us that lowered the asking price to 2.6 million. Additionally, I broached the idea of the unification of the two congregations. *Lord if you give me an opportunity, I will take it.* Me and my prayer life!

What was God doing? Were we trying to force an issue or was *He* doing only what *He* can do, namely the impossible. A local church was selling the property. Their people were hurting over the death of their shepherd, a well-respected Bishop. As a result of his death, their congregation had dwindled from many to few. Morale was low. People were angry, confused, disappointed and those who remained were also pondering whether to find spiritual sustenance elsewhere. On the other side of the county line was *The Fountain of Pembroke Pines*. Simply put, there were dozens of failed attempts to purchase property. There had been at least five fundraising efforts with no results. There was the unpalatable Dade County option for several longstanding members of the church. There was the complexity of the deal and the difficulty explaining it in understandable terms combined with the changes that were occurring on a daily bases. Then there was a lease that had grown from 24 thousand to 35 thousand dollars per month in 2009. The lease was the death angel. I felt that God was pushing us to walk out on faith! At that astronomical amount, we could not afford to renew a lease for another three to five years; and the church that had recently lost their Bishop could not afford to lose their building to foreclosure. Here we had two local churches in difficult situations that could help each other if they could find the mettle to work together. It would be very difficult, but it was a kingdom move rather than a church move. We decided to seize the opportunity this time! We would become one congregation with two campuses.

OUT OF THE COMFORT ZONE

Unbeknownst to us, this decision created a Kingdom mess! The comfort we had all known evaporated instantly. The expenses were greater than the income and the opposition was louder than the affirmations. The uncertainty was greater than the expertise as none of us had ever experienced anything like this before. The Miami congregation had to submit to new leadership, a new style, and a new influx of people on their campus. They wanted to grow but did not imagine a change in the building, new paint, new pictures, new staff, a different order of worship, new rules and the Pembroke Pines congregation wanted property but not necessarily in Miami-Dade County. Many did not like the smaller parking lot, the longer drive, a loud air conditioner in the sanctuary or a sound system that needed an upgrade. Difficulties notwithstanding, some people began to work together in spite of the challenges. They decided to adopt an attitude that God is greater than all of our problems and fears. They resolved to follow a shepherd into the unknown; so the rebuilding process began.

We were twelve months into the process and all seemed to have settled down when... there was a knock on the door as I was leading a staff meeting. *"A courier is here to deliver foreclosure papers,"* a wide-eyed but clear vocalist shared. The unimaginable had happened! The bank that held the mortgage had executed a forbearance clause in the mortgage contract that allowed them to foreclose on the property if we failed to find financing in twelve months. At this point we decided to do one thing: press forward in spite of what it looked like. For twelve months, we sought financing only to receive rejection letter after rejection letter. However, on Friday, March 18th, 2011, a reporter from the *Florida Business Journal* caught wind of the foreclosure and called me for an interview. We chatted and by late afternoon the article was on the World Wide Web. By Saturday evening it had gone viral amongst the members from the Pines congregation. I had not disclosed the forbearance clause because I was confident that we would have secured the financing before the twelve months expired. Well, it did not happen and God apparently had other plans. He wanted to pull the curtains, close the blinds, turn out the lights and let the sun set over our situation. Talk about an emotional rollercoaster ride! We were in a place where we had taken extreme risks. We had invested large amounts of money; we had cast a vision of hope and we were staring at despair - but God was still in control. He wanted to challenge us to believe, to trust Him and to walk in the dark trusting that He would lead the way. It was hard considering what it looked like in the natural, but what else could we do other than trust Him? The Psalmist says with confidence that even the darkness is light to Him.

THE ANSWERED PRAYER

Forward we went. Some did not come along for the ride. Sadly, some left the church. Some stayed but stopped financially supporting the church. Some stopped supporting the church emotionally. Some thought I had betrayed their trust, mis-communicated information, failed to communicate information and poorly communicated information. Others thought I was a blatant liar. Then there were others who had trust in me as their leader and chose to wait and see. Some made appointments with me to gain clarification. Some sent cards that said "press forward". Others just prayed and believed that God was in control. When asked publicly about my plans if we did not get the financing, my response was, *I do not know how God is going to do it, but I believe that He will do it. I have no other plan. I have no other options. That is it.* On April 24, 2011, I proudly announced to the congregation that we had received financing from a local bank. That would settle all of the foreclosure issues. True to their word, the bank closed the loan on June 17, 2011. For many it was a day of rejoicing. For some it was just another day. For me, it was many lessons learned. Faith does not guarantee results, it demonstrates conviction. Loan or no loan, I still believe.

It is impossible to walk with God and always know what the final destination will be. If we always knew what the end would be, then we would not need faith. I share this story with you because I want you to understand that God has called you to something that is beyond your individual abilities. He has called you to the edge of the cliff and He is telling you to jump with the security of knowing that he will bring his purposes to pass. The Apostle Paul said to the church at Rome, "If God is for us, who can be against us?" Make no mistake about it, it is God who answers your prayers - in His timing. That will not happen if you choose to have all of the answers rather than trust Him to guide you to the destination that He has chosen. There are many who may be fatigued by the *perseverance* that faith sometimes requires. Faith can produce very heavy burdens. The attacks can become vicious and the accusations vociferous and venomous. Family members will dismiss you as fanatical. Friends will delete your name from their address books and unfriend you on their Facebook accounts. You may be penalized for doing the very best that you can for the cause of the Kingdom of God. But in spite of all of this, I encourage you to fight the good fight of faith. (2 Timothy 4:7) Even if your hope remains unfulfilled and your prayers unanswered, continue to believe and trust God. Why would I advise this? I say this because I am confident that God is not simply trying to answer prayers in times of distress. God uses the faith walk to build a deeper relationship with us. God is not in the land business. God is in the relationship business. He used every step of the journey to draw me closer to Him. Believe me, this is better than an answer to any prayer. If He did it for me, He will do the same for you! So when it is your turn and God pulls the curtains shut, closes the blinds, turns out the lights and lets the sun set over our situation, press forward. Beyond the darkness and despair is the God of Abraham, Isaac, Jacob, Mary and Jesus of Nazareth; who walked the rugged road of faith but reaped an even richer reward. Press Forward!

ABOUT THE AUTHOR

Pastor Dwayne Richardson was born and raised in Miami, Florida and is a product of the Miami-Dade County Public School System. He graduated from Miami Northwestern Senior High School in 1989 and matriculated to the University of Central Florida in Orlando, Florida where he majored in Criminology with a minor in Religion. He is a graduate of The Union Institute where he received his Bachelors of Arts Degree in Liberal Studies. He is currently pursuing his Masters of Science degree in Administration and Supervision from Nova Southeastern University.

Rev. Richardson was licensed to preach in August of 1992 and ordained in august of 1993 at New Mt. Moriah under the leadership of Rev. Richard P. Dunn II . In 1994 Rev. Richardson joined the New Hope Baptist church under the leadership of Bishop Randall E. Holts, where he served as youth Pastor.

In 1998, Rev. Richardson founded Greater Love Missionary Baptist Church which was later changed to Greater Love Full Gospel Baptist Church. In a span of thirteen years under Rev. Richardson's leadership, the church has experienced tremendous growth and has established a viable Primary Learning center, Summer Camp, and a Before and After Care Program.

Rev. Richardson Whole heartedly believes that the Best is yet to come! He also believes that with God and through Faith, all things are possible. Rev. Richardson has two handsome boys Daniel Rashad,10 and Daylan Ahmad, 7.

Greater Love Full Gospel Baptist Church
18200 NW 22nd Avenue
Miami Gardens, FL 33056
Rev. Dwayne Richardson, Senior Pastor

Chapter 4

The Cost of the Anointing
Written by Pastor Dwayne Richardson

"Before I shaped you in the womb, I knew all about you. Before you saw the light of day, I had holy plans for you. A prophet to the nations that's what I had in mind for you."
(Jeremiah 1:5)

Before Jeremiah was born, God had already determined that he would be a prophet. Just as God had a plan for Jeremiah, God has a plan for you and He had a plan for me. My Christian journey began at an early age at New Covenant Presbyterian Church. When I was just a baby in my mother's arms, the late Dr. Irvin Elligan placed his hand on my head and said: *"This baby is going to preach."* That prophetic word was spoken over me over 38 years ago. The destiny began unfolding when I was about ten years old as I began going to church with my father, who attended a Baptist church. Since I had been exposed to the Presbyterian Church, the Baptist experience was new for me. It was vastly different from the Presbyterian Church in many ways. Generally, when people go to any church, they enjoy the choir and the various programs that churches have, but my favorite part of the service in the Baptist church at such a young age was the sermons that were preached. I so enjoyed hearing that good ole' Baptist preacher sing and then preach the Word with fire! The more I would visit, my desire to return back the next Sunday grew stronger. Then, one Sunday morning at the age of sixteen, I found myself walking down the aisle of the church excepting Christ as my personal savior. At that moment, I knew that I had developed a love for the Lord and a hunger for more of Him. I felt in my spirit that He was calling me to greater service in His kingdom. For the next two years, I became very active in church. I even found myself attending revival services during the week. No doubt, God was moving in my life, but trying to walk the Christian walk was not easy at such a young age. I was a teenager, a high school athlete, and ironically, I was dating the pastor's daughter. Upon graduating from high school, I received a four year football scholarship to the University of Central Florida. Like so many others, my dream was to play professional football and I figured that I was on the right track to getting there. The desire to continue learning about the Lord was still in me, so upon entering my freshman year, I immediately began seeking a local church to attend on Sundays. However, none of my peers seemed to have that same agenda. Friends my age were just excited to be away from home at college and their agendas were to party, find girls and get as much as they could out of the college life. Nobody was thinking about any church, nobody except me.

One day while walking to class through the campus courtyard, I saw a group of people on a platform stage who were singing gospel songs. The school was hosting a symposium that day displaying all of the different organizations offered at the school. I inquired about the group singing and it happened to be the school's gospel choir. Needless to say, I joined the choir and it turned out to be a great blessing for me. It afforded me the opportunity to connect with other people who were on fire for the Lord and a chance to fellowship at other churches in the city. During this time, I also connected with one of the fraternities on campus, Phi Beta Sigma. This organization was truly about brotherhood and service and being a part of it was an enhancement to my life. I formed a bond with other young men of whom I am still connected with to this very day. As I look back, I can see how God knew that the desire in my heart was to continue receiving the Word and to grow stronger in Him. He navigated the circumstances for me to connect with individuals who would help me to grow in Him because they loved Him the same way I did. *...that we henceforth be no more children, tossed to and fro, and carried about with every wind of doctrine, by the sleight of men, and cunning craftiness, whereby they lie in wait to deceive; But speaking the truth in love, may grow up into him in all things, which is the head, even Christ* (Ephesians 4:14-15).

However, as the time went by, I found myself being pulled in two different directions. One foot was in the world while my heart wanted to please God. The pressures of being a college athlete, the constant parties, my knack for getting on the DJ's mic and hyping up the party and just getting caught up in the pleasures of the world seemed to overwhelm my desire and obligation to grow in Christ and follow His commandments; yet, I was still in the gospel choir and felt His closeness and love every time I sang a worship song to Him. We were singing often at different churches, which gave me a chance to hear the Word and listen to some good preaching. God was definitely moving in my life. In spite of what I was doing, I knew and felt that there was a heavy anointing upon me.

The day came when my life took a drastic turn. It was August 1991, a hot summer morning as I was walking to the field for football practice. Out of nowhere a voice spoke to me and said, *"This is it. Your football career is over."* I immediately walked to the coach's office and asked to speak with him. As I began to talk to him thanking him for the opportunity that he and the University had given me, I began to tear up and explain that I would no longer be playing football. He and other coaches tried to convince me to take a few days off to think about my decision then come back. However, I explained to him that my desire and love for the game was gone. I knew that God had a greater calling on my life and it did not involve football. My decision to give up football and pursue what God was calling me to do came with a price. Needless to say, it cost me my scholarship, an opportunity to fulfill my dream of playing professional football, and ultimately, the social life that I had been enjoying. This period in my life was very difficult and challenging. I was going through a personal transition and inner struggle that no one understood - not even me. Unfortunately, at the same time, my parents were going through a divorce, so all of these things happening at once had me frustrated, discouraged, and confused. As a twenty year-old college student away from home, this seemed too much to bear. As the Christmas break was drawing near I was preparing to return home.

When I returned home to Miami I connected with one of my cousins who had just been called to pastor his first church. I shared with him where I was spiritually and mentally. He immediately took me under his tutelage and began to mentor and guide me into the direction that God was leading me. As months went by and I began to grow spiritually, I finally answered my call into the ministry. On August 9, 1992 I preached my first sermon, 'Life's Turning Point.' I knew that I was finally walking into my destiny to preach. It felt right. As time progressed, I had become the Youth Minister at my cousin's church. As a twenty-one year old young minister, it was not an easy journey. As the apostle Paul says in Romans 7:21: *"When I would do good, evil is always present."* The challenges that I had began to face were new and sometimes very strong. I had never experienced such temptation on the level that it had begun to come. The more I preached and the more the Lord would use me, it seemed as though the enemy came at me stronger. He was coming in all shapes, forms, sizes and circumstances and from all angles. For instance, women (particularly older ones) would literally place their phone numbers in my hands after service. There was even a time that I was invited to a home to perform a house dedication, but found out through prior conversation that there were no other guests invited. It was a trick of the enemy. As time went by and

I continued to grow in wisdom and faith, the Lord allowed me to see that the enemy was trying to destroy my anointing.

In 1993, I met a young lady who I fell in love with. She was humble, graceful and truly loved the Lord - much different from the other women whose paths I had crossed. However, she and I attended different churches, but I knew that something was going to have to change because we needed to worship together. Surprisingly, I ended up joining her church. Her Pastor graciously welcomed me and shortly thereafter, I became a part of his ministerial staff. As I started working in ministry and demonstrated my faithfulness, I became the Youth Pastor there. It was a wonderful opportunity for growth, experience, and exposure. Additionally, I graciously accepted the opportunity to preach at least once a month on youth Sundays and I also began preaching at other churches throughout the city. About a year and a half later, she and I got married. Marriage was great. Ministry was great and God was using me to bless many lives. I was finally in a place of peace of knowing that I was where God would have me to be at that time. At that time of my life, I had gotten through the storms of uncertainty, the sadness of my parents divorcing and the temptations of the enemy to destroy me. About three years after marriage, a wonderful leadership opportunity came up for me. After discussing ways to expand the ministry with my pastor, he shared his vision of having one church in two locations. He presented the opportunity for me to oversee the outreach location and expressed that he had been watching me and felt that I was mature enough, gifted, anointed, and ready to handle the task. I humbly and gladly accepted the task and in a few months went to work. The leadership support that was supplied by my pastor was a tremendous help to me and much needed. The ministry began to grow fast. New souls were coming to Christ and connecting with the church and Sunday after Sunday the church was full. The level of growth surpassed my expectation.

As with all things, there were some challenges. The goal of the outreach campus was to bring "new" souls to Christ, but too many members from the home church began worshipping at the outreach campus during the same time as service at the home church. Some even expressed a desire to remain at the outreach location for their own personal reasons. I knew eventually that this would pose a problem because the intended purpose of this ministry was not to swap members from one location to another. *What do I do?* was the question that played in my head. *How do I stop people from worshiping where they are comfortable?* I began to feel a struggle in my spirit. I couldn't grasp what was happening, but the ministry was being blessed. The worship experience was awesome, lives were being changed, but something still was not right. My spirit was not at ease. Eventually I began to feel a separation from the vision of the house. So as I prayed and God revealed some things to me in from the spirit. The things revealed to me confirmed that my assignment there was over and it was time for me to operate in a different manner and walk in a higher calling. Out of ultimate respect for my pastor and the church, I humbly resigned. In time, God allowed me to organize my own church: 'Greater Love Missionary Baptist Church'. We started out with 25 faithful souls. However, there were 75 souls who came to our first worship service. After service, more people walked down the aisle and united with the church. I literally saw God moving powerfully that day. As weeks and months passed, more souls were connecting to the church. Both the unsaved and the already saved were coming. In about a year's time, we had a consistent 400 worshipers. God's hand of approval was upon us and my heart was full of gratitude and thanksgiving. It was amazing to watch the growth and development of the church. At the time, I was only 27 years old, but the foundation and support I had was strong. My wife was the praise and worship leader, my mother and brother-in-law managed the finances and I had a very strong, experienced and dedicated group of deacons. The church was young and vibrant and after two years, the Lord opened a door for the church to purchase a location. The ministry grew so much that we started a second service. The ministry had really taken off and great things were being done for the enhancement of the kingdom. We were also doing various community outreach initiatives which compelled the community to the church as well.

People were excited about the ministry that was making a positive impact in their lives. Needless to say, there were still challenges and obstacles that we had to face as a church. Some of these obstacles included unfaithful members, non-tithing members, gossipers in the church, jealousy and envy and those who were always complaining about the pastor - just to name a few. The devil was not going to let us do all of this ministry without raising his ugly head. Peter reminds us that, *"Our adversary the devil, walks about as a roaring lion, seeking whom he may devour"* (1peter 5:8). One thing you must keep in the back of your mind is that the devil is real and he never ceases being busy. For this reason, we must stay busy as well and always try and stay one step ahead of him through prayer. Nevertheless, God was still blessing our church in a tremendous way. Seven years had gone by and we were strong in operation, in ministry, and also in numbers with over 1,000 members including 22 deacons, 22 deaconess over 60 choir members, over 35 ushers and over 100 youth. I have always kept in mind however that it was not about numbers, but to see God use me as His chosen vessel to be a blessing in the lives of people. What He had done for me was amazing. I would often ask God *why me?* I know there were many others that He could have used, but I have learned that what God has for you is for you! I enjoyed pastoring God's people. Although I had my share of church challenges, I was not faced with the same challenges that some of my colleagues were dealing with and for that, I was grateful.

Although God had moved mightily in our ministry; had blessed me abundantly and allowed His anointing to flow from me, I still felt lonely and incomplete. Although I had a beautiful wife, two delightful sons, and a beautiful home, there was something missing. We drove luxury cars, traveled at will, had season tickets to all of the local athletic events and life was great, but emotionally I was struggling. I was confused and numb at the same time until I came to grips with the fact that I was not happy at home. My wife and I never argued, finances were not an issue, and we attended many social events together. From the human eye, we looked like the ideal couple, but something had changed in me. I prayed. We prayed. We went to counseling, but the numb feeling and nonchalant attitude that I had became stronger and would not go away. At this point and in all fairness to my wife and to myself, I felt a need to make some decisions. Again, I went to God in prayer, knowing that prayer changes things or prayer changes us to handle different things. After fervent prayer and a peace from God, I decided to separate and file for divorce. I knew that this would not sit well with many of our church congregants. This was one of my biggest fears. I knew that my decision would cost me a lot. Yes, the church lost some members in the interim which resulted in a temporary setback. I personally experienced financial hardship, people formulated their own opinions relating to the reason for the divorce and this created gossip and unsubstantiated lies. However, knowing the adverse impact it would have, I was still willing to suffer all for the sake of my peace and happiness. I knew God had not brought me this far to leave me. As I look back, I can see how I became so engrossed in the things of the church, the people in the church and the external possessions that came with the power of the position. I allowed the enemy to come in and speak to my mind, causing me to lose the most important things to me, next to my salvation. Charity begins in the home, but in my home I had failed to communicate early on the feelings that I had begun to experience. I hid my feelings behind material possessions and used them as a sense of comfort. I also poured my assistance into helping with issues of church members, and put my own feelings on the backburner until it was too late.

I am now a young, divorced pastor dealing with a whole new set of temptations as a single man. When we resist the devil, he does flee, but when he comes back, he comes with a whole new set of temptations and we must recognize him. The devil never stops and he won't stop until he has ultimately destroyed everything you have. So I encourage you to trust God with everything and He won't let you down. Be vigilant and watchful because the enemy desires to *sift you as wheat And the Lord said, Simon, Simon, behold, Satan hath desired to have you, that he may sift you as wheat* (Luke 22:31).

As time progressed and the dust was settled, those who were meant to be a part of our church family were still there. God was still God! However it felt like starting all over again, which was not a bad thing. New members who were joining brought a breath of fresh air to the church. During this same time, God gave me the vision to start a pre-school and to expand the aftercare services we were offering. The anointing was still flowing and God was still blessing. I learned that subtraction does not mean failure, but sometimes that is God's way to bring real success. So as I close this chapter, I say to you guard your anointing, and know that it comes with a cost. As the apostle Paul says, *"If God be for you, who or what can be against you"* (Romans 8:31). Always remember this verse because it is real and it is true: *I can do all things through Christ who strengthens me* (Philippians 4:13).

ABOUT THE AUTHOR

Pastor Gaston E. Smith is the Senior Pastor/Teacher of the Friendship Missionary Baptist Church of Miami, Florida, where they are "Moving Mightily to Fulfill the Master's Mission." He is married to Kimberly Smith and is the proud father of Antoinette, Jasmine, and Gaston Everett II.

Pastor Smith is a proud native of Houston (fifth ward), Texas. He was educated in the North Forest Independent School District, where he graduated from M.B. Smiley Senior High School. He furthered his educational quest as a Political Science major at the University of Houston, and a student of Evangelism and Pastoral Studies at Houston Bible Institute and Moody Bible Institute of Chicago. He was awarded a Fellowship to Oxford University in London, England for the summers of 2006, 2007 and 2008 to further his biblical studies. An honorary Doctorate of Divinity degree was bestowed upon him in 2008 by Smith Chapel Bible University.

In 1990, Rev. Smith accepted his calling to the Gospel Ministry. He currently serves as the Executive Vice Moderator and Bible Expositor for The Seaboard Baptist Association of Florida and as President for The Baptist Minister's Council of Greater Miami and Vicinity. Additionally, he has delivered the invocation for the State House of Representatives and the Congressional Black Caucus. Pastor Smith has been honored with commendations, proclamations and certificates of appreciation from various civic organizations, such as Congress of the United States, State of Florida, City of Miami, Miami-Dade County, Congressional Black Caucus and Bethune Cookman College but one of his most memorable moments was attending the inauguration of the 44th President of the United States of America, President Barack H. Obama. Pastor Smith has appeared on national and international television broadcasts, such as CNN Headline News and MSNBC and has appeared in national publications, such as the New York Times, the Miami Herald and the Washington Post. Pastor Smith has had a weekly television and radio broadcast that reached Miami-Dade, Broward, Palm Beach and Monroe Counties in Florida as well as the Bahamas.

Chapter 5

No Test, No Testimony!
Written by Pastor Gaston E. Smith

That the trial of your faith, being much more precious than of gold that perishes, though it be tried with fire, might be found unto praise and honor and glory at the appearing of Jesus Christ:
(1 Peter 1:7-8)

It was nearly twenty-five years ago that my then Pastor and father in the gospel ministry, the Reverend Harvey Clemons Jr., Senior Pastor of the Pleasant Hill Baptist Church of Houston, Texas said to me *"Gaston, the gospel is not fully realized, nor is the preaching of the gospel effective until it transitions from the theoretical to the experiential."* As a young zealous warrior, I did not quite comprehend the value or the validity of that statement at the time, but now, a quarter of a century later, I can attest to the living proof and power of that profound yet prophetic statement, *"The gospel must move from theory to experience."*

Many biblical perspectives have prepared me for life's ups and downs. In fact, the bible is pregnant with warnings and witnesses regarding trials, tribulations, temptations and tests that every believer must endure and embrace on the this earthly pilgrimage. King David declares in Psalm 34:19 *"Many are the afflictions of the righteous; But the Lord delivers him out of them all."* The Apostle Paul says it this way in Romans 8:37, *"Yet in all these things we are more than conquerors through Him who loved us."* I have known these and other passages for nearly three decades, but nothing in print (theory) has been able to compare to what I learned through life's experiences. As a young boy I heard over and over again that *"more is caught than taught"* and I can truly say that experience is no doubt the best teacher. I had to discover that for every "testing" there's a "blessing". In fact, God uses tests not to destroy, but to develop His people. Show me an under tested believer and I will show you an under developed believer. While the enemy is set out to destroy us, God is always developing us. In fact, God takes delight in flipping the script of the enemy. Genesis 50:20 says *"But as for you, ye thought evil against me; but God meant it unto good, to bring to pass, as it is this day, to save much people alive."* There is no doubt in my mind that God always takes you *through* something in order to get you *to* something. Oftentimes we encounter discouragement, disruption, drama, disaster, even death in route to our ultimate deliverance and destiny.

My story is an awesome and living example of the presence, power, and promise of God! I was born in a Christian home with a devout mother and a semi-believing father, James and Dorothy Smith. I did not have the option or luxury of skipping church or Sunday school. Mother Smith was NOT having that! I learned all the tenants of the traditional Baptist church; baptized at the age of six; immediately became an usher and served until becoming president of the usher board as a young adult; served in many capacities, i.e. Director of Transportation, Media Ministry, Trustee, Deacon, and all before professing my calling to the Gospel Preaching Ministry in 1990.

Although I had extensive experience in church as a youth, unfortunately the church was not always in me. I have come to realize that it really doesn't matter how many times you've gone through the Bible, the question is how many times has the Bible gone through you? I have had many tests in life starting from early childhood, but the majority of my most excruciating tests started after my calling into the Gospel Ministry. It did not take me long in ministry to see that I would always be tested on what I preached and even more specific, tested on "what I believe'. My painful pilgrimage of preaching began twenty-one years ago. Of course, many see the precious glory of preaching, but few realize the painful story of preaching. Preaching is an intriguing combination of bitter and sweet, and the awesome task of Pastoring bares an even greater balance of blessings and burdens. I would love to say that it has been all "Seasons of Success", but I have also had my "Seasons of Sorrow". Ministry is co-mingled with highs and lows, ups and downs, and joy and pain. I still concur with the late, great Rev. Paul Jones who penned a song that I have been quoting and singing for over twenty years *"I've had some good days, and I've had some hills to climb, I've had some weary days, and some sleepless nights; but when I look around and I think things over, all of my good days outweighed my bad days, but I won't complain!"* Sometimes when the clouds hang low and I can hardly see the road, I ask the question, "Lord, why so much pain?" But He knows what's best for me, although my weary eyes, they cannot see, I'll just say Thank You Lord! I WON'T COMPLAIN!

    I believe that the Apostle James said it best in James 1:2-4, *"My brethren, count it all joy when you fall into various trials; knowing that the testing of your faith produces patience; but let patience have her perfect work, that you may be perfect and complete, lacking nothing."* This passage says to me in short, first comes pain, then comes patience, but it is all working towards perfection. Even in our state of deep imperfection, God is always trying to navigate us closer to Him. For the believer, it is not what we go through, but rather *how* we go through what we go through. There are at least four things that I have discovered in my journey about the "Test of Life."

1. Tests are Personal
2. Tests are Periodic
3. Tests are Purposeful
4. Tests are Painful

What I like about the apostle James is that while he may not be as meticulous as Luke, as radical as Peter, nor as prolific as Paul, but James is real, raw, and relevant. In this first chapter of James, he gives a moving message on pain management. Let's take an examination of James 1:2:

My Purpose Is Greater Than My Pain

James 1:2

One really does not learn the value of life until they come into the revelation of how valuable their own life is. The value of life is not measured by wealth or health, position or possession, status or stature, but rather by how well we glory in tribulation; how changed we are by our life's changes when we face challenges.

Since early childhood I can remember being taught the Word of God and having to go to church, but not just go to church, I had to be active in service - as in becoming a servant. For many years, I learned about God through explanation, however it was not until I began to face my own adversity, that I came to know Him through experience. It is one thing to *hear* about God, His wonders, His Son Jesus, Jesus' miraculous power, His resurrection and His return. But it is something totally different to be a recipient of God's grace and mercy, and then to be favored with an increasing faith that allows you to participate in your own life-changing miracle! That is what James admonishes every believer to do; not only to *hear* the truth which is the Word of God that we believe by faith, but rather put it into action. James teaches us that living faith is what makes the difference between just living and living by faith. Our faith is more than just a statement, but it should result in action. God allows us opportunities to put our faith to work by sometimes allowing a trials, tribulations and temptations. When I am faced with what seems like a plethora of problems, I must be mindful that my purpose is far greater than my pain. As a mature believer, I have learned and I am still learning that pain comes for few reasons:

1. to keep me grounded; it makes me pray harder and more consistently;
2. to develop my growth; it makes me patient
3. to depend on His grace; it minimizes my pride and
4. to deliver unto Him glory; it maximizes my praise!

In order for me to stay grounded, my pain forces me to pray. In other words, I really do not have a choice in the matter. Sometimes life's situations will blindside you and will bring you to your knees. Things may catch us by "surprise" but nothing ever catches God by surprise. James is very clear in letting us know not *if*, but *when* trouble comes, how we are to respond. Our trials are never by chance; they are either ordained or orchestrated by God. Nevertheless, it is possible to profit from them. What do I or we profit or gain from our pain? Glad you asked. When we face trouble with the right perspective, which is an attitude of gratitude, it means that God sees something in us to trust us with trouble. This should bring about genuine joy. The point is not to pretend to be happy or "fake it 'til we make it", but despite the pain, we make a conscious choice to have a positive outlook and do our best to remain optimistic through it all. The joy of the Lord becomes your strength and your burdens become lighter. You may not be able to change anything about your situation, but you can have an optimistic attitude about it regardless of what it looks like. You may be going through pure hell, but you do not have to look like what you are going through.

In order to remain optimistic or joyful about my grief, I turn to the Word of God which I believe by faith will see me through it all. When I take God at His Word and trust Him to deliver on His promises, I am encouraged because I know the outcome. The outcome for me and every other believer is victory. So I, or we, do not have to crumble in the face of troubles when they come. As you grow in the knowledge, wisdom and grace of our Lord, you will learn to joyfully embrace troubles knowing that your prayers will prevail. My prayers prevail when they are effective and effectual. My prayers are effective and effectual when I pray the will of God over my trials, troubles, tribulations, and hardships. Since I know that God has a purpose for my life, I know there has to be divine purpose for my pain. God has a divine plan for your life too and the only way that He can get you to the victorious destiny that awaits you, is to take you through the pain of living in this earthly realm. You must endure the trying of your faith, trust in God, stand on the Word, and persevere. God will never leave you nor forsake you. He will deliver you out of all your troubles in His time.

    I no longer believe in the old adage that says we are to never question God. Growing in maturity has taught me that I can question God. Whether or not I get an answer is a different story. When I do question God, it is not out of lack of faith or disbelief, but more out of my wanting and needing guidance and wisdom, to know what I need to do now for this particular storm. What course of action do I take …am I to go on a fast? If so what kind of fast? Is this something You have given me the power to overcome on my own Lord? Wisdom has also taught me that there are some things that God will empower us to do ourselves. What prayer or which prayers should I be praying over this? In case you didn't know, there are different elements or types of prayers. There are prayers of intercession (on behalf of others); supplication/petition (making our request made known unto God); warfare (when we recognize the attack of the enemy) and general (when we pray for everyone and everything). I do this so I do not pray or ask amiss. When my pain becomes debilitating, my prayers becomes deliberate! Staying grounded is natural because I am dependent upon God to show Himself strong on my behalf. I am kept grounded by prayer, but secondly, my growth is developed by patience and perseverance. I successfully overcome adversities when I allow God to grow me up by proving my character. Character skills are those little nuggets or lessons for life we learned as children, such as:

> ***Integrity***: We learned this as honesty
> ***Compassion***: We learned this as caring for others
> ***Accountability***: We learned this as responsibility
> ***Perseverance***: We learned this as patience.

These are seeds that were planted and should have caused us to blossom or flourish into purpose-driven and productive individuals. When we have gotten off course or our character became tainted or tilted for one reason or another, trouble was a sure way to get us back on track. We do not really know the depth of our own personal character until we see how we react to adversity, that is, until we are under pressure - like a tea bag in boiling hot water. It is God's desire to perfect and mature us and make us complete. He wants us to be "more Godly". He wants us to be wise enough to understand that we are to use our painful experiences as opportunities for growth. We are strengthened and our faith is fortified when we trust God with our whole heart for an expected outcome. In the believers case, it is the victorious ending that is promised to us. *Eye hath not seen, nor ear heard, neither has entered into the heart of man, the things which God hath prepared for them that love him. But God hath revealed them unto us by his Spirit* (1st Corinthians 2:9-10). Since God is the only one who can do it, we have to wait it out or P.U.S.H. - **P**ersevere **U**ntil **S**omething **H**appens. We wait patiently on the Lord to bring us through to an *expected end* because we know without a doubt that He is right beside us strengthening us by either helping us solve the problems or helping us to endure the problem. No matter what, the Lord is there helping us grow in grace by producing patience within us.

As I wait it out, my resolve is that I am coming out of this better than I was before. I give God permission to perform a work in me as I surrender my will to His. Therefore, whatever He chooses to purge out of me, I accept so that I may be complete in Him. At the end of the day, one thing I do not wish, and that is to repeat a trial by wrestling with God. When God orchestrates or allows problems in our life, if we do not take the time to learn the lesson, we are doomed to repeat it. The best thing for us to do is persevere and allow patience to have its perfect work in us. My pain keeps me grounded, develops my growth and causes me to depend on God's grace by minimizing my pride. Where I have been, the Lord has brought me, where I am now, He is sustaining me, and where I am going, He is taking me. I am absolutely nothing and can do absolutely nothing without the grace of God in my life. It is in Him that I live, move, and have my being.

It is when you face adversity that you realize even more that you are a miracle because of the grace of God. Not only are you a miracle but it is a miracle that things are not worse because it could be. We have not dotted every "i" and crossed every "t". God could have allowed our worst nightmare to come true. For this reason, we must be careful with pride. Pride not only comes before destruction, but the enemy uses our pride to literally sift God's glory. Pride hinders our giving God total credit for all the great things He has done and continues to do for us. Pride is deceitful and will have us thinking that we could have done it on our own; that all we have accomplished was due to our own intellect, experience, or connections. If it were not for death, disaster, divorce, disease, disappointment, or devastation, we may still be blinded by our pride. When we are faced with the feelings of no-way-out, sometimes this is the only way God can get us to acknowledge His Kingship and Lordship over our lives. Regardless to what we have foolishly led others to believe, God is definitely the source of our existence. I can never afford to become puffed up and risk the enemy devouring me and causing me to not be triumphant over my trials.

Lastly, not only does the purpose of your pain keep you grounded, develops your growth and causes you to depend on God, but it also causes you to render unto the Lord glory by maximizing your praise. Praise is what I do sincerely when I am going through and through and then through some more. I know that God does inhabit the praises of His people, because there have been so many times when all I had was a sacrifice of praise and I offered it unto the Lord. He not only turned the situation around for my good, but He did it right in the presence of my enemies! The pressure of my pain prompts me to praise the Lord. The power of my praise increases my joy, lifts my burdens, gives God glory and at the same time confuses the enemy. Satan expects me to walk around with my head hung down, depressed, devastated and in despair. Yes, the fact of the matter is that I am experiencing pain, but I can never allow gloom to overshadow God's glory. God has been too good to me and His perpetual blessings are too awesome for me not to offer up praise. My praise is not predicated on what's going on or what's happening around me because then that would mean I only glorify God if and when something happens. God is worthy of glory, honor and praise simply because He is God! Paul says in I Thessalonians 5:18 *"In everything give thanks; for this is the will of God in Christ Jesus for you"*.

I have been tested beyond measure in a myriad of areas from one extreme to the other, but I can truly say that though my tests have been great, my testimony is far greater! I now know that the anointing of the Almighty is greater than the attack of the adversary.

ABOUT THE AUTHOR

Bishop Isaiah Musgrove is the husband of one wife, Lady Stacey-Ann Musgrove, the son of, Bishop Dr. Artglee Musgrove and Apostle Dr. Almada Musgrove, founders of Jesus Christ Is Lord Miracle Deliverance Center.

Ordained as a Minister and Youth Pastor in January of 2000, his ministry was instrumental in reaching the youth of the church, some of whom are ministers and leaders in the kingdom today. Another important duty served by Bishop Musgrove, was as the praise and worship leader. Through his talents of singing and songwriting, the JCIL Praise Team became second to none in the city.

In 2004, Isaiah was elevated to the office of an elder, after achieving valedictorian status, when he graduated from ministers training. After serving faithfully as an Elder, Youth Pastor, and Praise and Worship Leader for six and a half years, Isaiah was elevated to the office of Senior Pastor and General Overseer of Jesus Christ Is Lord Miracle Deliverance Center, in August of 2006.

As Senior Pastor and Teacher, Pastor Isaiah Musgrove became a scholar of the Word of God with the desire to bring the heart of God to His people through the word.

In March of 2008, Isaiah Musgrove was consecrated as Presiding Bishop, in which capacity he serves to this day.

If anything would be said of this man of God, let it be known that Bishop Isaiah Musgrove preaches and teaches the truth, in season and out of season, without compromise.

Jesus Christ is Lord Miracle Deliverance Center
6306 Pembroke Road
Miramar, FL 33023
bishopisaiah@realworld.com
Bishop Isaiah Musgrove, Senior Pastor

Chapter 6

Answering The Call

Written by Bishop Isaiah Musgrove

Walk in the Spirit, and ye shall not fulfill the lust of the flesh. For the flesh lusts against the Spirit, and the Spirit against the flesh: and these are contrary the one to the other: so that ye cannot do the things that ye would.
(Galatians 5:16-17)

Allow me to ask you a few questions: Have you been resisting the call of Almighty God on your life? Have you been making excuses of delay and procrastination? How many times has God given you warnings, only to fall on seemingly deaf ears and your stubborn will to do your own thing? How long have you been allowing the enemy to deceive you and rob you of the rewards that God has in store for those who willingly and obediently serve Him? How many times have you cheated death, but still refuse to surrender to His will? How long will God's voice be ignored and His call on your life goes unanswered? What have you gained from trying to function on the outside of God's perfect will, plan and purpose for your life? If you know that you have been called by God and have not yet surrendered, then this chapter is for you.

Answering the call of God on my life was not easy, but it was the greatest, most important and rewarding decision I have ever made. The experiences, the struggles and the trials I encountered on the journey that brought me to where I am today, has taught me lessons that can never be unlearned. God took me from the pit of contempt as I struggled in resistance from Him, to a place in Him that I vow never to allow the enemy to move me from. I have discovered true deliverance by the spirit of the Lord that is upon me and have made it my mission to *...preach the gospel to the poor, heal the brokenhearted, preach deliverance to the captives, recovering of sight to the blind and to set at liberty them that are bruised* (Luke 4:8). This is my story!

"Go mommy, go!" I shouted with excitement from the back of my father's 1980 Chevrolet pickup truck, encouraging my mom to pass us as we drove along the single lane airport road. It was a Saturday afternoon during our summer vacation from school on the island of South Caicos in the Turks and Caicos Islands. We were returning home from a family cookout at the beach. I stood up cheering as my mom's Cadillac passed us, without even a thought of what was about to happen. Just as she passed us and attempted to pull in front of us, off of the shrubbery on the side of the road, my mom's car aimed across the single lane road right in front of my dad's truck, which my brother-in-law was driving. A screech and a big bang is what I heard as my brother-in-law who was driving, uselessly applied the brake before the truck smashed into the driver's door of my mother's Cadillac where she was behind the wheel.

Just as my brother-in-law swerved to the left to avoid the accident, I fell over the side of the truck. It could only have been the hand of Almighty God on my life that allowed me to grab hold of the side of the truck instead of hitting the paved road surface below. Hanging from the side, my knees dragged on the ground as I watched the spinning tires, under which I thought I was about to fall and be crushed. Those few seconds felt like an eternity as the truck came to a screeching stop. Letting go of the rail, I fell onto the road. The pain in my knees drew my attention to the scrapes and bruises I had sustained.

Being helped up by my family, I was led across the road to the house, in front of where my mom's car had stopped, just a few inches shy of hitting a huge rock in the front yard. Thanks to God, apart from my parents having both of their vehicles involved in the same accident with some shattered glass, minor cuts and bruises, none of us suffered any major injuries.

A MESSAGE FROM THE LORD

We made it home that evening shortly before my father did. He worked long days as a fisherman. Dad was happy that we were okay, but I do not think he wanted to tell us how he really felt about both my mom's car and his truck being crashed. Later in the evening, Elva, a fourteen year-old a young lady who was staying with us while she attended high school, came to me with a prophetic Word from God. *"This is a warning from God."* she said. She told me that God had a call on my life and that I was wasting my young years running from Him, but that the near death experience was meant to be a wakeup call. I knew immediately that it was a true Word from the Lord as I began to feel His presence surrounding me. However, I still did not surrender.

I was disgusted with myself to know that I was born and raised in a Christian home and even at the age of fifteen, I still did not know Jesus as my Lord and Savior. From the time I was old enough to understand, just about every adult who knew me would call me the little prophet that was born out of the favor of God and would someday preach the gospel of Jesus Christ. My grandmother Louise would never let me forget it. She constantly reminded me that there was a great calling on my life. My mother, who was a minister at the Church of God of Prophecy, was well known in the community as a street evangelist who won many souls to Christ. But I, my mother's own child, did not know the Lord.

THE PROMISED CHILD

Several weeks later, I was walking down the hall from my bedroom and met my mom in the dining room. She told me that she needed to talk to me and that I should have a seat. I pulled out a chair and sat down while she leaned over the chair in front of her and began to speak to me. *"You are my promised child."* She said, as tears filled her eyes and she pulled the chair out from the table in front of her and sat down. *"I've waited all this time to tell you to be sure that you would understand the call that is on your life."* Then she began to tell me the story of my birth and started revealing things to me that I had never heard before. She told me that before I was born, she had given birth to six babies and had two miscarriages, all of which were girls. Living in the Bahamas at the time, she preached throughout the islands, winning souls and casting out demons, but still her petition to God for a son went unanswered. *"One night"* she said; *"When your sister Sherry, was about three months old, the Lord spoke to me and told me that if I would go to the island of Inagua and preach the gospel, He would give me not only one, but two sons."* Hearing those words brought tears to my eyes. As I learned her story, I knew that all I had heard before about the call of God on my life, was real and not just the wishes and desires of others. As she continued to talk, I learned further that my brother and I were given names that very night, even before our conceptions, which were written in a Bible awaiting our births: Moses Isaiah and Daniel Elisha Musgrove.

Recanting these events in my life reminds me of Hannah, the mother of the Prophet Samuel in the book of 1 Samuel chapter one. Hannah petitioned God to open her barren womb and bless her with a son. At an early age, Samuel was given back to God. God called and anointed him to be a prophet to the nation. Honestly, I was not looking to be a prophet, pastor, preacher, or anything that had to do with church because I had seen and heard from an early age, the many persecutions my mom went through as a preacher and prophetess and I did not want to endure those things. That was not something I wanted for my life. At fifteen years of age, I already had plans to become an English professor or a certified public accountant. I did not mind being a Christian, but I didn't want to have to do that preaching stuff.

As I continued to listen to my mom speak to me, she took me to an emotional place that I had never known. The weight of the responsibility seemed almost unbearable, and somehow I knew that they were more than just words, but it was God urging me to accept His call on my life. The story went back to the Friday evening of June 27, 1969. *"It was just before midnight"*, my mom said, *"I was out on a street corner praying for people."* During this time, she was in her ninth month of pregnancy with her ninth child, the son that God had promised to her, the child whose name was written in a Bible, awaiting his arrival. Mom continued to tell me that in the middle of praying for someone, God told her to go to the hospital. In obedience, she left the street meeting and headed for the hospital experiencing no pain. Arriving at the Rand Memorial Hospital in Freeport, the nurses who saw her every year when she came to give birth to another child, thought it would be another lingering situation as was her previous pregnancies. However with no pain, as she laid on the bed in the posture of delivery, a bright light entered the room and flashed from one end to the other. And, as if someone had pressed on to her abdomen, the baby came out and was caught by a nurse who was entering the room at the time. *"That baby was you!"* she said, *"My promised child!"*

NOT ENOUGH

Sadly, as moved and emotionally touched as I was, it was not enough to move me to surrender to God. It just was not something I wanted for my life. Well, at least I thought it was my life and I could do with it what I wanted. Writing this, I am reminded of the talk Jesus had with His disciples in John 15:16; *Ye have not chosen me, but I have chosen you and ordained you, that ye should go and bring froth fruit and that your fruit should remain, that whatsoever ye shall ask of the Father in my name, He may give it you.* Unfortunately, I did not get the understanding that God had chosen me. I did not get it that even before the beginning of time, God had a plan for my life. My mind at that time could not comprehend that God had seen me worthy of the favor of being separated from among many to carry out His will in the earth. What was so special about me that God wanted to use me to fulfill His purpose?

READY TO SURRENDER

After cheating death in the accident, getting a warning from God, and learning the miracle of my birth, there was an awakening in my spirit. For the first time in my life, my spiritual consciousness came alive with a desire to be satisfied. I soon learned that there was a youth revival going on at the Baptist church in the middle of town and I knew I had to be there. I remember sitting on the right side in about the fourth or fifth row. I remember the minister who was an invited guest minister from the Bahamas saying that she could not read when she became a Christian, but the Holy Ghost taught her. That was simply amazing to me. By the time she had ended the sermon, I was ready to surrender my life to God and I did it that very evening.

There were many of us who made the decision to follow Christ that evening, but in just a few short months, most had backslidden, including me. Somehow it seemed too difficult to stay saved. The temptations were too strong and I didn't even want to resist them. So like a coward, I gave up on God and walked away from Him, returning to my old ways. I had become a backslider, one of those I heard my mother preach to, time and time again saying; *"Repent and return to God before it's too late."* But I was determined to live my life the way I wanted to, rejecting God's call and doing my own thing. Someone must have been praying, because soon after that, I returned back to God, but my spirit was still not satisfied. There was yet the matter of answering the call.

Thinking back on the time I walked away from God, I cannot even imagine what could have been if it were not for God's mercy and grace that continued to shelter, protect and keep me, even in my sin. I just cannot help but give my God praise, thanksgiving, honor and glory for what He has done for me. David said in Psalm 107:1 *O give thanks unto the LORD, for He is good: for His mercy endureth for ever. 2: Let the redeemed of the LORD say so, whom He hath redeemed from the hand of the enemy;*

STRUGGLING IN THE FAITH

After graduating from high school, I migrated to the United States to be with the rest of my family who were residing in Miami, Florida. I became a covenant member of the body of Christ when I joined the Miami Church of God of Prophecy. For the next seven years, even though I struggled hard behind the scenes to keep my faith alive and to not fall into sin again, I wasn't always successful and as a result, I felt like a hypocrite. I was teaching Sunday school and I was also one of the lead singers in the youth choir. However, I felt as though God had abandoned me because I grew tired of praying and begging and pleading with Him and still ended up in sin. I had not yet learned changing power of not just reading, but studying the Word of God for myself. It's like being sick and going to the doctor, but refusing to take the prescribed medication, then blaming the doctor when you don't get well.

THE ANSWER TO ALL

The Word of God is *the* antidote to every ailment we will ever experience in our lives, but unless we apply it, we will not get well and we cannot blame God because of it. He has given us His Word, but it is up to us to use it. In John 17:17-19, it is written: *Sanctify them by your truth. Your Word is truth. As you sent me into the world, I also have sent them into the world. And for their sakes I sanctify myself, that they also may be sanctified by the truth.* I was not yet sanctified and the old nature of Adam, which represents the core of sin and the temptation to commit it, still had root in me. I needed a daily encounter with the Word of God, which I spent almost no time studying. We should never expect to be changed if we refuse to do what it takes to be changed. It is only the power of the Word of God that can change us. Without the Word rooted and grounded in us, it can only mean that something else is rooted and grounded in us. The Word will keep us from fulfilling the sinful desires the enemy brings on us. David said in Psalm 119:11 *Thy word have I hid in mine heart, that I might not sin against thee.* David knew that the antidote to sin was the Word. I wish I knew then, what I know now. *For the word of God is quick, and powerful, and sharper than any two-edged sword, piercing even to the dividing asunder of soul and spirit, and of the joints and marrow, and is a discerner of the thoughts and intents of the heart.* (Hebrews 4:12-13)

After struggling with the darkness of my flesh for so long, I allowed the enemy to deceive me into thinking that God didn't care. And once again, when I was twenty four years old, I left the church and walked away from God. This time I found myself doing things which I swore I would never do. Apart from the fornication, I found myself drinking and smoking cigarettes as well. I hated beer and smoking, but I thought I would fit in better if I did what everyone else was doing. At this point, answering the call of God on my life was only a distant thought. I had gone against everything I was raised to believe and was angry at God for allowing it. For the next four years, I spent as many nights in the clubs around Miami as I could afford to go to. Unfortunately, those four years were the worst four years of my life. Within those four years, I felt as though I had lost my family. I had alienated myself from my mom, dad, sisters and brother because I was too embarrassed by the life I was living. I lost my apartment and found myself moving from place to place, sleeping on couches and floors.

My car was crashed then repossessed because I had lost more than 33% of my income and could not afford to keep it. My perfect credit rating had plummeted and everything around me had fallen apart. God was not playing games with me anymore.

One night, I left a night club drunk after drinking three beers which I didn't even enjoy. While driving home, I fell asleep at the wheel on I-95. God woke me up just in time to steer me away from me hitting the guard rail of an overpass more than 100 feet high. For the rest of the drive, He kept me awake. I knew then that God was keeping me alive because of the *call* upon my life. At this point, I really wanted to change and submit to God, but I could hear the voice of the enemy telling me that I couldn't do it this time. He tried to tell me that I would never be delivered and set free. He tried to make me believe that I would only be just another hypocrite with a double life - in church on Sundays and in the world on Monday through Saturday. The tone of his compelling whispers caused me to doubt that God would ever come through for me.

We must understand that the negative and ungodly thoughts we experience on a daily basis are well orchestrated plans by the enemy to control our thought life. The enemy knows that if he can control our thoughts, then he can control our destiny. Every effort must be taken on a daily basis to ensure that we guard our minds from the constant stream of attacks the enemy is unleashing against us. The entire sum of his mission is to kill, steal and destroy. He wants to kill your passion for life and for living for Christ. He wants steal our identity and leave us confused as to who we are, living outside of God's favor because of our disobedience to answer the call. And he wants to destroy our character and make us feel like we have gone too far and done too much wrong for God to forgive and save us. Philippians 2:5 gives us a command when it says: *Let this mind be in you, which was also in Christ Jesus.* The mind of Christ can only be developed through the Word of God. It is the only weapon that can effectively combat the forces of evil in our minds. One thing I have learned is this: A thought entertained is a deed committed. We cannot allow evil thoughts to linger in our minds. We must *...cast down imaginations and every high thing that exalts itself against the knowledge of God and bring into captivity every thought to the obedience of Christ (2nd Corinthians 10:5)*. We must learn to use the Word as our defense against every contrary thought the enemy brings to our minds. Looking back at this period in my life, I can clearly see the truth that the devil is a liar and the truth is not in him. The Word says in John 8:44: *Ye are of your father the devil, and the lusts of your father ye will do. He was a murderer from the beginning, and abode not in the truth, because there is no truth in him. When he speaketh a lie, he speaketh of his own: for he is a liar, and the father of it.*

If I could advise anyone who is in the position I was in during my season of contempt against God, I would say: Do not allow the enemy to deceive you. Give no space to the devil. Disallow him from interfering with your destiny in God. Reject the cunning devices he is using to frustrate you and hinder you from walking in God's call on your life. Satan wants to rob you of ever experiencing the revelation of Ephesians 3:20, which tells us that *God is able to do exceeding, abundantly, above all that we ask or think, according to the power that worketh in us*. The enemy knows that if he can get you to doubt the Word, he will succeed in preventing God's power from taking root in you. It is the working power of God in your life that he's afraid of. Don't believe his lies. Denounce every word he has spoken to keep you separated from God. Don't let the enemy kill your desire to please God with your life. Delay no longer in answering the call on your life. Agape!

ABOUT THE AUTHOR

Pastor Jimmie Brown, Ph.D has served as a United Methodist Pastor for over 37 years, retiring in July 2011. He is married to Michelle Brown. During his tenure as Shepherd over God's sheep, Rev. Brown led the congregations of Saint Paul UMC, Mount Sinai UMC, Kerr Memorial UMC, Ebenezer UMC, and Harris Chapel UMC.

Reverend. Brown is a veteran of the U.S. Air Force (1962 - 1969). He received the Bronze Star and the Air Force Commendation Medal for his service during the Vietnam War. He is a retired Division Chief of Miami-Dade Police Department with over 30 years experience in Law Enforcement. During his tenure, Reverend Brown rose through the ranks of Police Officer to that of Division Chief. Upon his retirement in 1999, he was Chief of the Special Investigation Division. He has hosted the ever-popular talk show "HOT TALK' on WHQT-FM Hot 105 for over 21 years. He is currently an adjunct professor at Barry University. He is also the President/CEO of JLB Consulting, Inc. Reverend Brown is a frequent motivational speaker and workshop facilitator at schools, banquets, and correctional institutions.

He holds a Doctor of Divinity Degree from International Seminary, a Doctor of Philosophy Degree in Public Administration from Pacific Weston University, a Master of Science Degree in Human Resource Management from St Thomas University, a Master of Science Degree in Management from Colorado Technical University, a Bachelors of Science Degree in Public Administration from St. Thomas University, and an Associate of Science Degree in Police Science and Criminology from Miami-Dade College.

Reverend Brown is a member of Phi Beta Sigma Fraternity, The Society for Human Resource Management (SRHM), The American Legion, The American Civil Liberties Union, The American Association of Christian Counselors, American Society for Industrial Security (ASIS), Kiwanis Club of Oakland Park, and a life member of the NAACP. He has received over 300 awards from civic, professional and fraternal organizations and was inducted into the Miami-Dade College Hall of Fame in 2006.

Chapter 7

Walking in the Calling
Written by Pastor Jimmie Brown

And we know that all things work together for good to them that love God, to them who are the called according to his purpose.
(Romans 8:28)

It is amazing how we can look back over our lives and clearly see the hand of God in every situation we have encountered. God sits on the throne and will forever be with us - especially when we ask for His guidance and His leading. He never leaves nor does He forsake us. As His servant, I have served as a pastor over 37 years and I am blessed for the journey of winning souls for Christ as the Shepherd that He called me to be.

My journey as a veteran pastor has allowed me to see, experience, and learn from many things. This walk has enabled me to preach over 3,000 Sunday sermons, eulogize over 400 funerals, officiate over 300 weddings, perform over 500 baptisms, and win over 1,000 new souls into a relationship with Jesus Christ as their personal Lord and Savior. As the songwriter says, *"I never would have made it without you (God)."* I am grateful for the journey that I have travelled, the road that I have walked, the lessons I have learned and even the disappointments and frustrations through this journey of pastoralship. Thirty-seven years of ministering the gospel of Jesus Christ led me to the date of June 19, 2011, which is the date that I preached my last sermon as a pastor. This was the culmination of a journey that entailed many ups and downs, trials and triumphs, victories and defeats, as well as some failures.

My life began its journey as a young adult in my late twenties. The beginning of the journey would lead me into a calling to save souls for Christ. It all began on June 16, 1974 when at the tender age of twenty-eight, I was appointed as the new pastor of St. Paul United Methodist Church in Deerfield Beach, FL. Needless-to-say, there were many questions in my mind and of course there was some trepidation. Would I be able to meet the expectations of my new congregation? Would I be able to take on this monumental task of leading the people of God with effectiveness? Would my schedule as a law enforcement officer interfere with my pastoral duties? These questions flooded my mind, but when there is an appointing, there is an anointing and with God's appointing comes His provision. He always makes a way. On June 17, 1974, the next day after being appointed as pastor, I was promoted to Sergeant within the Miami-Dade Police Department. This was a major accomplishment for me at that time. As mentioned, the promotion came one day after my first appointment as a United Methodist pastor, so it seems that God was opening up the windows of heaven and showering me with His blessings and favor. Throughout the duration of my time with Miami-Dade Police, I served as pastor of churches in Deerfield Beach, Hallandale, and Perrine. For twenty-five years, I simultaneously served the Miami-Dade Police Department and served as a pastor for a congregation in the United Methodist Church. Many could not understand how I could be both a Law Enforcement Officer and also the pastor of a church all at the same time. And so there were some who did not take my pastoral position seriously. They simply could not find logic in how God could His children for His purpose, anytime, anywhere, and in any capacity. *The natural man receives not the things of the spirit of God, for they are foolishness to him, neither can he know them because they are spiritually discerned.* (1st Corinthians 2:14). *With man this is impossible, but with God all things are possible!* (Mathew 19:26)

During my first appointment as pastor, I grew tremendously in leadership abilities, in intellectual capabilities, and most importantly in my spirituality, particularly my relationship and walk with the Lord. Reflecting upon my learning experiences and leadership preparation, I can look back now and see the value of my four years of study at Emory University's Candler School of Theology. This learning exposure had a significant impact upon my Christian foundation. Taking courses such as Systematic Theology, New Testament studies, Old Testament studies and Pastoral Counseling, laid the foundation for my pastoral ministry. These courses were deeply meaningful and enhanced my knowledge of theology and Christianity. They helped to equip me to become an effective spiritual leader to my congregation. *Study to show thyself approved unto God, a workman that needeth not to be ashamed, rightly dividing the word of truth.* (2nd Timothy 2:15). There are many who feel a pulling in their spirit to minister to the people of God. The calling that God has upon your life is real. However, once you accept your calling to preach the Word as God's Shepherd, there is a preparation time. You do not accept you calling today and preach tomorrow. It does not and should not work that way. Premature leadership can lead to a devastating and humiliating downfall. You must sit and learn after accepting the calling. You must study the Word to *show yourself approved.* Take classes and sit under the leadership and tutelage of those with spiritual knowledge and allow them to impart that knowledge into you. This way, when the time comes for you to stand before the people of God, you are ready. If you do this, then your sermons will be a miracle and not a mockery!

Notwithstanding my spiritual preparation and studies, as a rookie pastor it was not easy. There were bumps and hurdles as well as obstacles and oppositions. However, God was always there and several factors helped me to overcome such challenges. I began to truly appreciate the fact that prayer and my study of the Bible made a difference in my personal growth, change, and leadership. Being mentored and encouraged by my spiritual father in the ministry, the late Rev. E J. Sheppard, Sr., provided me with the encouragement, advice, support, and counsel I needed to continue walking the Pastor's walk. His mentorship and guidance was priceless for me. Everyone needs a spiritual father or spiritual mother in the ministry. Having been nurtured in Rev. E J. Sheppard, Sr.'s ministry at Kerr Memorial United Methodist Church as I wrestled with my calling, provided me with focus, clarity, and a readiness to accept the call that God had upon my life. Being under the tutelage of this great man was a great blessing for me. That foundation prepared me for my first appointment as pastor at St. Paul United Methodist Church.

LESSONS

One of the first shocking, yet real lessons I learned is that everyone who comes to church is not necessarily coming to worship the Lord. Respectfully, some come out of pure habit that has been imbedded in them since childhood. Going to church on Sunday morning is routine for them and sadly, many who have been going to church for ten, twenty, and even thirty years are still babes in Christ. From childhood, the habit was formed and unfortunately, that's all it is - a habit. As such, some do very little for the work of the ministry or building up the kingdom in terms of growing and saving souls. Frankly, many of them cause problems instead of helping to edify the body of Christ. In like manner, some come to church just to see what the latest fashions are. Some come to see whose hand the pastor is going to shake the longest; and quite honestly, some come only because they have miserable or boring jobs where they are not recognized, so they come to church, assume a leadership position, and then feel validated and important.

Through my many years of observation, learning, and acquiring wisdom, I have also learned that the 80/20 rule not only applies in private and public sectors but it applies in the church as well. That is to say that 20% of a church members take up 80% of the pastor's time. From experience, I discovered that 20% of the membership supports the ministry financially, prayerfully, and by way of being positive. But in many instances, the other 80% still believe that one dollar is a good offering, but that their opinions are worth a million dollars. My ministry at Saint Paul helped me to grow, understand and benefit from the power of prayer while seeing and experiencing these eye-opening things. As a pastor, I could not have made it through some of those difficult times without it. Through my discovery was the realization that no ministry or personal life can reach its full potential without prayer and study time in the Word of God. *In the beginning was the Word and the Word was with God and the Word was God.* (John 1:1) Therefore, every time we spend time in the Word, we are spending time with God! These spiritual sacrifices provide the foundation for developing loving, peaceful, and harmonious relationships with the congregation. There were many experiences at Saint Paul that proved to me that prayer, coupled with faith is a powerful combination! One simply cannot have one without the other. There are many incidents where this biblical principal has demonstrated to work, but one in particular clearly stands out in mind. One day as I was arriving to the church after the usual one and a half hour drive from Richmond Heights, one of the older saints ran up to my car, crying out, *"Rev Brown come quickly. The girl is possessed by a demon!"* I quickly proceeded to the dwelling next door to the church where the girl was. Demon possession was something I certainly had not been exposed to nor was I properly trained to handle. There on the screened-in porch sat a teenage girl whose eyes stared straight ahead, talking in a deep base voice that certainly was not the voice of the girl. The demon was speaking of a desire to kill her mother. I immediately began to pray. I had never experienced anything like that before. After several minutes of prayer, the young lady began to speak in her natural voice and had no recollection of the time she was "possessed".

Lesson learned: When you don't know what else to do pray!

There will be many times in life when we will encounter things we have never seen or heard of. Those are perfect opportunities to take it to the Lord in prayer and watch Him move in the situation. He has every answer to every problem and when we seek Him for the answers, he will reveal them. When dealing with things and people you do not understand, take them to the Lord in prayer. Prayer does change things!

When I arrived at Saint Paul United Methodist Church in Deerfield Beach, it was a framed structure with a 2x6 piece of lumber holding up the porch. I remember going to the bathroom in the small pastor's office and being able to see the ground through the cracks. Needless-to-say, the congregation was extremely desirous of a new sanctuary and I was in total agreement. Shortly after my arrival, the church leaders and I met. We chose an architect, drawings were constructed and a design for the new sanctuary was chosen. After the meeting, I drove back to Richmond Heights with a heart full of thanksgiving that we had been very productive in the meeting. We had voted on a design and were well on our way toward to the start of a new building. By the time I arrived home, a little more than an hour later, I started receiving calls telling me that the design was not what the members wanted. They wanted a church that "looked like a church".

Lesson learned: Sometimes the meeting after the official meeting can really change things!

In an effort to overcome our diverse opinions on how the new church building should look, we had a twenty-four hour prayer vigil. I believe this prayer vigil was the catalyst that made our new sanctuary possible; but the next roadblock was the fact that the bank was hesitant to loan us money (they said the reason was that they would not want to foreclose on a church). That was over thirty years ago, and I am told that banks still generally use that line as they deny churches the financing needed to build or improve existing structures. However, prayer and faith changed the banker's mind.

Lesson learned: It's not over until God says so!

Therefore, on April 28, 1978, we victoriously marched from the old decrepit sanctuary into a modern church that "looked like a church."

Lesson learned: Never underestimate the power of faith!
Confess your faults one to another, and pray one for another, that ye may be healed. The effectual fervent prayer of a righteous man availeth much. (James 5:16).

As everyone else, I have certainly been through some challenges, disappointments and struggles in my life, but the greatest tragedy I have ever gone through was the death of my daughter on October 21, 1974. At the time, I did not know how I could survive that tragedy. I could not see how my family would be able to move on; but I prayed, asking God to give me the strength to help my family and myself through that tragedy. I promised the Lord that if he helped us overcome that disastrous and disheartening time in our lives, I would never let anyone or anything defeat me. Yes, I've had many challenges over the years, both personally and professionally, but I have persevered. To God be the glory! *God is our refuge and strength, a very present help in trouble.* (Psalm 46:1)

When the Lord takes you through the valleys and shadows of death, we are to *fear no evil*. Another imbedded memory of mine is that of being awakened by a frantic call from a new mother who was in the hospital and had been told that her newborn male son would never walk on his own. Having worked the midnight shift at the police department, I immediately began to pray for both her and the baby. The last

Sunday I was at Saint Paul, the little boy who was "never supposed to walk" ran down the center of the church to give me a hug!

Lesson learned: The power of prayer is not limited by location. We can send the word of prayer and it will go to where it is sent and heal if you just believe! God is omniscient, omnipresent, and all powerful!

After being promoted to police lieutenant, one of my newly assigned sergeants, an Anglo male, shared with me that someone had told him that I would never reach a rank higher than that of a lieutenant. Interestingly, the person who made the comment retired as a police sergeant, but I retired as a Police Division Chief. It is not about what people say. Instead, it is about what God can and will do. He will prepare a table before you *in the presence of your enemies!* I spent twelve years at Saint Paul United Methodist Church and during that time, the congregation prospered with significant financial and membership growth. It was difficult for me to leave because I was torn. I prayed that the Lord would move me when it was time for me to move on because I never wanted to be a part of a divided congregation and the congregation had become divided. My prayer was always that the Lord's work would be blessed through me as He leads and guides me during my tenure. For thirty-seven years, He has never led me astray. *To every thing there is a season, and a time to every purpose under the heaven:* (Ecclesiastes 3). It was the season for my change.

The next pastoral appointment given to me from the Bishop was at Kerr Memorial United Methodist Church, located in Perrine, FL. This had been my home church, so I had a personal connection there. It is the church where I accepted Jesus Christ as my Lord and Savior, the church where I had attended Sunday School and worshiped every Sunday. Once again, questions flooded my mind. Could I go back and serve as the pastor of the church that I had grown up in? Would I be respected and appreciated by the older members who had watched me grow up (an perhaps misbehave)? Through prayer, faith, and a God of power, my questions were answered and I spent thirteen years as the Pastor of Kerr Memorial. The Lord's work was blessed and under my leadership, the church flourished - through God's leading of course. An after school program completely staffed by volunteers blessed the lives of many children in West Perrine - for free. The church also had a mentoring program for boys with the support of community leaders, church members, and the Dade Community Foundation. There were weekly bible studies and other community-based ministries operating at the church as well. Unfortunately, major damage to the sanctuary was done in the aftermath of Hurricane Andrew. That was the only time that I facilitated a church service in my police uniform. The Florida Conference of the United Methodist Church and the United Methodist Committee on relief (UMCOR) designated Kerr Memorial as a warehouse and distribution point for supplying food, clothing, and other essentials to the West Perrine community resulting from the hurricane. Hundreds of lives were blessed during this most difficult time. Also, during my tenure as pastor of Kerr, the church was blessed with membership and financial growth. Additionally, the seating capacity of the sanctuary was doubled. While Pastoring at Kerr, I also served as a consultant to the United States Justice Department's Office of Juvenile Justice and Delinquency Prevention (OJJDP). This position enabled me to teach and interact with police officers all over the country. I also served as the senior police consultant to with the Webster-Williams Commission in the aftermath of the Rodney King incident in Los Angeles. This commission was empowered by the Board of Police Commission to investigate and provide recommendations to prevent future incidents like that of Rodney King from happening in the future. Through God's favor, grace and mercy, I received three more promotions within the police department while at Kerr Memorial: Police Bureau Commander, Police Major, and Police Division Chief. Throughout the years, I have returned to Kerr Memorial to preach funerals and other church celebrations. It is always a great feeling to be able to go back home and do God's work while blessing the lives of others. My life has truly been blessed as a result of putting God first.

Lesson learned: Take care God's business and He will take care of yours!

My next appointment by the Bishop was Ebenezer United Methodist Church in Miami Florida. Ebenezer at that time was the largest predominately African American church in Florida, with a documented membership that exceeded 1,000 members. Once again, the questions flooded my mind. At this time, I should have known that God was going to work everything out as He always had, but still I questioned myself: Could I handle a church of this magnitude? I have learned that regardless of how big a challenge you face, with God's help you can make it. Ebenezer was a church deeply rooted in tradition. This certainly was a challenge for me because getting people focused on God rather than having them hold on to religion and tradition was a challenge. Many pastors face this. Many congregations forget or do not realize that being Christ-centered is the only way a church can be the church that God wants it to be. The previously described 80/20 rule was very pervasive at this church. Because of its huge physical structure, Ebenezer presented great challenges in managing the physical structure. The operating costs were enormous! Many church members could not seem to comprehend the fact that just like their homes and businesses, the church has maintenance expenses as well. Additionally, sometimes church members oftentimes do not see the benefit in partnering with other non-profits to build partnerships and reduce operating costs. Unfortunately, the governing board of Ebenezer voted not to extend a very lucrative contract with a Metro-Dade County entity (Metro-Dade Action Plan) and the Children's Home Society, which would have been extremely beneficial for us as a church. This was a great disappointment to me.

Lesson learned: Sometimes people will not see the long-term vision that a pastor sees. A pastor must steadfastly defend doing what he or she perceives is right in God's sight, even if they are not supported by church members.

One of the most impactful ministries that was implemented at Ebenezer was called 'Exodus'. This ministry was started to assist those who were trapped by addictions - particularly substance abuse. It grew into a partnership with other ministries including the Miami Rescue Mission, which eventually helped hundreds of people with addiction problems, domestic problems, immigration problems, and court problems. Share Florida Food Network, a community-based food co-op ministry was also started under my auspice. Partnering with organizations such as these made it possible for persons to purchase food at dramatically reduced prices. And the greatest part about it was that they did not have to be a member of the church in order to get help. A Family Night ministry was also started. Once a month food, fun, movies for all ages, and crafts for all ages were available for free on a Friday night. For me, this was another example of how church families can have as much fun as any other "secular" group. Periodically, we teamed up with healthcare providers and others to conduct health fairs for the church and community. In my opinion, healthcare should be a ministry for all churches, especially African American churches when taking into consideration the number of health issues faced by African Americans. Workshops were presented in many areas to enhance the lives of church and community members. Church leadership, parenting, motivational speakers (including presentations by noted motivational speaker, Les Brown), and other types of seminars and workshops were available to all, members and non-members.

The Lord is concerned about the whole person: mind, body and soul. God cares about *all* of our needs and can meet *all* of them. Whatever you need, God's got it! We also had days of celebration called "Fun Day". These days were filled with fun and food with prizes, games and activities for all ages. Similar to Kerr Memorial, during the six years of my tenure at Ebenezer, the church grew financially as well as in membership. Once again with God's help, I left the church better off than it was before I was appointed there. My next pastoral appointment was Harris Chapel United Methodist Church in Oakland Park, Florida. Based on past experiences and after careful study, I drafted a plan for ministry at Harris Chapel. The plan included a basic foundation of teaching and preaching the Word. A church that makes a difference must have prayer warriors and dedicated Bible students. In order to experience a truly changed life and a close relationship with Jesus Christ, prayer and comprehensive study of the Bible are the foundation. An ongoing after school program and affordable summer camp were an integral part of this ministry. A food and clothing bank blessed the lives of many people in the community who were not members of Harris Chapel. Goal Setting, Financial Planning, A couples ministry called 'Happily Married for a Lifetime' and a ministry for parents called 'Smart Discipline' were offered. Annual health Fairs and a Community Easter Egg Hunts were also part of our community events. The church attendance doubled and the ministry as a whole was blessed. The spirit of the Lord flowed in the services. This was my last appointment as a pastor. To God be the glory!

Time goes fast and if we are not doing something meaningful with our lives on a daily basis, the time will pass us by and we will find that we have done very little for the kingdom and very little for ourselves. We are all called to minister. Some do it from the pulpit and some do it in their everyday lives to varying degrees. We were not sent on this earth to enjoy life and contribute nothing to the kingdom. We were sent here with a predestinated assignment to fulfill the call and will of God on our lives. Everything else is extra. When you walk down the path that God has marked for you, you will find favor, wisdom, prosperity, and blessings on that path. Yes, there will also be some obstacles and detours along the way, even some frustrations and disappointments, but with God by your side, there is no need to fear. You will always come out triumphantly. *The Lord is my light and my salvation, whom shall I fear? The Lord is the strength of my life. of whom shall I be afraid?* (Psalm 27: 1-2)

LESSONS LEARNED FROM 37 YEARS OF PASTORAL MINSITRY:

- Everyone who comes to church is not necessarily coming to worship the Lord.

- The 80/20 Rule: 20% of a church's membership takes up 80% of the pastor's time.

- When you don't know what else to do pray!

- Sometimes the meeting after the official meeting can really change things!

- It's not over until God says so!

- Never underestimate the power of faith.

- The power of prayer is not limited by location. God is omniscient, omnipresent, and all powerful!
- Take care God's business and He will take care of yours!

- Sometimes people will not see the vision that a pastor sees.

A pastor must steadfastly defend doing what he or she perceives is right in God's sight, even if they are not supported by church members. *So shall the knowledge of wisdom be unto thy soul: when thou hast found it, then there shall be a reward, and thy expectation shall not be cut off (Proverbs 24:14).*

ABOUT THE AUTHOR

Pastor Kevin Williams, Ed.D is the husband of the First Lady, Denise P. Williams. At an early age, Pastor Williams received the Lord as his personal Savior, and by the age of 16, he began preaching the Gospel of Jesus Christ. He has worked in the Ministry in manifold capacities preaching the loving, but unadulterated Word of God.

In the year of our Lord 2000, Pastor Williams launched out to begin a weekly Bible Study in his home. After months of seeking the face of God, the vision was given and True Praise Family Worship Center, where he serves as Founder and Pastor, was birthed out of his Spirit. True Praise Family Worship Center is a Non-denominational Ministry with a Pentecostal flavor.

Pastor Williams received his undergraduate degrees from Florida Memorial College, where he finished Magnum Cum Laude with two degrees, an A.S. in Elementary Education and a B.S. in Elementary Education; Masters of Science in Urban Education/TESOL from Florida International University, and his Doctorate Degree in Educational Leadership from Nova Southeastern University.

Pastor Williams expresses a unique and powerful approach of preaching, especially to young adults. He has traveled both nationally and internationally to Saint Croix and the Turks and Caicos Islands. Through his Prophetic Ministry, the unique gift of Wisdom, and other Spiritual gifts, he has ministered to the needs of hurting men and women, utilizing the Word of God to dispatch blessings and deliverance.

True Praise Family Worship Center
1524 NE 147 Street
Miami, FL 33161
305-957-0031
Rev. Kevin Williams, Senior Pastor

Chapter 8

Thanks for the Push!
Written by Pastor Kevin Williams

I am Joseph your brother, whom ye sold into Egypt. Now therefore be not grieved, nor angry with yourselves, that ye sold me hither: for God did send me before you to preserve life.
(Genesis 45:4-6)

We all have at some point in our lives endured tragedy, trauma and pain, but the perspective from which we see these situations determines its hold on our ability to survive or perish. Perception is an awesome thing given to mankind. How we view things and respond accordingly has a lot to do with our successes and failures in life. We can all see a glass of water filled to the halfway mark. One would see the glass as half full and another would see that same glass as half empty. The strangest part about it however, is that both individuals would be correct. Yet, the one who sees it as half empty already has a negative outlook about it. He or she feels that something has been withheld from them and thus, will never be fully satisfied with that water. The other person sees this same glass of water as half full and fulfilling their thirst. This person feels blessed to have something that is almost full. In this person's mind, *"I am only halfway there!"* And so it is with problems in our lives, we can either grow from them or become forever stunted by them. I choose to grow. How about you?

Psalms 1:3:
And he shall be like a tree planted by the rivers of water, that bringeth forth his fruit in his season; his leaf also shall not wither; and whatsoever he doeth shall prosper.

This psalm shares with us that empowered to prosper is the man that remains focused. This individual must be like a tree planted by the rivers of water, that brings forth fruit in its season. This particular tree is planted, which indicates that it was placed there by the owner, creator or vinedresser and it rests upon a foundation. As believers, we must learn to blossom where we are planted. The tree has no choice in its supply source; neither does it have control of the conditions that may come where it is planted. Yet, it has the obligation to continue bringing forth fruit *in its season*. The operative term that is worth noting is "in its season." We want what we want right now, but nature teaches us that there is a seedtime and a harvest time. There is a season for planting and plowing, toiling and sweating. In the life of the Christian, this equates to fasting and praying, working and sacrificing. And then in "due season" the seeds planted shall bring forth fruit after their kind. Another operative term here is "after their kind." Worth noting here is the fact that we only get back the harvest from what we have planted during seedtime. You will not get back anything that you did not first plant. If you planted seeds of discord and confusion, then that is what you will get back. If you planted seeds of joy and peace in the lives of others, then that is what you will get back.

Galatians 6:7-8:
Be not deceived; God is not mocked: for whatsoever a man soweth, that shall he also reap. For he that soweth to his flesh shall of the flesh reap corruption; but he that soweth to the Spirit shall of the Spirit reap life everlasting.

Being from Miami, I am accustomed to seeing Palm Trees everywhere, even by river banks. Although we see the tree standing tall and powerfully poised, we do not know all that it has had to endure to stay rooted and in place. We are just awed by its beauty, but we must understand that this tree has deep roots grounded in the place where it has been planted. Though the water supply may be within feet or miles away, the roots of that tree continue to grow until they reach that supply no matter the conditions or circumstances that it has to go through. So must we as believers. We must continue to grow in the grace and knowledge of the Lord Jesus Christ, no matter the opposition or obstacles. We cannot choose the hand that is dealt to us in life, but we must learn to play with the cards we are given.

PUSHED INTO DESTINY

The story of Joseph is an awesome example of being pushed into destiny. Throughout his life, Joseph experienced seasons of loss and seasons of favor. When full revelation of his destiny was revealed, his family was blessed, and a nation was saved. Joseph finds himself going through a five step process that we all must also go through: Separation, Preparation, Anticipation, Manifestation, and Revelation.

SEPARATION

Joseph, whose name means "to increase" is the son of Jacob (Israel's love). His mother dies in child birth while having his youngest brother Benjamin whose name means the "son of my victory" or my right hand. As we examine the life of Joseph, many things become apparent to the reading. One thing that stands out is the fact that Joseph was a dreamer. Hopefully as a believer, and more importantly, a leader we are all dreaming of a greater day, and we should see ourselves in a greater light than our current circumstance.

Although Joseph is a dreamer, he has an issue that a lot of believers suffer from. Joseph talks too much! I recall

growing up as a child hearing this song with the following lyrics: *You talk too much, you worry me to death. You talk too much you never shut up. You talk too much you even worry yourself. You talk about people you don't even know. You talk about places you don't ever go. You just talk too much.* Joseph's immaturity with life causes him to tell his dream too soon to people who did not and could not understand the destiny that God had upon him, and as a result of his untamed mouth, warfare came upon him starting first with his own brothers. Just because people are in your family does not mean they will understand the anointing that is upon you. To be honest, your own family are usually the last ones to accept your calling, because they know almost all of your past sins, so they are less inclined to sometimes think that you are serious.
He came unto His own and His own received Him not (John 1:1).

Although Joseph's brothers were older, they lacked the discernment to see through the eyes of God. Often time in the kingdom we find this to be true. Many believers lack the discernment to see the Hand of God on individuals who God is anointing for purpose. Joseph tells his dream, which makes his brothers mad to the point that they could not (not would not, but could not) even speak peacefully of him or to him. In all that Joseph dreams he does not see the process he must endure for the promise. Isn't it amazing how God can show you the end result before you begin, but does not give you the details of what shall happen in the middle?

Genesis 37:20-24: *Come now therefore, and let us slay him, and cast him into some pit, and we will say, some evil beast hath devoured him: and we shall see what will become of his dreams. And Reuben heard it, and he delivered him out of their hands; and said, Let us not kill him. And Reuben said unto them, shed no blood, but cast him into this pit that is in the wilderness, and lay no hand upon him; that he might rid him out of their hands, to deliver him to his father again. And it* *came to pass, when Joseph was come unto his brethren, that they stripped Joseph out of his coat, his coat of many colors that was on him; And they took him, and cast him into a pit: and the pit was empty, there was no water in it.*

Joseph is thrown in a pit and sold. This was not part of his dream. People get jealous of people who are going somewhere, when they themselves are satisfied with less. People seem to be alright as long as you are dependent on them, but when you desire more, they seem to develop a problem with you. People who you thought would love you, will be the very ones to hurt you. The real desire of the enemy is to destroy you and your dream. John 10:10 puts it this way: *The thief cometh not but for to steal, to kill, and destroy.* The stripping of the coat was what they thought as the removing of the anointing, but you cannot kill what God wants alive. Many people may have conspired to destroy you, your reputation or your spirit, but you are still alive and kicking. How is that? Because God is the source of your strength; He is a very present help in trouble. Later in the text, we discover Joseph's brothers throw him in a pit. Notice the pit was dry which means there was nothing in it to sustain life. The enemy wants to get all of us to a dry place spiritually so that we may whither away and die, but I declare we shall not die, but live to proclaim the Word of the Lord. Joseph's eldest brother Rueben (whose name means misery) plots the pit, but the other brother Judah (whose name means praise) pulled him out. Note the chain of events and the lesson here: Misery may place you in a bad situation, but praise will always pull you out!

PREPARATION

Genesis 39:2-6: *And the LORD was with Joseph, and he was a prosperous man; and he was in the house of his master the Egyptian.³And his master saw that the LORD was with him, and that the LORD made all that he did to prosper in his hand. And Joseph found grace in his sight, and he served him: and he* *made him overseer over his house, and all that he had he put into his hand. And it came to pass from the time that he had made him overseer in his house, and over all that he had, that the LORD blessed the Egyptian's house for Joseph's sake; and the blessing of the LORD was upon all that he had in the house, and in the field. And he left all that he had in Joseph's hand; and he knew not ought he had, save the bread which he did eat. And Joseph was a goodly person, and well favored.*

Regardless of the obstacles that you must cross, it is all part of God's success plan for your life. Joseph had to realize that no matter what situation he found himself in, there was one common thread throughout: *"And the Lord was with Joseph"*. As long as the Lord is with us, we can handle the test. *Many are the afflictions of the righteous, but the Lord shall deliver us out of them all* (Psalms 34:17).

If God be for us, who can be against us (Romans 8:31)?

When the Lord is with you, success happens, even in unlikely places. God even blessed Joseph while he was in prison. He gave him favor with the guards and other inmates! Success is not what you are becoming, it is a product of who you are. Success is in you doing what God has called and anointed you to do, and go through. Many people never realize when they reach success because they are too busy measuring themselves according to the standards of man instead of the standard of the call of God that is on their life.

The bottom line is that success is really measured by how much *hell* you go through and still come out saying, *I trust God, and I will bless the Lord at all times. His his praise shall continually be in my mouth* (Psalm 34). Or you will be as my friend Job who, in spite of all the hell he went through, still proclaimed: *The Lord giveth and the Lord has taken away, blessed be the name of the Lord!* (Job 1:21) Many are called, but few are chosen. The word chosen in the Greek means "one who endures being tried." Joseph was walking in success before his dream ever came to pass. You must know friend, that whatever you may be going through right now, that is a part of your success process.

Genesis 39:7-9: *And it came to pass after these things, that his master's wife cast her eyes upon Joseph; and she said, lie with me. But he refused, and said unto his master's wife, Behold, my master wotteth not what is with me in the house, and he hath committed all that he hath to my hand; There is none greater in this house than I; neither hath he kept back any thing from me but thee, because thou art his wife: how then can I do this great wickedness, and sin against God?*

Joseph is set up by the enemy called flesh. No matter how anointed you are, there will come a time in your walk with God where you have to take or refuse to take. You have to make a choice. Choose ye this day, who you will serve - flesh or spirit? *Walk in the Spirit, and ye shall not fulfill the lust of the flesh. For the flesh lusteth against the Spirit, and the Spirit against the flesh: and these are contrary the one to the other: so that ye cannot do the things that ye would. But if ye be led of the Spirit, ye are not under the law* (Galatians 5:16-18).

You must maintain your integrity. Holiness must be maintained. Untested holiness is no holiness at all. It has to be tried to see if it is real. Oftentimes believers brag about all that they have stopped doing, not realizing that just because you have not done something in a while does not mean you are delivered from it. Sometimes you just lacked opportunity to get into the thing. True holiness is the lifestyle of God being lived out in you, not by you, but by God. We must learn in hard places of choices to maintain, abstain, reframe, and contain. Then we can call it the holiness of God. Joseph had such a relationship with God that he proclaimed, *"How can I do this thing and sin against God?"* No matter what friend, do not allow the pressures of the problem to cause you to compromise your walk with God. It is is more than people and their views about you. It is about pleasing God and doing His will.

ANTICIPATION

Genesis 39:*20:* *And Joseph's master took him, and put him into the prison, a place where the king's prisoners were bound: and he was there in the prison. But the LORD was with Joseph, and shewed him mercy, and gave him favour in the sight of the keeper of the prison. And the keeper of the prison committed to Joseph's hand all the prisoners that were in the prison; and whatsoever they did there, he was the doer of it.*

Joseph ends up in prison which of course was not a part of his dream. Following the dream, God will oftentimes place you in some obscure places; but the text encourages us that the Lord was with Joseph. Being locked in dark places develops your relationship with God. The best pictures are developed in a darkroom. Everyone cannot enter that dark room with you either - other those who have been approved to enter and they are very few. Dark places without light allows you to learn to hear the voice of God and sharpen the gifts that God has placed inside of you. Even in this strange place, Joseph receives favor. Know this friend, where you are right now may seem to be strange and different from what you are used to, but be confident in this very thing: that the favor of God is with you, and causes all you do in this season of obscurity to prosper. While in this place, you are commissioned to help others while you are going through yourself. These types of assignments do not come to stay, they come to pass, but you must allow God to shape, mold, refine and purge you while you are in this place.

Joseph gave a word to the chief butler and the baker. In your *going through* process (which was the prison for Joseph), you still have a word from the Lord for someone. Do not allow the prison to overshadow your gift and your assignment. David declared in the 23rd Psalm, *"Yea though I walk through the valley of the shadow of death, I will fear no evil for thou art with me."* I want to encourage you again believer to know that God is with you. He is Jehovah Shammah, which means: The Lord is There. God is a present help in times of trouble.

Genesis 40:23: *Yet did not the chief butler remember Joseph, but forgot him.*

Joseph had a word for the chief butler, but he forgot all about Joseph once he himself was released from prison. I am so glad that God remembers when others forget. Joseph had to stay in prison with anticipation that one day God is going to deliver him. I can imagine him thinking: *This was not part of my dream and it certainly doesn't end like this.* I know right now friend, it seems that it's been a long time, but the dream doesn't end like this.

Jeremiah 29:11: *For I know the thoughts that I think toward you, saith the LORD, thoughts of peace, and not of evil, to give you an expected end.*

God has your end in mind and it is going to be better than your beginning!

MANIFESTATION

Genesis 41:25-43: *And Joseph said unto Pharaoh, the dream of Pharaoh is one: God hath shewed Pharaoh what he is about to do. The seven good kine are seven years; and the seven good ears are seven years: the dream is one. And the seven thin and ill favoured kine that came up after them are seven years; and the seven empty ears blasted with the east wind shall be seven years of famine. This is the thing which I have spoken unto Pharaoh: What God is about to do he sheweth unto Pharaoh. Now therefore let Pharaoh look out a man discreet and wise, and set him over the land of Egypt. Let Pharaoh do this, and let him appoint officers over the land, and take up the fifth part of the land of Egypt in the seven plenteous years. And let them* *gather all the food of those good years that come, and lay up corn under the hand of Pharaoh, and let them keep food in the cities. And that food shall be for store to the land against the seven years of famine, which shall be in the land of Egypt; that the land perish not through the famine. And the thing was good in the eyes of Pharaoh, and in the eyes of all his servants. And Pharaoh said unto his servants, Can we find such a one as this is, a man in whom the Spirit of God is? And Pharaoh said unto Joseph, Forasmuch as God hath showed thee all this, there is none so discreet and wise as thou art: Thou shalt be over my house, and according unto thy word shall all my people be ruled: only in the throne will I be greater than thou. And Pharaoh said unto Joseph, See, I have set thee over all the land of Egypt. And Pharaoh took off his ring from his hand, and put it upon Joseph's hand, and arrayed him in vestures of fine linen, and put a gold chain about his neck; And he made him to ride in the second chariot which he had; and they cried before him, Bow the knee: and he made him ruler over all the land of Egypt.*

Your suffering gives you an answer for the world and teaches you who God really is. Anyone can serve the God of the mountain top, but only true believers can worship the God of the valley.

Psalms 119:71: *It is good for me that I have **been afflicted**; that I might learn thy statutes."*

Genesis 42:9: *And Joseph remembered the dreams which he dreamed of them.*

It is important that while you are going through the season of tests and trials, that you remain focused on what God has said. In this hour you must forget what you have been through and remember your dream. It is the remembering of the dream/promise that will help you make it through the dark nights. As long as God is with you, you can make it and you will make it. An entire nation is depending on your going through the fiery furnace to get them an answer and bring them out. Deliverance of others is in your hands. When we look at the state of our nation, we know people are looking for an answer. Friend, the answer is in your mouth. God has processed you through life's afflictions, so that you could have an answer for times like these. The answer is not in government or education. The answer is not in the mouth of a president or national leader. The answers are in the mouths of believers like you and I who have gone through the fire, but have not been burned, who have gone through the river and it has not overtaken us. This is a season where your gift is about to make room for you. I prophecy right now that you will stand before great men and proclaim Jesus is still the answer for the world. All your suffering has not been in vain. Though your beginning was small your ending shall be great!

REVELATION

Genesis 45:4-8: *And Joseph said unto his brethren, come near to me, I pray you. And they came near. And he said, I am Joseph your brother, whom ye sold into Egypt. Now therefore be not grieved, nor angry with yourselves, that ye sold me hither: for God did send me before you to preserve life. For these two years hath the famine been in the land: and yet there are five years, in the which there shall neither be earring nor harvest. And God sent me before you to preserve you a posterity in the earth, and to save your lives by a great deliverance. So now it was not you that sent me hither, but God: and he hath made me a father to Pharaoh, and lord of all his house, and a ruler throughout all the land of Egypt*

The revelation of the entire process is unveiled. Joseph realizes that, *"They sold me, but God sent me."* What an awesome understanding! As for them, they did it for evil, but God did this for their good that he might preserve them a posterity in the land. Joseph was their deliverance in advance. The dream has now become a reality. The greater revelation is when you have completed the process that God will give you a Manasseh, and an Ephraim (the two sons of Joseph). Manasseh means "God has caused me to forget all the sorrows/toils of my father's house", and Ephraim means "God has made me fruitful in the land of my affliction". Work the process, and give birth to your Manasseh and Ephraim.

Which step are you on in the process? Find your enemies, haters, naysayers and tell them *Thanks for the push*. If they didn't do what they did, you would not have been able to do what you did, so therefore… THANKS FOR THE PUSH!

ABOUT THE AUTHOR

Bishop Dennis M. Jackson, Ph.D is God's under shepherd at United Christian Praise & Worship Center Church, Inc. AKA "Holy Ghost Headquarters USA" where he has served faithfully since 1996. God has consistently blessed United Christian to build and grow a spiritual assembly of Christian believers consisting of several ministries including Evangelism Outreach, Food and Clothing give away, and our one-of-a-kind Youth Scholarship Fund when we provide the children of God with savings bonds and stocks in various companies as well as monetary gifts to assist them as they embark upon their journey into college. Dr. Jackson was born in Moultrie Georgia to Mary Lee Jackson and the late Arthur Eugene Jackson. He married Jerry Ann Carr in September of 1969 celebrating 42 years of marriage to date. From this holy union was born Dennis M. Jackson II Pastor of New Mt. Moriah Missionary Baptist Church and Anitra R. Jackson, student.

Dr. Jackson is a graduate of Carver Heights High School in Leesburg Florida and attended Bethune Cookman College in Daytona Beach, Florida. After marrying Jerry, they moved to Miami where he attended Miami Dade North Community College studying Religion after his call to preach the gospel under the leadership of Rev. Dr. Billy Baskin of New Way Fellowship Baptist Church in Miami. He enrolled at North Florida Baptist Theological Seminary receiving an Associates and Bachelor's Degrees in Ministry, finishing at Jacksonville Baptist Theological with a Masters in Theology and a Doctor of Ministry Degree. Dr. Jackson has been blessed to have received many awards and accolades. He is presently the President and Owner of Green Leaves of Miami Inc. a Plant Rental System for over 40 years, Vice President African American Council of Christian Clergy, Executive Director 5Linx, Civic Past President and Charter Member Opa-Locka Rotary Club, Who's Who Worldwide Business, and Proclamations State of Fl Senator K. Meeks, Cities of Opa-Locka, North Miami.

Chapter 9

Becoming a Vessel of Honor
Written by Bishop Dennis M. Jackson, Ph.D.

"I am the good shepherd; the good shepherd lays down His life for the sheep."

(John 10:11)

When asked, *"What do you want to be when you grow up?"* I don't see many young children answering, *"a pastor."* A pastor's commission is a serious one that must not be taken lightly. We are called to be shepherds of souls and the stakes are extremely high. It takes a deeply dedicated individual with moral fortitude and perseverance to remain steadfast in the preaching ministry which God has called him. Needless-to-say, this task can be daunting and quite challenging at times. As I have closely examined myself by the aide of the Holy Spirit, I know that God Himself called *and chose* me to be the pastor of United Christian Praise and Worship Center Church Inc. *Many are called, but few are chosen* (Mathew 24:14). Before God gave me the assignment, He had me in training. As with all things, there is a training season after you are called. The actual appointment to the position comes *after* adequate training has taken place. God is a God of order and does everything decently and in order. He first prepares one for leadership and preparation. This preparation is highly essential in order for leaders to be effectual in leading God's people. Moses lived in the lap of luxury and enjoyed the splendor of pharaoh's palace, but God had other plans for Moses and began to disturb Moses in his spirit. *By faith Moses, when he was come to years, refused to be called the son of Pharaoh's daughter; choosing rather to suffer affliction with the people of God, than to enjoy the pleasures of sin for a season* (Hebrews 11:24-25). In order to prepare Moses for greatness, God allowed him to become a shepherd first. However, when God called Moses to lead the Israelites at the burning bush, what did he do? He did what I did and what most people do - run, make excuses, or try to hide, but we very well know that we cannot hide from God.

My mother questioned me at the age of 15 regarding my future aspirations. With me being an all-round athlete, I immediately told her that I was going to play ball. It did not matter whether it was football, basketball, baseball, or track because I was good at all of them. My mother looked me squarely in the eyes and said, *"Son, you are going to be a preacher."* My response was, *"Yeah right!"* I was a lady's man and had no intentions on becoming a preacher or pastor. But God chose me. Romans 10:15 questions future ministers and pastors, *"And how shall they preach, except they be sent?"* When one walks out into the commission of preaching, they must know beyond a shadow of a doubt that God has called *and sent* them to the office of Pastor. There is a difference between a minister of the gospel and a Pastor who has been called and ordained by God to lead God's people and yes, there is also a difference between *being called* to Pastor and going out on your own (self proclaimed). If a Pastor has not been divinely ordained and called by God, there will be grave consequences for stepping out into such a spiritual position without approval and covering from Almighty God. But when God calls you and you finally do embrace the call that He puts on your life to preach the gospel, you must then be *steadfast, unmovable and always abounding in the work of the Lord; forasmuch as you know that your labor is not in vain in the Lord.* (1st Corinthians 15:58) When you are not steadfast and unmovable, you fall into grim categories.

EYE-OPENING REALITIES

Statistics show that due to the complexities that come with ministry and pastoring, ministers are abandoning ministry at an alarming rate. The Schaffer's Institute Survey (FASICLD, 1998-2006) which distilled research from The Fuller Institute, George Barna, and the Pastoral Care Inc. (1989-1992) depicts a grim future for Pastors.

HOURS AND PAY:
- 90% of pastors report working between 55 to 75 hours per week.
- 70% feel grossly underpaid
- 57% said they would leave if they had a better place to go including secular work

TRAINING AND PREPAREDNESS:
- 90% feel they are inadequately trained to cope with the ministry demands
- 50% feel unable to meet the demands of the job

HEALTH:
- 71% of pastors stated they were burned out and they battle depression and fatigue on a weekly and even a daily basis
- 70% of pastors constantly fight depression, frustration and discouragement
- 50% of pastors feel so discouraged that they would leave the ministry if they could, but have no other way of making a living

CHURCH RELATIONSHIPS:
- 100% surveyed said they had a close associate or seminary friend who had left the ministry because of burnout, conflict in their church, or from a moral failure

- 75% report significant stress-related crisis at least once in their ministry
- 70% do not have someone they consider a close friend in the ministry
- 66% of church members expect a minister and family to live at higher moral standards than themselves
- 40% report serious conflict with a parishioner at least once a month
- 1,500 leave the ministry each month due to moral failure, spiritual burnout, or contention in their churches

NUMBER ONE REASON PASTORS LEAVE THE MINISTRY:

Church people are not willing to go in the same direction and vision of the pastor. Pastors believe God wants them to go in one direction but the people are not willing to follow or change.

LONGEVITY:

- 89% considered leaving the ministry at one time
- 50% of ministers starting out will not last five years
- One out of every ten pastors will actually retire as a pastor
- 4,000 new churches begin each year and 7,000 churches close each year
- Over 1,700 pastors left the ministry every month last year
- Over 1,300 PASTORS were terminated by the local church each month, many without cause
- According to one survey, only 23% of pastors' report being happy and content with their identity in Christ, in their church, and in their home

QUALITY TIME WITH GOD:

- 72% of pastors surveyed stated that they only studied the Bible when they were preparing for sermons or lessons leaving only 38% who read the Bible for devotions and personal growth study

The statistics are bleak. So a pastor must first be called and sent by God to a Church. Ministry has always been a part of me and I knew that God had His hand on me years ago. However, I wasn't in any rush to fulfill this duty. After a lifestyle of doing what I wanted to do and how I wanted to do it, God sent an angel to confirm my calling to preach the gospel. I remember vividly. It was in 1985 around 4:44a.m. An angel appeared in the doorway of my bedroom. I blinked and looked again thinking that I was dreaming, but it was as clear as day. I saw the silhouette of an angel! He was holding a big book in his hands similar to that of an old-fashioned big Bible. The angel walked toward my bed. I didn't move. He opened the book and took out a glowing white collar and placed it around my neck. He opened the book again and took out a purple robe and put it around me. (This is the very reason why I preach in my robes today.) While still in the spirit, I laid hands on my wife Jerry. I then leaped from my bed and laid hands on my son Dennis II who is now a pastor as well. I proceeded to go and lay hands on my daughter Anitra. After I had laid hands on everyone in the house, I went into the living room and rolled on the floor for hours crying out to God in praise and worship overwhelmed with joy and thanksgiving for Him choosing a wretch like me. I called my praying mother in Leesburg, Florida who had prophesied this when I was 15 years old. The praising and crying continued. She was overwhelmed with joy as she expressed to me how grateful and blessed she was to still be alive to experience the awesome power of God move so miraculously on my life. This marked the beginning of my ministry.

THE TIME OF PREPARATION

I spent several years under the watchful eye of the late Prophetess Lillian Mack. My family and I later became members of a local church in Miami, Florida for over eight and a half years. While there, I served as Youth Director, sang in the male choir, was a yoke fellow, and taught Sunday School. Billy Baskin, who was and still is the pastor at this church was a great pastor, preacher and teacher. Being led by the spirit of God, I quickly discovered what my ministry was: I was to do the work of an Evangelist. I was already ministering at one of the local jails three to four Saturdays a month with a long time friend and brother in Christ with me.

This time of preparation lasted over 15 years. I was blessed by the Holy Spirit to see two spiritual sons birthed from this assignment at the jail. One was a young man that I preached to for 18 months while he was incarcerated facing two life sentences. God moved in his situation and blessed gave him favor. He was found "not guilty" and was released from jail. He then went to seminary and later became a Pastor of an AME Church. God continues to show me daily that my labor as a Pastor is not in vain. God keeps confirming over and over that He called me into this great commission of saving souls. Not only do the angels rejoice when one sinner comes to Christ, but it warms the heart of a minister to see them go on to actually spread the Word! Just recently, I ran into another brother who reminded me that I had preached to him over 15 years ago while he was incarcerated. He was an ex-drug addict and robber. He is now a licensed and ordained deacon at a local Church in Miami as well. To God be the glory for the great things He has done!

I continued doing the work of an evangelist - preaching and teaching Evangelism from West Palm Beach to the Florida Keys. God also had me going to the Miami Rescue Mission, drug holes and street corners preaching and teaching the Word of God to the lost. I spent six months going to the Women's Detentions Center ministering. I continued ministering through the hedges and highways of life leading as many souls to Christ as I could. I counseled over 300 AIDS patients as well as the staff at North Dade Health Clinic for six years. I was doing what God had called me to do - leading souls to Jesus Christ as an Evangelist!

TIME FOR THE APPOINTMENT

God began to navigate the path of my life in December of 1996, when I was interviewed to pastor United Christian Missionary Baptist Church in Miami, Fl. I took the interview only at the advice of my pastor who expressed that he had all the confidence in the world in me and I quote *"I will put you up against the best of them!"* After the interview, the committee told me that they did not have to look any further because I was their new pastor. I stood up, and with a spirit of humility, thanked them for the votes of confidence they had in me *but* told them that God had not told me to pastor them. Everyone was astonished and tried to talk me into accepting the position, but I respectfully said *"no."* Word got back to my pastor and mentor and he called me into his office the very next day inquiring of me as to what was the matter. He told me that to have been chosen to pastor that church was a great honor and opportunity and asked what I was waiting on. As the question was asked again, *"What are you waiting on?"* I took a deep breath, not to offend my pastor and to speak to God before I spoke to him, (Proverbs 3:5-6 KJV) *Trust in the Lord with all thine heart and lean not unto thine own understanding. In all thy ways acknowledge him and he shall direct thy paths.* Being led by the Holy Spirit, I responded, *"Pastor I love you, and I don't know what God has shown you or told you about me, but I am waiting on my marching orders from the Lord."* He looked at me and smiled. After that, he never said another word about the interview until I came back to him two months later. I had been seeking God over and over saying, *"Lord, what will you have me to do? You showed me from the beginning and I know you will show me again."* And then one night God took me up in a vision and placed me at the front door of United Christian with a big brown key in my hand. I tried everything I could to not put that key in that door and God spoke these words into my spirit, *"I will give unto thee, the keys of the kingdom of heaven. Go in and possess the land."* (Matthew 16:19 KJV). The same key that I had in my hand in the vision was the same key that the late John Williams, who was a deacon in that church and also over the committee to select a new pastor gave me as I started my assignment as Pastor of United Christian. I know beyond a shadow of a doubt that God sent me to pastor United Christian Praise & Worship Center. My installation service was in February of 1996.

On this 26-year journey, God has used and manifested Himself through me in many ways, and although there has been some stumbling blocks and trials along the way, I am still grateful for each test and trial from which I have learned lessons and gain wisdom. In 1996, I fell out of my boat into the lake that is behind my house. I went down to the bottom of the lake some 30 feet deep and stuck on the bottom to my knees. It was there that I had an out-of-body experience. I saw my spirit floating up in the air while my physical body was floating on top of the water. I then saw my wife and daughter coming through the back gate of the house. I knew that I didn't want them to see my dead body, so I cried out to God, *"Lord save me!"* Within seconds, my spirit was back in my body I began throwing up. But as I began pulling my boat out of the water, I stepped on an electrical outlet. It began to burn my body all over. As the pain intensified, I tried to tell my mind to pick up my foot, but to no avail. I then cried out to God again JESUS HELP ME! Right then, the electricity turned me loose. This all happened within an hour. When the devil realized that he couldn't take my life in the water, he tried to take it when I stepped on the electrical outlet - But God! It was not my time to depart from this earth and God saved me after I called upon Him TWICE! *For whosoever shall call upon the name of the Lord shall be saved* (Romans 10:13). For years after that, I would have flashbacks of that day in the lake each time I tried to submerge my face under water, but thanks be unto God who gives us the victory! For some reason, God saw fit to keep me here on earth. Because of that, I feel that there is more work to be done for the kingdom and I avail myself to Him to move and work through me in all things. I am grateful to be alive to be able to tell this awesome miracle that happened to me.

As the pastor of United Christian Praise & Worship Center with all its challenges, I still thank God for choosing me. For each challenge there was a greater opportunity and blessing. I have discovered that when we humble ourselves, God will exalt in His own way an in His own time. In April of 2008, I delivered the eulogy for Cedella Marley Booker, world renowned singer and mother of the great legendary Bob Marley. It is written, *we will be as unknown, but yet well known* (II Corinthians 4:9 KJV). The heart of a pastor has to be in tune with the Word of God. Jesus said in Matthew 22:37, *"Thou shalt love the Lord thy God with all thy heart, and with all thy soul, and with all thy mind."* In order to love God, pastors have to love His Word and His people. His Word is the keeping power. When trials and tribulations come your way and when all seems hopeless and lost, it is the Word of God that sustains you. The truth of the matter is that God does call His pastors to higher standards. Pastors are considered the watchman. In Ezekiel Chapter 33, God gives a strong rebuff to the person He has put in charge over His people. God has high expectations for His leaders. But if the watchman sees danger coming and does not blow the trumpet and the people are not warned, and a sword comes and takes a person from them, he is taken away in his iniquity; *but his blood I will require from the watchman's hand.* (Ezekiel 33:6) Ezekiel delivered a series of messages concerning the chosen nation. The first message described the function and responsibilities of the prophet under the figure of a watchman. In the day of danger, a watchman then and now was appointed to give notice of the approach of an enemy. If he did his duty and his warning was not heeded, the blood of the slain would be on their own heads; but if he failed to give the warning and the people were slain, their blood would be on his head. He was then to declare to the people who were lamenting that Jehovah had no pleasure in the death of the wicked, but rather that the wicked would turn from his ways and live. We Pastors are the watchman of today.

God left specific instructions in His Word regarding the duties and characteristics of a Pastor:

1. **Acts 20:28:** Take heed to yourselves and to all the flock in which the Holy Spirit has made you overseer, to care for the church of God which He obtained with the blood of his own Son. (KJV)

2. **I Timothy 3:2:** A Bishop then must be blameless, the husband of one wife, vigilant, sober, of good behavior, given to hospitality, apt to teach. (KJV)

3. **I Peter 5:2:** Be shepherds of God's flock that is under your care, serving as overseers, not because you must, but because you are willing, as God wants you to be; not greedy for money, but eager to serve; (NIV)

4. **John 21:16:** Again Jesus said, "Simon son of John, do you truly love me?" He answered, "Yes, Lord, you know that I love you." Jesus said, "Feed my sheep."(KJV)

5. **Jeremiah 23:1-2:** Woe be unto the pastors that destroy and scatter the sheep of my pasture! saith the LORD. Therefore thus saith the LORD God of Israel against the pastors that feed my people; Ye have scattered my flock, and driven them away, and have not visited them: behold, I will visit upon you the evil of your doings, saith the LORD. (KJV)

It is important to understand the behind-the-scenes things that go on in a pastor's life. But as a pastor, it is important to understand what is expected of us. We *are* called to a higher level of accountability and responsibility. As we stand in front of the people of God as their Shepherd, we must stand firm, be strong, be wise, be patient and always ready to impart the Word of God with power and great authority. But the truth is that pastors do not always feel like that. Sometimes we don't want to preach. There are times when we want to stay home from church, but we cannot. I have found however, that when the enemy brings discouragement and frustration upon the man of God, God gives him a sermon. The pastor thinks that the sermon is for the people, but it is actually for him first. After preaching it, he feels better. How? Because the Lord strategically gave the pastor a Word to strengthen him, and the anointing on the Word destroys the yoke upon the pastor and blesses the people of God.

I thank God for this opportunity to share with the world a snapshot of what it is like to be a pastor and what God requires of us in order to lead His people effectively and with compassion. Once the call is answered, the walk will not be easy. There will be discouragements, frustration, hurt from members of the congregation, jealously, and many days of crying out to the Lord. But He is faithful. He will never leave you nor forsake you. Even though I have had some bad days as a pastor, I can truly say without any mental reservation or spiritual hesitation that my good days has out-weighed my bad days and I refuse to complain I live to please God. So I encourage you to *wait on the Lord and be of good courage and He will strengthen your heart. Wait, I say, on the Lord!* (Psalm 24:14). Love you in the Lord.

ABOUT THE AUTHOR

Reverend Fred Cromity, Senior Pastor/Teacher has a philosophy about God that prevails through everything that he does. In his Christian walk, he is consistently striving to pass on peace through love, which supports God's vision, which is so eloquently written in John 3:16. "For God so loved the world, He gave His only begotten Son".

Rev. Cromity was born in Jacksonville, Florida to the late William and Bernice Cromity and he has three children. He is happily married to 1st Lady Carol Harris-Cromity for 19 wonderful years and continues to live up to dad and husband daily. He graduated from William M. Raines High School in Jacksonville, received a Bachelor's Degree from Florida A&M University in Tallahassee, a Dual Master's Degree from Nova Southeastern University and a Master's Degree from Trinity Evangelical Divinity School in Davie Florida.

Rev. Cromity, through Word of Life Baptist Church, was licensed and ordained by Rev. Richard P. Dunn II, Pastor, of Faith Community Baptist Church as he serves as his spiritual father. Rev. Cromity is currently a licensed and State Board certified Educator where he instructs in the area of Mathematics and serves as the Director of After School and Summer School Programs.

In lieu of the many accomplishments and accolades that has been bestowed upon Reverend Cromity, the two most important accomplishments outside of his family is the appointment of the Homeless Ministry and being named the Pastor of True Love Praise and Worship Church.

True Love Praise and Worship Church
15600 NW 42 Avenue
Miami Gardens, FL 33055
Rev. Fred Cromity

Chapter 10

The Heart of a Pastor
Written by Pastor Fred Cromity

Whoso stoppeth his ears at the cry of the poor, he also shall cry himself, but shall not be heard.
(Proverbs 21:13-14)

Many people think that being a Christian or being "righteous" is only about memorizing scriptures and testifying in front of people; but I've discovered that being saved means living for and being obedient to Jesus. The foundation of our Christianity is predicated upon us loving God and loving people. The Bible is simply put by many as **B**asic **I**nstructions **B**efore **L**eaving **E**arth.

One of the things that intrigues me the most about our biblical instructions and our relationship with Christ is how people respond to adversity. When I first began my ministry, it started in a homeless shelter. I was amazed at how real and transparent people are when life has seemed to let them down. I vividly recall one day when I was volunteering at the shelter that it was testimony time during one of the sessions. A young lady walked down to testify about her faith in spite of all she had been through. She seemed to be about 89 pounds and her beautiful smile made her stand out to people. It was so warm and compelling that it made others feel at ease just looking at her. When she began speaking, she revealed that she was living with full blown AIDS and had a T-Cell count of zero. She stated that the doctors were shocked that she was still alive, let alone walking around talking and smiling. Before she came up to speak, hardly anyone had approached the microphone to share anything about themselves. However, after hearing her story, many began sharing their stories about hope and faith in spite of the trials and struggles they had and were enduring. With faith like hers how could anyone still lack their own faith I wondered. This was one of the incidents that catapulted my ministry with the homeless and challenged me to never forget my first love. We must remember - especially as pastors, that our first love is the love we have for Christ and we cannot love Christ without loving His people. I now have a passion and commitment to reach the lost, teach the found, and carry out God's plan for His people.

Many hurt people have a problem with Jesus' plan to love all people because they feel that they have not been loved themselves so why should they give love in return. However, the same DNA we carry to distinguish us from one another is the same DNA that allows us to be different from one another. When we were born, at that very moment our lives began to take different paths. Even if you are an identical twin, you are still different from your identical sibling in some way. It is impossible for all of us to have the exact same experiences, the exact same thoughts, the exact same anything. We are each different and each of us travel down different paths. Therefore, if I experience pain in a particular area of my life such as physical, sexual or emotional abuse and I am not counseled properly, that traumatic experience can follow me for the rest of my life. Was the abuse designed for my life by God? Did I allow it to happen to me? These are the questions I find myself answering for the flock on many occasions. If not careful, a pastor can become emotionally overwhelmed and psychologically drained by listening to so much pain that people have gone through, but God has given the pastor a very unique kind of heart and compassion for God's people.

A pastor must love Christ first and people second. There is no compromise there. This is the order. How can a pastor not have a love for people? If this is ever the case, then the pastor will end up doing more harm than good to the people of God and will cause the flock to go astray with broken hearts, broken faith and diminished hope. When a pastor does not have a love for the flock, he usually has a love for something else and that something else is usually himself. As a pastor, there is very little room for self. To be a pastor is to be selfless. As pastors, our duty is protect the sheep, guide them, lead them, teach them and comfort them. People have experienced some disheartening, traumatic and painful experiences in their lives and yet they are still holding on to their faith and trust in God. When they come to church, they are looking for a Word that will sooth their wounds, which are sometimes very deep. They need a Word that will give them strength to make it another day. We must remember that we were born for one purpose: To give God pleasure. How do we give God pleasure? By pleasing Him and praising Him. How do we please Him? By using the pleasure handbook and it is called the Bible. Many people have discovered how to play church. They know how to dance the dance, shout the shout and "Amen" their way during the pastor's sermon. They go around the communion table, pick up the elements and sit back down. The problem with this is that playing the part won't save you. Some of these same people will use profanity before they hit the last step on their way out of the sanctuary. By the time they get home, they have already had two beers and may be smoking a cigarette. They continue in their sinful ways and next Sunday morning get ready for church and play it over again. Once their sins catch up with them, they come to the pastor and cry that they did everything right and do not understand why things are still going wrong for them. They know full well in their hearts, that they have not been living right. They think that they are fooling me, but they are only fooling themselves and will remain in the same circle of mess until they change. Change starts in the heart. And it is the heart that God looks at. You can never fool Him!

One of things I always share with members is a quote from Dr. Phil, *"If what you are currently doing is working for you, then keep doing it, but if it's not, then change it."* However, the pastor's heart in me will not stop me from loving them as their Sheppard because they... use to be me! My goal is to never forget where I came from. The one thing that keeps me loving God's people is knowing that no one is exempt from sin. I have found myself very sympathetic to individuals in the homeless shelters where I volunteer because they really believe that their survival skills and internal fortitude learned while growing up is enough to sustain them. One of the things that has been successful in trying to change the mindset of the unsaved is getting them to agree to be baptized. I'm very pleased that in seven years, I have baptized more than 300 individuals. There was even a time after I had just finished baptizing someone that a young lady from Korea asked if she could be baptized. After we talked about her faith and she answered a few questions about Christianity, I went forward with the process. She asked for my information and has since emailed me and thanked me for taking time out to baptize her.

Having both a main church and an outreach ministry where I spend just as much time in one as the other can be very demanding. This also leads to one group sometimes feeling left out. Ironically, in my ministry, the side that feels that they are left out the most is not the homeless ministry where I volunteer, but the main church. Early on, we lost many members because they felt as though they were second seat to the Pastor behind the homeless. Through experiences - good and bad, I have learned that church members become very dependent upon the pastor to the point that they sometimes become jealous of one another. Their focus is all too often on spending time with the pastor in order to get a word from him to validate their feelings instead of seeking validation from the Lord. When they feel as though they are not getting time with the pastor quick enough or feel that he is not "accessible" enough for them, they leave that particular church. However,

God always replaces what has been lost with those who will share in the vision of the pastor to evangelize and extend salvation to those outside of the four walls of the church and not just those within the four walls. People who join our church now, realize that God did not just call me as their pastor, but He has called me to pastor to the lost outside of the church. They get it because they have seen my heart and that is why they are still there.

Part of growth in Christ is to step in and help those who are the least among you. It sometimes baffles me how people who have a place to stay, food on the table, and the ability to come and go as they please always seem to find something to complain about. Sometimes, I will ask the congregation to take a deep breath and discover that they are alive. I often find myself reminding them that there were many funerals over the weekend, but none of them were theirs. This, I feel should be reason enough for anybody to say *"I will bless the Lord at all times. His praises shall continually be in my mouth. (Psalm 34)* And the part I like is when David said: *"O, magnify the Lord with me."* The word *magnify* can easily be translated as "focus" because focus seem to highlight whatever is magnified because wherever focus goes, energy flows. If we just learn how to focus on God, we will be able to magnify him, to make Him larger in our life than what He currently is. If we have a big mountain and a little mustard seed, the one that gets the power is not necessarily the one that's the biggest. The one that get's the power is the one which attracts the focus of our faith. If the doctor tells me that I have cancer, either I can believe the doctor or I can believe my God and what HE has spoken over my life. My God said, *"No weapon, formed against me shall prosper."* Magic Johnson is a perfect example. He was told in 1992 that he had AIDS, but Magic did not focus on what was happening around him or what the doctors said was happening inside of him; his focus changed to believe that he was healed. Some may still believe that he is going to die of AIDS, but I believe that Magic has claimed in his heart that the God he serves is a healer and has and will heal him. Again, wherever your focus goes, energy flows.

Every Sunday when I stand before the church to address them as their pastor, both joy and sorrow grips my heart. Joy, because I know that God sent me and ordained me in His council for "such a day as this". Sorrow, because I know that some will choose to go home the same way they came in. Many are now coming to church to be entertained instead of focusing upon the unadulterated Word of God and how they can apply it to their lives. They seem to look for excitement and entertainment for their flesh. For this reason, I have often reminded people that church is very similar to a bank, not in the money aspect, but in the "deposit" aspect. What you put in, you will be able to withdraw at a time of need. The longer you let your deposits build up, the more of an interest you have to draw from. If you deposit love, then you can expect God to give back love to you, with interest. If you deposit serving, then God returns a greater investment that is more than what you gave, if you deposit your tithes, then guess what? He will prosper you in your finances. The problem we seem to have in the church with Christians making the right deposits is the devil's influence in their lives. The devil never wants a Christian to do too much, but always want them to complain about what they don't like. Every church has their share of complainers and every pastor has their "thorns" in the church. These people are strategically placed by the enemy to divide the people of God in the church. The goal of the enemy is to get God's people to focus upon foolishness instead of upon the cross and the meaning of that cross in each of their lives. Through wisdom, I have learned how to handle those types of people. Blind Bartimeus gave a great illustration to us in Mark 10:46 when they told him to be quiet, but what did he do? yell louder. That is what we need to do when we face our enemy. We need to call them out, but also to love more, serve more, and of course, pray more. After all, we need our enemy in order to help propel us to the next spiritual level. Psalm 23 tells us that God prepares a table before us in the presence of our enemies. He only prepares our table if we have enemies and they are before us. It took me a while to get this one, but it is certainly something to think about. If we can learn how to treat our enemies as His Word instructs us to do in Matthew 5:44 which states, "*But I say unto you, love your enemies, bless them that curse you, do good to them that hate you, and pray for them which despitefully use you, and persecute you.* Then we can pass one of God's tests in our lives. If we pass the test, then He says in His Word that He will anoint our head with oil and *our cup runneth over, surely goodness and mercy shall follow us all the days of our life.* The 23rd Psalm has been one of my favorite passages of scripture simply because in the seven years that I have had the opportunity to minister at the homeless shelter, the one thing that I see that has had a stronghold on them is unforgiveness. More often than not, most of them blame their failures in life on somebody else. Rape and molestation is very common in their history until it is very easy for them to talk about it in testimony in front of others. Nine times out of ten, others have experienced the same thing.

A 22 year old young lady once told me that she would like to be able to stop other young girls from becoming her. She had four children and was raising three of them. She had been raped, molested, and eventually turned to prostitution. She poured out her heart to me that she had slept with so many men that she couldn't remember half of them. However, she wanted to help somebody else because although she made lots of money on the streets, all she has to show for it now are four children and a life in the homeless shelter. As with many people, she too has someone in her life who she cannot forgive for a hurt or abuse done to her. In this case, it was her mother. Each week when I went to volunteer at the shelter, I tried to convince her through the Word why she should forgive. I give her the example of Christ on the cross. While He was yet dying, He said Father forgive them for they know not what they do (Luke 23:34). Then He continued with dying that ignominious death on the cross. So then, how can we not forgive and yet we are still alive? If there is someone in your life who has hurt, abused, lied on, betrayed or abandoned you in some way, can you stop reading right now and... forgive them for what they did to you? Just say this: *Father, forgive them. They know not what they did.* It will take time to feel it, but speaking the words out of your mouth is a great start. Not only do we need to forgive others, but we need to forgive ourselves and trust in the Lord for healing in our soul. Second Peter 2:20-22 tells us that if after we have escaped the pollutions of the world through the knowledge of our Lord and savior Jesus Christ, then are again entangled in them and overcome, the latter end is worse than the beginning. This simply means that if we do not learn how to trust, we will keep getting caught up in sin over and over again. Within the ministry that God has entrusted me with, I run across many people who have been hurt deeply. And unfortunately most of them choose not to forgive the one(s) who hurt them. Hurt people hurt people. Many people inside the church have been hurt by people within the church. That is why in most of the African American Churches, there is what we call the "back door". The back door is considered the door that new members/converts come in and go out of - never to return again.

    The church is considered a spiritual hospital. It is a place where the hurt, the broken hearted, the downtrodden and the sinner should be able to come and receive love and acceptance. Unfortunately sometimes, it is the very members in the church, the ones who are there every time the church doors open, who sit on every board and are in every ministry that run new people away. Many people do not go to church right now - not because of an offense or hurt they endured in the world, but one they endured from directly inside of the church. Many people come to the church for refuge or they are simply tired of the hustle and bustle of the world. When Christians set bad examples by getting arrested and allowing themselves to get "conformed by the standards of this world" and then are later humiliated for it, there are those in the world who say, "See, that's just why I don't go to church." Unfortunately, that excuse will not be acceptable to God on judgment day. There is a sure hell for all of those who had one excuse after the other and took pleasure in their unrighteousness. The world has grown so comfortable in sin until many rarely question people who dress as though they are going to a club while supposedly coming to church. We really push the button on modesty, integrity and the sacredness of the temple that God loans us while we are on this side of heaven. We make subtle attempts to pimp the church for how the church can and should bless us instead of how we can bless the church. President John F. Kennedy once challenged us to do the following: *"Ask not what your country can do for you; ask what you can do for your country."* We should have that type of love for our God. Instead of wondering what God can and will do for us, we should be concerned about what we can do for God.

    A pastor has so many obligations to God, his family, the church and to continuously spread the gospel as much as he can. When a person is called to the ministry to preach the gospel, a great deal of them think that the office of a pastor is what they have been called to do. Being called into the ministry does not necessarily have to mean pastoring. *And God hath set some in the church, first apostles, secondarily prophets, thirdly teachers, after that miracles, then gifts of healings, helps, governments, diversities of tongues. Are all apostles? Are all prophets? Are all pastors? Are all teachers? Are all workers of miracles? Have all the gifts of healing? Do all speak with tongues? do all interpret?* (1st Corinthians 12:28). Being a pastor reminds me of what my mother had to do to raise all ten of her children. Sometimes she would rather see her children happy before being happy herself. It is my opinion that if you are a pastor, you should love your flock as though they were members of your own family. It is a privilege and an honor to serve in this great position as Sheppard over

God's precious sheep. I know that I must handle them with care because as a pastor, I am called to a higher standard and responsibility. It never crossed my mind that one day I would be where I am.

When a person opens up their heart to another and reveals their emotions, feelings, fears, and aspirations, it is because they trust that person. In like manner, people trust pastors with perhaps more than they should at times. One thing that pastors must be careful about is not to judge people by what they do or are going through. Being a pastor is not thinking and making decisions by how the world prepared you to make them through their humanistic logic and reasoning, but more like God would have you to make them. *But the natural man receiveth not the things of the Spirit of God: for they are foolishness unto him: neither can he know them, because they are spiritually discerned. But he that is spiritual judgeth all things, yet he himself is judged of no man.* (1st Corinthians s 2:14-15). It is a lot like that old cliche....what would Jesus do? If more people made decisions with their heart and not their experiences, less people would be hurt. That's why the scriptures encourage us to *Trust in the Lord with all thine heart, and lean not unto your own understanding. In all your ways acknowledge Him and He shall direct thy path* (Proverbs 3:5-6).

It's now come a time in this world that people are finally thinking that maybe they should start examining their Christian life. Finally, the church has started seeing growth. It's tough to keep waking up every morning seeing things getting worst and not better. People have been waiting it out for many seasons trying to see if life would get better. Well, it's not. So when all else fails what do we do? We learn how to trust God again. When Paul was on his missionary journey to Rome, they were sailing on a ship which came under a storm called the northeastern by Crete. The ship took a violent beating and the crew did everything they could to save the ship. They tied straps around the ship, they threw the cargo overboard, but nothing would save it. Finally they decided to sit down and admit that everything they did had failed. When they came to the point of giving up, that's when God stepped in and blessed them. That is why we as people of God need to include Him from the beginning so we won't get to the point of trying everything else, then having to try God. Let's admit that only God can direct our paths. He is looking for us to turn to Him with all of our hearts and stop looking for answers from external things. He wants us to trust Him so much that even when the situation seems grim and impossible, we know that God is going show up, show out and work miracles on our behalf. We know it with every fiber of our being regardless of what it looks like in the natural. That's the kind of faith He wants us to have. Are you willing to have that much faith in Him? Are you willing to trust Him with every problem you face right now? Step up your faith and watch God come through for you. I'm a witness that He is able!

ABOUT THE AUTHOR

Pastor Ranzer A. Thomas is the Founder and Senior Pastor of New Generation Missionary Baptist Church in Miami, FL. He has been a pastor for more than twenty years and has served as leader of New Generation for the past 15 years. Pastor Thomas received a Bachelor's degree in Banking and Finance from Morehouse College in 1986 and a Masters of Arts degree in Religion from Trinity Evangelical Divinity School in 2002.

Pastor Thomas served as President of the Baptist Ministers Council of Greater Miami & Vicinity, Inc. from 2004 to 2007 and is a sought-after speaker for conferences in the areas of Leadership and Stewardship. He and his wife, Rev. Rhonda Thomas, have been married for 21 years, and they have two beautiful children, Roquonda and Ranzer, Jr.

Pastor Thomas is a God-fearing, humble man and through his obedience to God, the New Generation family has experienced glory to glory.

Pastor Thomas' favorite passage of scripture is 2 Chronicles 7:14, *"If my people, who are called by my name, will humble themselves and pray and seek my face and turn from their wicked ways, then I will hear from heaven, and I will forgive their sin and will heal their land."*

Pastor Ranzer A. Thomas, Sr.
New Generation Missionary Baptist Church
940 Caliph Street
Opa Locka, FL 33054
305-389-3308

Chapter 11

Walking in Humility
Written by Pastor Ranzer Thomas

Yea, all of you be subject one to another, and be clothed with humility. For God resisteth the proud, and giveth grace to the humble. Humble yourselves therefore under the mighty hand of God, That he may exalt you in due time:
(I Peter 5:5-6)

On this Pastoral Journey, I have come to realize that "walking in humility," has allowed me to be the recipient of many blessings from God. In the world that we live in today, many think that if you are highly esteemed, have many people serving you, honoring you, have a lot of money or fame, power and position, then you have it made. In the world that may be so, but in the spirit, those earthly things mean absolutely nothing. As a student of the Holy Spirit, the great Teacher, I have learned that it is humility that God honors. It is the humble whom He exalts and blesses. While traveling on this Pastoral Journey, I have come to realize that humility is the highest rank that one should aspire to possess. To walk in humility is to walk in lowliness. As we walk in humility, the world may perceive us as quiet, shy or even insecure from the natural eye, but the true humble in heart are aware that God is their strength, source, and supplier of all their needs. The word *humility* simply means to offer oneself as meek in a spirit of lowliness.

As the founding Pastor of New Generation Baptist Church, I initially secured our worship services in the auditorium of John F. Kennedy Middle School. We worshipped there as a congregation, for two and a half years. Although we did not have a sanctuary of our own, we never considered ourselves homeless because we believed that God would eventually provide a sanctuary that we could call home. During our search, we discussed the fact that there were very few existing churches for sale in Miami Dade County, but we were constantly praying for God to lead us to the building that He had chosen just for us. We knew that He would make a way because He always makes provision for the vision! As the shepherd, I constantly searched and inquired about buildings for sale. Then the day came that I was informed about a beautiful piece of property located in a residential area in North Miami Beach. Although it was not an existing church, I visualized it being converted into a beautiful sanctuary. This property sat on over three acres of land with over 5,000 square feet of indoor space. Additionally, there was a swimming pool and a tennis court with the potential to build a sanctuary there in the future. We stepped out on faith and purchased the property believing that we would receive an approval for a variance from the Miami-Dade County Zoning Department. The variance would allow the church to exist in the residential neighborhood.

As a baby church, we were excited about acquiring this new property. The church was growing and many members shared in the vision of acquiring our own property. We felt that this property was the answer to our prayers. However, a huge zoning battle was presented to us, not with the county but with the neighbors! Unbeknownst to us at the time of acquiring the property, we began dealing with all levels of racism.The attacks came at us from all levels and the church was persecuted. We knew that this was a spiritual battle designed by the enemy, so we stayed prayerful. *For we wrestle not against flesh and blood, but against principalities, against powers, against the rulers of the darkness of this world, against spiritual wickedness in high places* (Ephesians 6:12). As the Lord's blessings come into fruition, the enemy tries to attack those blessings. The church was vandalized and we had to deal with statements such as, *"You people are not wanted here."* Some of the neighbors even suggested that we relocate to the Liberty City area, which is an urban and economically deprived part of Miami-Dade County. We endured racist comments such as that on a frequent basis, but tried to stay focused on the Lord in spite of the enemy's fiery darts.

As a result of these disheartening challenges, we had to attend a zoning hearing. While at the hearing, the neighbors complained that the increase of traffic would decrease the value of their homes and that we were making too much noise. The zoning hearing started at 7:00p.m and we did not leave until 11:00p.m. that night. I did not think that people could be so cruel when people only wanted to come and worship the Lord. Considering the fact that prior to us purchasing the property, the building had been used as a home to grow marijuana, one would have thought that the neighbors would have been happy to have us in the neighborhood. Ironically, the neighbors had never complained about the marijuana house. But God! In His grace, mercy and favor, He allowed us to win the zoning hearing that night with some limitations and restrictions attached in order to please the neighbors. Although it was a bitter sweet victory for us, we most certainly gave God praise for the victory. Anything worth having is worth fighting for and then praising God for after you receive it. As a result of this victory, New Generation grew spiritually and we also in number. In spite of the challenges, we still hosted our first Women's Conference, Men's Conference, Marriage Conference and Youth Conference. The children enjoyed the space and the new programs that the church had begun offering them. They tremendously enjoyed being in a church that had a swimming pool, play area and a tennis court. Notwithstanding the rude awakening from the neighbors when we first arrived, we still reached out to the community and invited them to come take part in what God was doing. Some did, but the majority continued to do everything in their power to stop this awesome worship experience from moving forward.

There were times that they would interrupt the worship service and call the police. They would then stand on the walls that circled the building to videotape and take pictures of how many cars were inside of the gated and walled building. Unfortunately, the victory that we won at the zoning hearing did not seem to make a difference. The neighbors were still plotting for our dismissal from the property. They filed an appeal and we found ourselves in an ongoing legal battle. After much fasting and praying, we as a congregation felt that it was best to sell the property and move to a more peaceful location where we could worship without interruptions, limitations and restrictions. Needless-to-say, this was a very difficult and discouraging time for all of us - especially me as the pastor. It was a time on my pastoral journey that I felt as though I had missed the voice of God and had made the wrong decision in purchasing that particular property. Little did I know at the time that God was preparing the New Generation Church family for a greater blessing and an awesome move. From that zoning experience, God was breaking me so that I could learn to totally trust Him. I had to resort back to our church's founding bible verse, which was:

Whereas you have been forsaken and hated, so that no one went through you, I will make you an eternal excellence, a joy of many generations.
You shall drink the milk of the Gentiles and milk the breast of kings; you shall know that I, the Lord, am your Savior and your Redeemer, the Mighty One of Jacob.
Instead of bronze I will bring gold. Instead of Iron I will bring silver. Instead of wood, bronze, And instead of stones, iron. I will also make your officers peace. And your magistrate righteousness.

Violence shall no longer be heard in your land, neither wasting, nor destruction within your borders; but you shall call your walls salvation, and your gates praise.
(Isaiah 60:15-18)

I would read this passage daily having no doubt in my mind that God was with us as a church family. We leased space for six years after that experience and my mind was made up that New Generation's theme was, *"We Are About Ministry."* We worshipped God as if we were in a Cathedral. We took our eyes off of the physical building that we didn't have and focused upon kingdom building. We operated church functions in a spirit of excellence and settled for nothing less. My wife Rhonda, was and still serves as the lead servant of the Women's Ministry and every June, we would have some of the most anointed and blessed women's conferences around. My ears became more sensitive to the voice of God as I learned to totally trust Him with my vision for the church. Although we were leasing space, He told me to follow His word in II Timothy 4:5:

But watch thou in all things. Endure afflictions, do the work of an evangelist, make full proof of thy ministry.

As I continue to ponder upon humility and what it means to be a humble servant of the Lord, I reflect upon Moses. Moses was a man who displayed humility in the infant stage of his Ministry. It is written in
Exodus 3:11-14

And Moses said unto God, Who Am I, that I should go unto Pharaoh and that I should bring forth the children of Israel out of Egypt? And He said: certainly I will be with thee; and this shall be a token unto thee, that I have sent thee: When thou has brought forth the people out of Egypt, ye shall serve God upon this mountain. And Moses said unto God, behold, when I come unto the children of Israel and shall say unto them, the God of your fathers hath sent men unto you: and they shall say unto me, What is his name? What shall I say unto them? And God said unto Moses, "I am that I AM" and he said, thus shalt thou say unto the children of Israel, I AM has sent me unto you.

In his natural state, Moses did not feel as though he was worthy to lead the children of Israel out of Egypt. I have discovered that the humble never feel as though they are able or worthy to do great things for God. Although we may be anointed and gifted, humility will always keep us at the feet of Jesus. As a Pastor, I have learned not to walk in pride, for the bible reminds us in Proverbs 16:18: *Pride goeth before destruction and a haughty spirit before a fall.*

A prideful spirit can be destructive to a progressive church. Pride destroys a blessed home, but God has a way of humbling the proud and boastful. The thing that many do not realize is that pride does not come upon a person all at once. It sneaks up on you and often comes through promotion, honor, exaltation and praise if one is not careful. I am not saying that we should reject promotion, honor, exaltation and praise. What I am saying is that if we are not careful, we can get too caught up in those things. The "proudness" that we feel from having attained such accomplishments can turn into "pride". We must be careful. I often teach the following bible Story in Daniel 4:30-37 concerning King Nebuchadnezzar.

The king spake and said, is not this great Babylon, that I have built for the house of the kingdom by the might of my power, and for the honor of my majesty?
While the sword was in the king's mouth, there fell a voice from heaven, saying O king Nebuchadnezzar to thee it is spoken; The kingdom is departed from thee.
And they shall drive thee from men, and thy dwelling shall be with the beasts of the field; they shall make thee to eat grass as oxen, and seven times shall pass over thee, until thou know that

the most High ruleth in the kingdom of men, and giveth it to whosoever he will.
The same hour was the thing fulfilled upon Nebuchadnezzar and he was driven from men, and did eat grass as oxen, and his body was wet with the dew of heaven, till his hairs were grown like eagles' feathers, and his nails like bird claws.
(Daniel 4:30-33)

God had to isolate King Nebuchadnezzar because of his pride and place him on a spiritual lock-down in order to teach him a lesson in humility. The bible states that he ate what the beast of the field ate. When we disobey God, He can change the menu of our diet without taking our orders. What a humbling experience for the king to go from fine dining to eating what the beast of the field ate. This is what happens when we become too lifted up in pride. God has to humble us and this humbling can be quite humiliating. *Pride goeth before destruction, and a haughty spirit before a fall* (Proverbs 16:18). Disobeying God can also have an effect on your outward appearance. King Nebuchadnezzar's hair grew like eagle feathers and his nails like bird claws. When we become too puffed up with pride, God will allow you to miss some hair appointments. Humility has a way of calling one back to submission to God.

And at the end of the days I Nebuchadnezzar lifted up mine eyes unto heavens and mine understanding returned unto me, and I blessed the most High, and I praised the Most High, and I honored Him that liveth forever, whose dominion is an everlasting dominion, and His kingdom is from generation to generation.

And all the inhabitants of the earth are reputed as nothing; and He doeth according to his will in the army of heaven and among the inhabitants of the earth; and none can stay His hand, or say unto him. What doest thou?

At the same time my reason returned unto me; and for the glory of my kingdom, mine honor and brightness returned unto me and my counselors and my lords sought unto me; and I was established in my kingdom, and excellent majesty was added unto me. (Daniel 4:34-36)

It was not until King Nebuchadnezzar looked up to heaven and got it right with God that he realized that God is in control of both Heaven and earth and He only is to be exalted. We acquire nothing on our own. King Nebuchadnezzar began to bless the Highest God and praised Him forever after he learned his lesson. When God brings us out of the wilderness, we must have a continuous praise! The king realized that it was not about him or his status, fame, or power, but it was and is always about God Almighty!

Now I Nebuchadnezzar praise and extol and honor the King of heaven, all whose works are truth, and his ways judgment.
(Daniel 4:37)

God resists the proud, but gives grace to the humble. Don't you want more grace? Become humble. God has an unusual way of bringing down the prideful, conceited and arrogant ones, but He promotes the humble. As pastor and Shepherd over God's sheep, one of the most valuable lessons that I have learned is that walking in humility is vital for spiritual survival. When we exalt ourselves, pride can lead to being pulled down by God Himself. In the gospel of St. Luke 14:8-11, Jesus gives a beautiful parable that I often share with the people of God on the subject of self-exaltation and pride. In Jesus' day, people had status symbols, but in the eighth verse of St. Luke, it says, *when you are invited to the wedding feast, do not sit down in the highest room, lest a more honorable man than thou be bidden of you;* verse nine reminds us that one may come and ask you to give up your seat to a person of higher status and this can certainly bring about shame. However, the humble will adhere to verse ten that says, *but when thou art bidden, go and sit down in the lowest room; that when he that bade thee, cometh, he may say unto thee, friend go up higher: then shalt thou have worship in the presence of them that sit at meet with thee.*

The words *"Friend, go up higher"* are fitting for me and the New Generation Family. The journey certainly has not been easy. We must understand that although God speaks His words and they will never return unto Him void concerning His plans for you, He never says that the road will be easy. After our zoning trial issues and being persecuted by the neighbors from the purchase of the first property, then the humbling experience of leasing for six years, God saw fit to lead us to our very own building. In September of 2006, we began negotiations with the Pastor of a church that was for sale. In the same month on Labor Day, we took a tour of that beautiful sanctuary. We prayed and took ownership of the building in the spirit realm. We knew that the building was ours. We understood that we had to do our part in the natural realm until the vision manifested. We made an offer the same day and had a signed contract by the end of that day. What a Labor Day to remember! That Labor Day helped us to remember that, *our Labor was not in vain in the Lord!* The church body embarked upon a thirty day fast and went before God with much prayer. Our church congregation understood that *"The prayers of the Righteous availeth much."*

It is incumbent upon me to encourage you to stay the course. Hold on to God's Word concerning you. Yes, there will be some wilderness experiences, some trials, tribulations and temptations, but if you stay faithful to God, He will stay faithful to you. *These things I have spoken unto you, that in me ye might have peace. In the world ye shall have tribulation: but be of good cheer; I have overcome the world.* (John 16:33). God allows us to go through challenges in order to bring out character in us, increase our faith in Him and appreciate the blessings when they arrive. There is no test without a testimony, no glory without a story! I would not be being honest if I told you that I was entirely confident when I made the decision to step out on faith to start my own church. It can be a very intimidating and lonely decision taking that big leap of faith, but you must know that God will be with you every step of the way. Even when it seems that nothing is going right, God is right there. When you take one step, He'll take two. Be not discouraged. Know that as a child of the most High, God will see you through, as He did for me. You must believe that when God has called you to do something great, it is human nature to be a little scared, but God will give you confirmation after confirmation that He has called you to this worthy task. However, He does not make acquiring the vision easy because He wants us to appreciate what we have when we get it and He wants us to totally rely upon Him knowing that He is our provider and will meet every need. If He makes things too easy, then we will not have a deep level of appreciation for Him. So if you have taken a big leap of faith to do something great for the kingdom, know that as you pray, ask God for guidance and seek His face. He will lead you down the right path and in the end you shall be blessed. *They that wait on the Lord shall renew their strength. They shall mount up with wings as eagles, they shall run and not be weary, they shall walk and not faint* (Isaiah 40:31)! Wait on the Lord my friend!

ABOUT THE AUTHOR

Pastor Richard Dunn, II was born in New York and moved to Miami with his family as a young child. He lived in Overtown and Liberty City, both in Miami, Florida. He attended and graduated from Miami Northwestern Senior High School. He is happily married to his wife Daphne Dunn for over twenty years and they have two sons, Richard P. Dunn III and Brandon Dunn.

Richard Dunn was appointed to the City of Miami Commission by his colleagues on January 26, 2010 to represent the Citizens of District five in Miami-Dade County for the second time and was elected in November 2010. In 1990, he led and organized the largest boycott in Miami-Dade County's history and was one of the plaintiff's in establishing single member districts in the City of Miami and Miami-Dade County School Board. He was also listed as one of the 50 most powerful Black professionals in South Florida in 2011 by 'Legacy Magazine'.

He is the founder of two Churches, Word of Life Missionary Baptist Church and Cathedral of Hope Church. He is currently the Senior Pastor of Faith Community Baptist Church.

Reverend Dunn received a Bachelor of Science Degree in Business Management from Central State University, and a Master of Divinity Degree in Counseling and Pastoral Care from Morehouse School of Religion

Faith Community Baptist Church
10401 NW 8th Avenue
Miami, FL 33150-1010
305 691-3200
Rev. Richard Dunn, Senior Pastor

Chapter 12

No Cross, No Crown
Written by Pastor Richard Dunn

*If any man will come after me, let him deny himself,
take up his cross and follow me.*
Mathew 16:24

This topic defines my trust in God, my test of faith and my perseverance through the journey of my life as a Pastor. Because of my trust in God and the tests and trials that I have overcome and triumphed over, I have a testimony. Through God's grace, mercy and His Hand upon my life, I am still standing despite the trials and tribulations that have come my way. This, I believe has given clarity to my ministry, which dates back to July 22, 1979.

Over 32 years of officially acknowledging my calling from God into the gospel preaching ministry, I have been on a journey that contained trials, triumphs, disappointments and victories. However, this glorious calling has dominated my entire life of fifty years since the tender age of eighteen. I can honestly say, "I have seen the lightening flash, I have heard the thunder roll, I have felt sin dashing trying to conquer my soul, but I heard the voice of Jesus saying to me, no never alone, He promised never to leave me, never to leave me alone." This is why I have chosen to write about the topic, 'No Cross, No Crown'! It is clear to me that no real, authentic ministry can effectively operate unless there is "a cross".

A CROSS

A cross is defined as a structure of wood standing upright with a transverse beam commonly used by the ancient Romans for execution. This of course, is the literal meaning with Jesus Christ, our Lord and savior being its most recognized victim. The definition of the words "bearing the cross" means an affliction that tests one's virtue, steadfastness, faith, or patience. The definition of *crown* is a reward of victory or a mark of honor. One thing I have had to realize in this faith journey is the fact that as paradoxical and excruciatingly painful as the cross is, enduring it is necessary if you are going to obtain the crown. There is no legitimate situation where someone received the crown without first bearing the cross. In fact, it is the cross that justifies the crown. Every great person has stories of great tests, trials, failures and disappointments. Everyone at some point has their own cross to bear. In 1693, Thomas Shepherd penned the words to the hymn, "Must Jesus bear the cross alone and all the world go free, no there's a cross for everyone and there's a cross for me." Jesus Christ said in Matthew 16:24; *"If any man will come after me, let him deny himself, take up his cross and follow me."*

I can remember growing up in Miami, Florida as a child in the late 1960's attending New Covenant Presbyterian Church. I was boxed-in religiously because both of my parents, the late Richard Paul Dunn and the late Cecelia Sheffield Dunn were founding members of the church in 1966. Conversely, I was born the middle child. My sister was eleven months older than me and my brother was seven years younger than me. My mother was the minister of music and my father was an elder and lead tenor in the choir. Needless to say, I was a drug child. I was "drugged" to church every week - rain, hail or heat. In the book of Proverbs, Solomon gave parents some wise advise when he said to, *"Train up a child in the way they should go, and when they are old they will not depart from it."* (Proverbs 22:6) Well, I was certainly trained up and that training took root deep in my heart, mind and spirit. Not only was I boxed-in religiously with my parents, but I was also boxed-in through my grandparents, who organized and founded Drake Memorial Baptist Church also in Miami, Florida. My grandfather was the Senior Pastor and my grandmother was also minister of music. As I reflect back over my life, I can clearly see destiny written all over the situations that I encountered - the good, the bad and the ugly. I can see that the foundation that was laid for me even before I was old enough to understand the plan that God had for my life. Destiny is evidenced in my childhood upbringing from a parental to an ecumenical standpoint, which, because of my diverse religious background within Christendom prepared me for where I was able to lead and promote unity among church denominations when I served as president of the African-American Council of Christian Clergy.

The year is 1978. I graduated in the top ten percent of my class from High School and was selected by my peers as "Most likely to succeed". I was on my way to Central State University with a full football scholarship. I was only 17 years old when I entered college. I was able to start all four years on the football team and I still maintained a better than 3.0 grade point average. Life seemed to be going well. My freshman year in college was full of highlights and joys. In football, I received the 'Unsung Hero Award' and excelled academically. I was a student-athlete in the truest sense of the word. However, in spite of these achievements, my life took a turn. It began when my high school sweetheart and I broke up. I simply could not understand how my girlfriend, who I had been faithful to, had not been faithful to me. I kept asking myself how this could have happened when usually it was the other way around. I had put my trust in her and this was how my trust was repaid. Needless to say, I was heartbroken. I remember vividly, after returning back to college from the Christmas break sitting in my room in tears because of the hurt I was experiencing and asking the question, *"Who can I trust?"* Just then I heard a soft voice say to me, *"You can trust Me. I will never let you down."* Although this cross seemed unbearable at the time, I now realize in retrospect that God was setting things up for "the crown". I was only eighteen then, but this is what God permitted to happen in that season because it catapulted me into a personal relationship with Him and into the gospel ministry. I became so committed in my relationship with Christ at this time that after a few "hits and misses" I pledged a self-imposed vow to celibacy. I was able to remain true to that vow for over five years. However, I always give the disclaimer: It was not that I could not indulge sexually, but rather that I would not. During my senior year, I was co-captain of the football team and was a four-year starter, so finding a young lady to "be with" was not a difficult task, but my level of spiritual maturity and commitment was genuine. During this time, I was also a part of an active campus ministry. My plan was to enter into ministry after I retired from professional football. It is quite obvious now, that God had other plans that did not line up with mine. God sent Dr. Terry L. Hill, founding pastor of a church in Dayton, Ohio to help guide me as a spiritual father and mentor. His son Victor Hill, was a friend while in college and was also instrumental in keeping me on the spiritual path that God was leading me.

There is no doubt in my mind that Dr. Hill and his son had a significant impact on my calling. These relationships coupled with others helped encourage and sustain me during my college years. I knew that once I was called, if I was going to be able to teach and preach effectively, that I had to attend seminary. It was at this time that I began developing my goals. My love for football began decreasing and I started losing motivation for the game. There had been a time that football was all that I ate, drank and slept, but at this time of my life, I was totally sold out for Jesus. Because of my deep love for Him, His Word, and applying His commands to my life, I was able to remain true to my vow of celibacy. However, I was faced with trying to maintain my football scholarship so that I could stay in school. Amazingly, even though I was no longer as committed to football as I once had been, I was able to remain a starter and still compete at high-levels. I eagerly awaited graduation because I had a strong desire to attend seminary. I was accepted at Duke Divinity School, Union Theological Seminary in New York, Howard Divinity School and The Interdenominational Theological Center's Baptist affiliate, Morehouse School of Religion in Atlanta, Georgia. I received my on-the-job-training from a senior pastor from Atlanta, Georgia. Little did I know at the time that he would have the most profound and long-lasting impact on me personally and spiritually. I learned a tremendous amount from a practical perspective about pastoral ministry, counseling ministry, radio ministry, outreach ministry, visitation ministry, death and dying ministry, urban ministry, bus ministry, finance ministry, evangelism, marriage, fatherhood and life in general. This man had been strategically placed by God into my life to mentor me. There is no doubt in mind that God used Dr. J. Allen Milner, Pastor Cleo O. Albury and others to mentor me. Everyone needs a mentor. No man is an island and no man knows all there is to know about anything. While in Atlanta at that time, God gave me a great blessing, my wife Daphne which was and still is a joy and delight to me. As of this writing, we have been married for 25 years and have two sons. At this point in my life, I had earned a Masters of Divinity Degree. I felt that I was ready to conquer the world, tear down strongholds and be about my Father's business in Kingdom building. There was no question about my willingness to trust and obey God. The evidence is clear that I was totally committed.

THE HEDGE

Prior to this, I had been successful in college in Ohio and even more successful in seminary in Atlanta, so there was no reason why I would not do even greater things in my hometown of Miami. And initially, this was the case. Upon returning home, I began preaching all over town and eventually became my grandfather's Assistant Pastor at Drake Memorial Baptist Church. Many people felt that I was going to be his successor. There were many larger churches that had expressed interest in me and I was even offered the position of Campus Minister at Florida Memorial University, but did not accept the offer because it would have caused a conflict with Sunday Morning Worship Services at my church. At the time, I also had a very popular radio talk show that I hosted. Through this show, we were able to help lead the largest one-day boycott in the history of Miami-Dade County where more than 85,000 students could not attend school because the bus drivers helped us "shut it down". As a result of that and other things I was doing in the community, I was being asked to serve on boards and committees by politicians and I was not even 30 years old yet. No doubt, I was well on my way. However, I could not and did not foresee the enemy coming. His severe attacks upon my life blindsided me with such fierceness that I did not know what hit me. From being called a "church thief" to enduring children drowning at a church picnic. I did not realize at the time that the test and the cross must come first.

THE HEDGE REMOVED

In Job 1:10-11, Satan asks the Lord, *"Hast not Thou made an hedge about him, and about his house, and about all that he hath on every side? Thou hast blessed the work of his hands, and his substance is increased in the land. But put forth Thine hand now, and touch all that he hath, and he will curse thee to Thy face."* I am convinced that all of us will have our hedge removed so that we could be tested. How will you handle your test or bear your cross? Will you crumble in the face of adversity or will you trust God to bring you out? I must admit that I did not do very well at first. Many things started happening all at once and became a domino effect, for it was one thing after the next. My father died and my uncle committed suicide the night of my father's homegoing service.

Then my grandmother died, who practically lived vicariously through me. All of these things happened seemingly at once. After my grandmother passed, my grandfather remarried a woman over 30 years his junior. Needles-to-say, I was shocked, hurt, confused and angry about this, but reluctantly accepted his decision. All of a sudden, my once loving and nurturing relationship with my grandfather was strained. It was evident that I was being attacked from an unseen level and became more obvious when the manifestations began to show up in my life. My grandfather and I no longer shared the close loving relationship we once had. He became very critical of my actions and our relationship became tense. This relationship hit an all-time low in the later part of May 1991 when I resigned from the church, Drake Memorial Baptist Church as his Assistant Pastor. When I left, there emerged all kinds of rumors as to why I resigned. It was rumored that I was forced to resign because I stole money from the church. This was the furthest thing from the truth and the lie hurt me deeply. I was under no pressure to resign. In fact, my grandfather and the church leaders asked me to come back, but I refused. This, as one can imagine almost became a permanent "cross" for me because whenever I ran for political office or was under consideration for a major appointment, this allegation would be used against me. And the funny thing about it is that people who knew nothing of my situation at Drake Memorial, who never met or knew me, would speak on the matter as though they were there. It was simply a rumor that had been started by someone and the lie spread like wildfire. It is a hurtful thing to have a lie circulate about you when you know you are innocent and when individuals do not have all the truth. Being labeled as a church thief is one of the worst accusations in the Black church that one could be accused of. People are more willing to forgive for adultery than they are for stealing from the people of God. This was a hard pill for me to swallow because it was my reputation, my character and my name that had been tarnished.

That lie was like a dark cloud over my head that tried to keep haunting me whenever I would aspire to do something impactful. The devil seeks to distract, discourage and ultimately destroy us. Dr. Martin Luther King once said, *"no lie can live forever"*. Believe me, God will always make sure that the truth is eventually revealed. Jesus says in John 8:32, *"And you shall know the truth, and the truth shall make you free."* To this day, I have preached at that same church over fifteen times since leaving and I am always welcomed there. There are many who know the truth.

THE HUMILIATION

As a result of this public humiliation, I was deeply wounded. The issue became a very public matter since I was a public figure. Luke 12:18 says, *"To whom much is given, much is required."* I went from the "golden boy" to now being labeled and branded as the "church thief". I was talked about and ridiculed, especially by those who desired to see me fall. As I look back over my life at that cross that I had to bear and the humiliation and betrayal, I clearly see that God was purging and preparing me. He needed to humble me and teach me to totally rely upon Him. It is the same with each of us as children of God. Things will happen that will knock you to your knees. You will be blindsided and not understand why such things are coming your way. This is the time to seek the Lord, to pray for humility and guidance and to ask God, *"What lesson do you want me to learn from this?"* We can sometimes cut our struggles in half when we do this. God will answer and we must be in position and ready to hear Him when He does.

THE CROWN

One thing is for certain on this faith journey for all of us, and that is that humiliation always comes before honor. No cross, No crown! No test, No testimony! No crucifixion, No resurrection! No story, no glory! Romans 8:28 says, *...and we know that all things work together for good, to them that* *love God, to them, who are the called according to His purpose.* Beloved, if we can grasp this biblical principle, it will help us to know that at the end of the day, we have the victory. The good news is that this is not how the story ends. One thing about God is that in Hebrews 13:5, He says, *"I will never leave nor forsake you."* God placed family members, friends and pastors in my life who supported, encouraged and helped me get through this season of cross bearing. God began to raise people up who would speak up for my character and dispel the lies that the enemy was trying to perpetuate. Testimonies started coming out of nowhere. God was preparing multiple crowns for me. He stepped in and vindicated me. After resigning from Drake Memorial Baptist Chruch, I submitted my resume' to another church and was called to pastor the New Mount Moriah Baptist Church in Miami, Florida on July 3, 1991. Yes, God showed up on my behalf and placed the hedge back around me. Since that time, I have served as founding pastor of Word of Life Baptist Church and Cathedral of Hope Baptist Church. God began to do great things for me once I learned to totally rely upon Him and humble myself. For instance, Word of Life Community Development Corporation was the first church-based African-American Community Development Corporation to build detached single-family homes in Miami-Dade County for first-time home buyers in 2001. I was then "appointed" to serve as Senior Pastor of Faith Community Baptist Church without a church-wide search in October 2008, where I am currently serving as senior pastor. This was unheard of in a main-line denominational church, But if God is for you, who can be against you? God can restore your reputation! During this period of restoration, I was named by Ebony Magazine as one of the nation's 30 'Black Leaders of the Future for persons 30 years old and younger in the November 1991 issue. I was appointed to the city of Miami Commission in September 1996, as the youngest African-American at the age of 35. I was appointed again to the city of Miami commission in

January 2010 and was elected out right for the first time without a runoff in November 2010. In 2011, I was recognized by "Legacy Magazine" as one of the 50 Most 'Powerful African-Americans in South Florida', which includes Miami-Dade, Broward, and Palm Beach Counties.

This is living proof that once we line up with God, stay faithful, endure the tests and trials and totally trust Him, He will grant you His favor. Once God's favor is upon your life, He will use you to do a great work in the earth realm. And it does not matter what antics, fiery darts, rumors or lies the enemy throws at you, *"No weapon formed against you shall prosper."* says Isaiah 54:17. Yes they can, and will mean it for evil, but God will make it work together for your good.

As I close, I want to remind you that we all have our crosses to bear. The road won't be easy and the burdens will not always be light; but each experience that you go through is designed to enhance you, strengthen you, and purge you. God will never leave you nor forsake you. There is no one on this earth who will escape the trials and struggles that come with this life, but when you trust in God, you will see how everything was tailor-made just for you. However, it all works out for your good. I have been through a lot in my life and although much of it hurt me to my core, I am a better man because of it and it has taught me to increase my faith in God, because He has taught me that He will be with me always - even until the end of the world. When we endure the cross, we get the crown, but no cross, no crown. *May God bless you and keep you* is my prayer.

ABOUT THE AUTHOR

Pastor Ricardo Peters is the Pastor of Glendale Baptist Church in Miami Florida. He is native of New York City and has served as Pastor for the past two years. He attended the "Fame" school Fiorello H. LaGuardia High School of Music and Art in New York City, NY and his love for music allowed him to sing at various events in the city of Miami.

In 2003 Reverend Peters sang and recorded with the Miami Music Workshop Choir. He is a veteran of the United States Navy with a total of six years of service. In 1993, he answered the call to preach the gospel and was licensed at Bible Baptist Church in Miami FL. He has been employed by the Department of Juvenile Justice since 2004 and is presently serving as Assistant Detention Center Superintendent while there. On September 7, 2008, Reverend Peters was ordained and appointed as Assistant Pastor of the Faith Community Baptist Church. On June 24, 2009, he was introduced to the Glendale Baptist Church of Brownsville Miami Florida and assumed the Pastorate on October 25, 2009.

In 2010, he was selected to serve on the Board of Directors for the Miami Youth for Christ. He also serves as the Regional Chaplain for the Department of Juvenile Justice. He is married to his best friend, Odetta. They have four great children, Felicita, Ricardo II, Benjamin and Gloria. His favorite biblical scripture is *Romans 5:8: God commended his love towards, us in that, while we were yet sinners, Christ died for us.* He feels that this captures how much God loves us.

Reverend Ricardo Peters
Glendale Baptist Church of Brownsville
4501 NW 22 Avenue
Miami Florida 33142
305 - 638 - 0857
Pastorrick1964@comcast.net

Chapter 13

From Altar boy to Pastor
"An Unlikely Progression"
Written by Reverend Ricardo Peters

For my thoughts are not your thoughts, neither are your ways my ways, saith the LORD. For as the heavens are higher than the earth, so are my ways higher than your ways, and my thoughts than your thoughts.

(Isaiah 55:8-9)

A look at my journey would reveal how an unlikely and farfetched situation can become your reality when God has a purpose for your life. As an altar boy in the Catholic Church, I practiced the Catholic tenets which differ significantly from the Protestant church. The two denominations share the belief in the Father, the Son and the Holy Spirit, but the worship is structured differently. Another major difference is the manner in which a person comes to give their lives to Christ. The qualifications that one must have in order to become a spiritual leader are also vastly different in the Catholic church from the Protestant Church. The scripture says in Colossians 1:12, ...*giving thanks to the Father, who has qualified you to share in the inheritance of the saints in the kingdom of light.* This scripture has helped me to understand that I could be what God has called me to be under His qualifications.

I am Reverend Ricardo Peters, Senior Pastor/Teacher of the Glendale Baptist Church of Brownsville in Miami Florida. I am the youngest of four children born to John and Felicita Peters. My father was of Haitian decent and my mother was from Puerto Rico. The primary language spoken in our home was Spanish and as far as I knew, I was Puerto Rican and Haitian. My father assimilated so much into my mother's culture that we did not learn much about the Haitian culture. At an early age, my mother told me that I was an unplanned birth. At the time, I could not see the blessing in being told that information. Since my parents were catholic, an abortion was unspeakable at the time of her pregnancy; so all throughout my childhood, the constant thought that I was not planned was a frequent cloud over my head. I also wondered why my mother would share this information with me. However, the look in her eyes was not one of regret or disdain. When I became a parent, I then understood the look. It was the look that comes from amazement at what God has done. I would later learn Psalms 139:14 *I will give thanks unto thee; for I am fearfully and wonderfully made: Wonderful are thy works; and that my soul knoweth right well.* I was not a mistake after all.

A GRIM-LOOKING FUTURE

In my early years, I was an altar boy at St Luke's Catholic Church, which is located in one of New York's five boroughs called the Bronx. I served faithfully until I was twelve years old, which was when I had a crisis of faith. I had never seen God, never felt God and felt as if my many prayers were never answered. The borough I lived in was one of America's poorest ones. Food stamps and Medicaid was a normal part of the households in my community. As a matter of fact, when I reached high school and met friends who did not live that way, it was quite strange to me. As a child, I would hear the priest talking about living a better life and following God's ways. However, it was far from reality for me. God or no God, my view of life was bleak. In 1977, President Jimmy Carter called my community the "worst slum in America." Not able to hold it in any longer, the plight of my community, the criminal activity and the suffering in the world caused me to speak out one day. I remember declaring *"There is no God!"* I did not know that the bible called me foolish, for it is written in Psalm 14:1, *The fool hath said in his heart, There is no God.*

The year 1978 was my first year at the famed New York school, Fiorello H. LaGuardia High School of Music and Art. While in high school, I met many classmates who called themselves "saved." I remember those who sang in the gospel choir singing in the auditorium one day. The song was 'A change has come over me'. I was amazed by their talent. For some reason, listening to them sing pricked my heart. During this time, there was a friend of the upstairs neighbor who would always come to the neighborhood and talk to me about Jesus. I remember telling him that the things he was talking about were not for me because I was Puerto Rican and a Catholic. My upstairs neighbors would also share the gospel with me every opportunity they had, but my ignorance to what they were sharing was a result of the Roman Catholicism with which I had been indoctrinated. As a Catholic, my understanding was that if all else failed, my family could pray for my soul and I would get into heaven. That is the reason that what the neighbors and their friends were sharing with me seemed unimportant. It was something that African-Americans did, not us Puerto Ricans. I felt that I could pay my way into heaven.

THE END OF MY WORLD!

My second crisis of faith occurred in the month of November in 1978. My world as I knew it had come to an end; my mother died. I recall going into the bathroom and falling on my knees crying to God, *"If you are real, then give me the power to make it through this."* I felt His presence in that bathroom that very moment. I was able to go out into the living room where there appeared to be utter chaos. There was screaming and wailing. It was *my* mother, but her brothers and sisters were taking it just as hard. I felt that I had no one to comfort me from the pain of losing my mom. My aunt and uncles were emotionally wrecked. They could not provide me with the comfort I needed at that time because obviously they needed comfort too. However, I felt comforted without really understanding why. Psalms 120:1 says, *In my distress I cried unto the LORD, and he heard me.* I can honestly say that that scripture was true for me.

A NEW BEGINNING!

In 1979, I decided to join the gospel choir at my high school even though I did not understand the message behind the singing. I just really liked the sounds and what I found out later to be the anointing on the singing. While in the choir, we would travel to different churches and events to sing. On one particular rehearsal, I remember hearing a voice telling me that I had been wrong. I thought the voice was talking to me about my musical notes but "the voice" went on to say that the way that I was living was wrong. The lyrics of the song that was being rehearsed at the time was: *Why do you wait my brother, why do you tarry so long? The savior is waiting to give you a place in his sanctified home. Why not give your life today!* As I listened to the song, the emotions and thoughts that emerged in me were overwhelming. Some months later, I heard my brother say that he had gotten "saved". There was an evangelistic event at a neighborhood church and he had given his life to Christ while there. So I decided to check it out for myself. That night I heard the gospel preached and I too accepted Christ. I could not wait to go to school on Monday to share this great news with my friends. It seemed that what was thought to be unplanned was actually in God's plan all along. As stated in Jeremiah 29:11, *For I know the plans I have for you," declares the LORD, "plans to prosper you and not to harm you, plans to give you hope and a future."* I recall that I wanted to read the whole bible right away so that I could know all about what my classmates were talking about. My best friend in high school brought a used (lost and found) bible to school and gave it to me. I started to read it, but it proved to be a bigger task than I was prepared for. However, somehow I felt that this was something that had to be done, especially since I was getting a late start at it.

PREPARATION FOR THE CALL

After graduating high school, I joined a community choir where I was in constant contact with the protestant way of life. In 1982, I enlisted in the United States Navy. However, I could not go to boot camp because of a back injury. I continued singing with the choir and getting closer to the Lord. Many of the places I visited people would assume that I was a preacher, which always fascinated me, but I did not know what a preacher was. Obviously, I was already carrying the mantle in the spirit realm and just didn't know it. Being raised under Catholicism, I knew what a priest was, but I had no inclination or desire to go that route - especially after I learned that they could not marry! That was enough for me to leave it alone. There was no need for me to inquire any further after learning that information. During church visits I would watch the preachers very closely. I eventually came to the conclusion that I would never be good enough of a person to be used by God as a preacher. In the winter of 1985, my back was finally well enough to go to boot camp. One of the most remarkable things that happened to me while there was being chosen to be the religious Petty Officer. This position called for me to pray for the unit every day. My shipmates would often ask if I was a preacher or the son of one - especially when I prayed for us to win competitions and we would win. Like Mary, the earthly mother of Jesus, I would ponder these things in my heart. However, my sensitivity to my sinful nature was growing stronger and I said to myself, *"not me, God can't use me."* After boot camp, I became very wild being away from home. The freedom was too much to handle. Even though my parents were not religiously strict, they were strict in other ways, such as not allowing me to openly have a girlfriend or drinking; so alone and away from home, it was party time for me! I partied until one night I got so drunk in the city of Groton, CT. that I had to be carried back to the barracks. The next Sunday, I decided to go to church because this was no way of living. I drove around New London, CT until I found a church with a familiar name: Trinity Missionary Baptist Church. I walked up a long flight of stairs wondering what was going to happen to me when I got inside. Thank God I found them to be a warm and friendly bunch of people. This was the beginning of church life for me. The Pastor of the church was a giant of a man both in stature and spirit. He took me under his wings and mentored me. I always say that he taught me how to be a man. All of my extra time was spent with him learning about Jesus and the Christian way of life. New London was only two hours from home and prior to joining Trinity, I went home almost every weekend. During my stay in New London CT, my life became predicated upon the Christian way of living. I learned church songs and the structure of the Baptist church as it relates to the different leadership positions and their functions. With this church I travelled to Philadelphia and experienced my first revival. 2 Timothy 4:2 says to *Preach the Word!* This revival experience was something I had never experienced as a Catholic. Looking back over my life, I can clearly see that God was preparing me to preach the Word as a pastor. Those years of serving under the tutelage of the pastor of Trinity were my training years, my years of preparation for ministry.

ACCEPTING THE CALL

In the fall of 1987, I acknowledged my call into the gospel ministry, but then human nature took over and I got scared. I was scheduled to re-enlist in the US Navy, but I decided not to reenlist. In December of that year I went to visit my father who had moved to Miami, Florida. I was intrigued by the ambience of the Miami lifestyle, but I still had the fear of pursuing the call of God in my life. However, in January of 1988, I moved to Miami. It is written in Psalms 37:23, *The steps of a good man are ordered by the Lord, And He delights in his way.* During this time, I still was not convinced that I was good enough to preach the Word. I worked at several places and would run into Christians who invited me to their local churches. Some of the churches were too large for my taste; others at that time were unfamiliar to me as a result of my ignorance of the doctrines of what I now know to be mainstream Protestant churches. I worked for a local security company and my life began to take a turn when a friend invited me to his church where he was the minister of music. I visited and became acquainted with others my age. As young Christians, we fellowshipped and had a good time in the Lord. However, both the minister of music and the pastor's daughter felt that I should meet a nice girl. They told me that there was someone interested in me. However, I later found out that the young lady was told that I was interested in her as well. Neither was true. When I did meet her, she did not appear to be my type and I was definitely not her type. Nevertheless, she had a very friendly personality and we began to converse frequently. It would soon become apparent to me that the decision to move to Miami was not mine. It seemed as though my life was being orchestrated by a greater power. As she and I were conversing one day, she happen to mention that God had showed her that she would marry to a minister. I became angry with her for two reasons: I thought I had left all that preacher talk behind me. Secondly, because it sounded like a line I had heard before. When I got over the initial shock from what she had just said, I later told her about the call of God upon my life. God was beginning to show His hand and His presence in my life. Needless-to-say, in the summer of 1989 I married her, the former Odetta Burgess.

ALL THINGS WORK TOGETHER FOR GOOD

Like so many young people in Christ do, we make many mistakes because we rely upon our own reasoning in challenging situations which is often contrary to God's purpose. This is why the word tells us in Isaiah 1:18 to, *Come now, and let us reason together, saith the Lord: though your sins be as scarlet, they shall be as white as snow; though they be red like crimson, they shall be as wool.* My wife and I made the decision together to dedicate ourselves and our marriage to God. I would begin to learn the stark realities of the called. We dedicated ourselves to the Lord with all our heart, soul, mind and strength. This however, did not keep us from trials and tribulations. This call on my life required different demands and different ways of dealing with problems of being young, married, and not financially well off. However, I simply could not choose the way of the world to handle my situations. If I was short of money in my before Christ days, I could come up with a scheme to get some. But as a Christian, I knew what the bible says in Hebrew 11:6, *without faith it is impossible to please God*...meaning that if what I do is not done in faith, it is displeasing to God. The worst of the trials always seemed to be financial. I have had my share of tests, trials, and struggles in life. For instance, I have suffered foreclosures, repossessions, family illnesses and two premature births. My wife and I had a total of four children and we both felt that God had called my wife to leave work to stay home with our children. During this time, I was a member of Bible Baptist Church and the Pastor would often preach about going through trials. I always felt that God was giving me comfort through the preacher. I once heard him preach the following scripture in Romans 8:28: *And we know that all things work together for good to those who love God, to those who are the called according to His purpose.* I would often ask God, *"You mean all these trials that I am going through are going to somehow work out for my good?* If you have ever been there, I would like to encourage you by saying that yes it ALL things work together for good. I eventually informed the Pastor of my calling. He cautioned me that the calling involved a call to prepare. So he ensured that I had preparing opportunities. I was assigned to the group that went to the Juvenile Detention Center on Sundays to conduct worship service. I was later elected to be the President of men's ministry called 'The Brotherhood'. This was a totally unfamiliar experience for me. No other church I had been involved in had anything like this - especially as a Catholic. I had never heard of men getting together to do ministry. This was a ministry that witnessed to the lost, conducted nursing home visits and prepared baskets for the less fortunate during Thanksgiving and Christmastime. Here I learned that I had to go even if no one went with me because I love giving back as a servant of Christ. It warmed my heart. I also learned that God never leads you to where He cannot keep you.

STEPPING INTO DESTINY

Some years later, I became a founding member of a new ministry, Faith Community Baptist Church. Needless-to-say, this was too a brand new experience for me. However I saw how when God orchestrates something, it leads you to a new appreciation of His power. I remained there until I was approached by the Pastor and told that Glendale Baptist Church of Brownsville was seeking God for a Pastor. I always told God that wherever He led me, I would go. I was offered the position. My first Sunday there would have discouraged a person who already had little faith. There were only a few members left. It was not a big building and they had very little funds. Nonetheless, I was still overwhelmed thinking that a Catholic altar boy from "The Bronx" was now entering into ministry as a Pastor. It felt good walking into what God had called me to be. As a boy, I never had imagined being the Pastor of a church. In my wildest most outlandish dreams, this would not be found there. Now here I was the new Pastor of Glendale Baptist Church. Of course I started out as an interim Pastor. The church and I used this time to pray and seek God's will. It soon became apparent that God wanted me to Pastor the people at this church. There were several people who gave their life to Christ under my leadership. Members were beginning to return. The outreach ministry became active again and on October 25, 2009, I was installed as Pastor. The altar boy was now an official Pastor! Unlikely to world, but with God *all things are possible.*

    We came into this world to do the work of the Lord. He gives us other things to enjoy, but we must embark upon and complete the assignment that God has given to us. It is amazing and utterly astonishing how we think we know what *we* are going to do with our lives and God steps in and disrupts all of those plans. In my own reasoning, I never in a million years would have even considered being a pastor - especially in a Baptist Church, but God will step in, navigate the circumstances of your life and turn you in another direction. In the beginning it can be confusing and frustrating not knowing what God is doing, but in His timing, all things will come together and will be revealed. It is a great feeling to know that you are in Gods' will when things finally do come together. So seek God and be faithful. *Trust in the Lord with all your heart and lean not unto your own understanding. In all your ways acknowledge Him and He will direct your paths.* (Proverbs 3:5-6). He will make His will known to you. Embrace your story. It is the building block to your glory.

ABOUT THE AUTHOR

Pastor Kenneth D. Duke, a native of Dallas, Texas, journeyed to Miami, Fl. at the age of three and has since been actively involved in promoting Godliness wherever he resides. It was at the age of five that Elder Duke accepted Christ as his personal Savior, and at the age of sixteen he accepted his call into the ministry.

Elder Duke graduated from Miami Carol City Senior High School and received his college degree in Religion and Philosophy from Morehouse School of Religion in Atlanta, Georgia. Elder Duke has been blessed with many outstanding preaching and teaching opportunities and has had the awesome privilege of speaking on countless panels, with his most memorable, being with the late Dr. E.V. Hill of Los Angeles, California.

In Miami, Fl., Elder Duke was actively involved, with his home church, New Jerusalem Primitive Baptist Church, where his Father is the Senior Pastor/Teacher. There, he promoted a holistic ministry for young Christians. His dedication and love for teaching and preaching the Word of God has gained him an undisputable reputation, which he humbly appreciates. As Elder Duke continues to grow in grace and in the knowledge of God, he aspires to reach a higher standard among God's people for the glory of God and his son Jesus Christ. Elder Duke is a powerful gospel singer and credits his vocal quality to his mother, Mrs. Avis Stevenson Petty.

Under the divine authority and will of God, Elder Kenneth D. Duke was ordained in October 2010 and was installed as the Pastor of the St. John Primitive Baptist Church in Delray Beach, Florida on November 13, 2010.

He is the eldest son of Elder Kenneth A. Duke and Evangelist Julia A. Duke. He is the sibling to a twin brother, Elder Kelon Duke and sister Aheisha Duke. He is also the proud father of Kennedi Duke.

Chapter 14

The Power of an Anointed Sermon
Written by Pastor Kenneth Duke

Preach the word! Be instant in season, out of season; reprove, rebuke, exhort with all long suffering and doctrine.
(2 Timothy 4:2)

Living in this post-modern era, a host of pastors/preachers have found themselves dealing with the strain of trying to balance the success of social affairs in the natural and the sanctioning of the spiritual. In dealing with a task such as this, surrogates of the anointing have been put into practice with its prominence and focus being shifted from preaching *in the atmosphere*, to *producing the atmosphere*. We observe the producing of atmospheres daily as we watch church leaders attempting to gratify the trends and the trendy only to end up yearning to go back to the basics. Our teachings have taught us that the anointing destroys the yoke, not our own self-confidence, self-assertiveness, or our own influence. And it has been a proven fact throughout the years that preaching is neither effective nor life-changing without the anointing. Without the anointing, it is merely inspirational words yielding little or no fruit.

I must admit that in wanting to be great, we sometimes bend the rules to get us where we desire to be. We believe that we have to do something out of the norm to be exceptional. We believe we have to formulate fancy verbiage in order to sound spectacular. It has become a resounding effort to engage in over-enthusiastic activities in order to give the impression that we are super expositors of the gospel in order to enhance powerful, anointed sermons. However, the truth is, *we ain't got to do nothing but operate under the anointing that God has already blessed us with!* So then, after the trends are no longer allowable and the producing of the atmosphere by way of distraction is no longer acceptable, when people would rather the power of an anointed sermon rather that the penmanship of an aggravated one, what should one do? Because the power of an anointed sermon is what convicts and changes the lives of individuals, it is extremely important that pastors understand the need to be led by God who anoints us in His power to speak and represent His Word. In my personal life, I have gained knowledge in knowing that the power of an anointed sermon is nurtured by:

       1.) one's relationship with God
       2.) dedication to bible preaching
       3.) preaching in transparency and
       4.) building a rapport with the people of God.

    The most vital area in developing powerful sermons with the anointing is to have a relationship with God. The bible declares in Luke 4:18-19, *"The Spirit of the Lord is upon me, because He has anointed me to preach the gospel to the poor; He has sent me to heal the brokenhearted, to proclaim liberty to the captives and recovery of sight to the blind. To set at liberty those who are oppressed; to proclaim the acceptable year of the LORD."* Certainly, God has called pastors to preach His Word. He has given His people the anointing to liberate and call into order things that have been out of order. However, like all other gifts He has bestowed upon us, being in direct contact with Him will keep us in the anointing. In my years of preaching, I would often hear people say, *"He had a good Word, but it didn't flow under the anointing."* My mission thereafter was to differentiate the anointed sermon from the un-anointed, stale sermon, and I did. I have come to understand in my walk with Christ that my preaching the Word of God is only effective to the degree in which He intended it to be when I have consulted Him, prayed alongside Him, conveyed that I needed Him, and consistently asked Him to anoint me anew and afresh every day. Let's be honest, even in our relationship with mortal men, we only thrive and grow when we are in constant relationship. That is why our prayer life is important and the time we spend with the body of Christ is important as well. I cannot imagine endeavoring to write a sermon without operating under the anointing of God. The power of an anointed sermon when you have a relationship with God is knowing that the people of God will hear from Him through you, that He will be speaking through a human vessel with power and clarity in spirit and truth.

One thing that remains classical in preaching is preaching the bible within the appropriate context coupled with the appropriate content. Though there may be a plethora of inconsistencies, what we know to remain consistent is the fact that *we* do not change lives; preaching the Word of God with biblical application is what changes lives. It is the Word of God that brings about the anointing in a powerful sermon. Again, let's be honest, we have all heard preaching that does not line up with the Word of God. It yields no fruit, causes many to question if the truth is the "actual truth" and it leaves the people of God confused. The power of an anointed sermon derives when the authenticity of the bible is being delivered effectively. It is not about one's opinions, ones thoughts, or even ones experiences, but it is about the unveiling of the Word of God - period! Nowadays, people want to preach what feels good. They want to stand in God's pulpit speaking words that will celebrate the people in their wrongdoing rather than convicting them in their willingness to do. I know, I know, I know that we have the right intentions at times, but the wrong submission at times as well. For some strange reason, people like to think that biblical preaching means to preach the bible using a certain style or a particular structure. However, in order to preach the bible and understand the content and context of it, one must first understand the culture of the bible. How can you preach an anointed sermon using the bible if you first do not understand it?

In reading a commentary on biblical preaching from the *'Core of Biblical Preaching'*, Author William D. Thompson stated the following: *"Biblical preaching is when listeners are enabled to see how their world, like the biblical world, is addressed by the Word of God. It is important not to be superficial when it comes to what makes preaching biblical. How many Bible verses a sermon has does not determine whether or not it is biblical. You can have a hundred verses in a sermon and misinterpret them all. Biblical preaching occurs when people listen, are enabled to hear that God is addressing them as God addressed the world of the scriptures and are enabled to respond."* Therefore, the power of an anointed sermon is brought forth when the bible is preached with clarity and causes application to take place in people's lives. No additions, no subtractions. The power in an anointed sermon comes alive when the *truth* is being preached.

In the book of 2 Corinthians 12:7-10 Paul lays claim to these words: *And lest I should be exalted above measure by the abundance of the revelations, a thorn in the flesh was given to me, a messenger of Satan to buffet me, lest I be exalted above measure. Concerning this thing I pleaded with the Lord three times that it might depart from me. And He said to me, "My grace is sufficient for you, for my strength is made perfect in weakness." Therefore most gladly I will rather boast in my infirmities, that the power of Christ may rest upon me. Therefore I take pleasure in infirmities, in reproaches, in needs, in persecutions, in distresses, for Christ's sake. For when I am weak, then I am strong."* As a growing preacher and now pastor, this passage of scripture has always been dear to my heart. As I went through growing pains both in my personal life and with my call to preach; having a baby out of wedlock, dealing with my own insecurities about whether or not I could fulfill this vision that God had given me, the one man I knew could help me capitalize on this pain was Paul. For fear that people would think my sermons were obsolete, I began to write sermons under my own leadership. Can I be transparent? I mean, really, who wants to hear about grace being sufficient in times such as these? Who wants to hear about thorns in our flesh when in fact, for many of us, those very thorns make us live in the corrupted and cryptic life we, for some weird reason have grown to love? Being called at the age of 16, I didn't comprehend a lot of the pain I was dealing with. I used to ask God as I got up in age, *"If I am this confused and feeling so frustrated about what I am dealing with now, how will I ever get any better?"* All types of questions were going through my mind. Who will believe I can even be called with such a jacked up resume? Will my openness be accepted or rejected? I didn't think I could write anointed sermons with a life story like mine. But, that grace response that God gave to Paul, He also gave to me. God gave me grace and a double portion of His anointing to use my testimony to invest in the power of anointed preaching. The bible declares in Romans 8:28: *"And we know that all things work together for good to them that love God, to them who are the called according to his purpose."* Truly this is the case. The power of an anointed sermon lies in the transparency of the pastor. Had I not gone through the things I did and explicitly share my story throughout my sermons, lives would not have been liberated. God has anointed me to touch the lives of men and women. When my relationship with God is tight, when I preach the unadulterated Word of God, and when I am able to be transparent in my sermons, God moves mightily! When all these components line up, then God shows up. It always amazes me how God gives me such power when I begin to talk about this old wretched man that I am. He pours His spirit out onto the people when I am yet able to be identifiable. In my church, I have some male members who are co-parents with a woman they did not initially marry - been there. I have some people who were broken by problems they created but could not carry - been there. I minister to men and women who do not know whether they are going to the left or to the right - been there. I can feel the pain of people whose self-esteem has dropped to a critical low - been there. But whatever I do, whether it is preaching, teaching, counseling, praying, laughing or crying, it is under the anointing. The anointing makes the difference in our lives. Without it we can only go so far and the most powerful thing about it, is the fact that it cannot be duplicated, replicated, or imitated. You either have the anointing or you don't!

An anointed sermon is distinctively different from a sermon that has no anointing. Believe it or not, many of God's people are readily discerning enough to know whether or not one has a relationship with God, is a bible based preacher, is transparent and carries an anointing. These qualities are the ingredients that makes a powerful, anointed sermon. However, let me add one more facet to what makes a powerful anointed sermon: building rapport with the people of God. In my short-lived moments of pastoring, I have discovered that people are looking for a shepherd who is concerned with them as individuals, making them more than a number on a roster. You may be wondering, "What does the power of an anointed sermon have to do with building rapport with God's people? Well, I am glad that you are pondering such a thought. It has been my personal experience that when I get to know what my congregants are going through, their hardships and pain, it is then that I began to pray for them. As I stand in the pulpit preaching, the anointing begins to flow. I then look out at the faces of those I have prayed with and for. It is then that I am able to remember the spiritual needs of God's people. It appears that something that is unexplainable, yet supernatural happens to me. Only God knows what it is begins He gives it to me. As I draw from Him, the people of God draw from me.

The anointing reaches places that I cannot reach. It touches what is intangible. The anointing that God gives is powerful.

Within this chapter, I have vividly discussed how being a bible-based preacher, having a relationship with God, being transparent, and developing a rapport with the people of God are all foundational components that make a powerful and anointed sermon. I feel that I can convictionally and emphatically tell you these things because I have integrated them into my own life and have experienced the supernatural results. For this reason, I testify that I have felt the power and anointing of God in the sermons preached by the Lord through me. At St. John Primitive Baptist Church, where God has blessed me to be the shepherd over His people, there has been over 50 people to join within one year. The people of God have been liberated because of the anointing that flows. I know the difference between preaching a powerful and anointed sermon and simply preaching a sermon. In all honesty, I have had days where I was not flowing in the anointing, and I knew it and felt it. At those times, I was going through my own personal struggles, tests and trials. I was too busy allowing my mind to become dominated by my own problems that I did not provide God's people with the tools needed to think and meditate on the Word of God for themselves. However, the anointing never left me. The anointing never leaves you! I just was not allowing it to operate though me, but it was still there.

In closing, I want it to be emphasized that my thorns pushed me into a deeper anointing. Those thorns allowed me to express the power of God in the midst of them. The power of an anointed sermon destroys yokes, liberates the people of God, motivates them to apply the Word into their lives, increases their faith in God, and blesses the one that brings that powerful anointed sermon forth! An anointed sermon is birthed when there is a relationship with God; when bible-based preaching takes place; when the preacher demonstrates transparency and when one builds rapport with the people. I cannot reiterate those key points enough! It is my heart's desire that God's people continue to operate under the anointing in everything they attempt to do. The goal is for pastors to preach *in* the atmosphere, as opposed to trying to *produce* the atmosphere which is created with activities, antics, and entertainment for the flesh. I have noticed that the body of Christ as a whole has parted from thriving under the anointing because so many things convolute and/or takes precedence over our responsibilities to God.

God is serious about His people getting free and liberated in Him. It is only in Him that we can walk in spiritual authority and be able to use the power of the Holy Spirit given to us. Therefore as the man of God stands in the pulpit to deliver a Word to the sheep, He should have sought the will of God through prayer, having asked for guidance for a message to give to the people. As the spirit of God increases, the flesh will decrease and the anointing of God will be on the sermon and bless the souls of the people. This is what God wants in a sermon. This is how you get the power of an anointed sermon - by seeking the Face and the will of God!

ABOUT THE AUTHOR

Pastor Tracy L. McCloud is the Pastor/Teacher of Peace Missionary Baptist Church in Miami, Fl having served over eight years as Senior Pastor. Reverend McCloud is also an administrator for a public school district in South Florida. As a leader, he also serves as President of the Congress of Christian Education for the Seaboard Baptist Association and 1st Vice Present of the Seaboard Baptist Association's Union.

Reverend McCloud has a Bachelor's Degree from Florida Memorial University, a Masters Degree from Nova Southeastern University and a Doctor of Divinity Degree from Jacksonville Theological Seminary.

Dr. McCloud has been happily married to First Lady Sheryl McCloud for over 20 years. They have five beautiful children: Talithia, 27, Keniesha, 26, Tracy Jr. 21, Tratasha, 20 and Dan, 12. His favorite passage of scripture is, *"And we know that all things work together for good to them that love God, to them who are the called according to his purpose. For whom he did foreknow, he also did predestinate to be conformed to the image of his Son, that he might be the firstborn among many brethren. (Romans 8:28-29)*

Peace Missionary Baptist Church
11700 NW 17th Avenue
Miami, FL 33169
305-681-4681

Chapter 15

Steadfast, Unmovable Always Abounding!
Written by Reverend Dr. Tracy McCloud

Before I formed thee in the belly I knew thee; and before thou came forth out of the womb I sanctified thee, and I ordained thee a prophet unto the nations.
(Jeremiah 1:5)

Throughout the course of my life, I have experienced many episodes of transformations through gratification and aggravation. Growing up as a pastor's child was very taxing and filled with spiraling events. On several occasions, I witnessed my father's heart severely broken by the very people he loved and was shepherd over. Through these experiences, I quickly grew to detest the rational for preaching, yet alone pastoring. However, as a young boy, I honored and looked forward to following in my father's footsteps in ministry. That urge swiftly began to shift as I matured and the adolescent naiveté began to diminish. It was during this time of maturing that I started to concentrate my focus more on the career of education rather than pursuing the call to minister.

STRUGGLING WITH THE CALL

My call into ministry began as a child. At the age of twelve, God visited me in a dream and called me to preach the gospel. However, I ignored my call because of my inner conflicts in ministry which my father and mother suffered at the actions of members and leaders within the very congregation that they provided spiritual leadership and guidance. The actions of adults can have a devastating effect on young children. Although I knew I was called to preach, I delayed because of my immaturity and the things I had witnessed my parents endure when I was just a child. Those things stuck with me all those years. Instead of preaching, singing and playing the organ became my focus in the church.

My experiences as a musician would take me through both secular and gospel arenas. In fact, I would sing in the clubs and participate in various contests in nightclubs around Miami to chase money and women. On Saturday night, one foot would be in the devil's backyard and on Sundays, I would transform into the "appearance" of the model Christian I was supposed to be in church. Little did I know that God had an assignment designed especially for me, despite my transgressions. It is written in the scriptures that, *God chastens those He loves* (Hebrews 12:6). Despite how many times I had disappointed Him, He kept forgiving me and continued dragging me out of the predicaments I had managed to keep placing myself in. As I reflect upon these incidents, I can clearly see that God was shaping me for my appointment to Kingdom work. In spite of how many times I wanted to remain in a secular domain, God said No! I'm reminded that I did not choose Him but that He chose me. *Ye have not chosen me, but I have chosen you, and ordained you, that ye should go and bring forth fruit, and that your fruit should remain: that whatsoever ye shall ask of the Father in my name, he may give it you (John 15:16).*

STRUGGLING WITH CAREER

And he said unto them, *render therefore unto Caesar the things which are Caesar's, and unto God the things which are God's (Luke 20:22).*

I am both a full time administrator within a public school system and a full time pastor. Often, I am engaged in conversations with people who are curious as to how I manage working in the secular world while serving as pastor of a church at the same time. My answer is always an enthusiastic and resounding, *"God has called me into both assignments."* It seems difficult for people to understand that I actually enjoy operating in excellence in both positions. Looking at my role as a school administrator and my role as a pastor, I find that both assignments are related to ministry. Every day I have the awesome task of helping young and older individuals reach their potentials. As a young child, my parents would frequently admonish my brother, my sister, and myself to lead by example. Their words took root in me and I try to remember always that I am to, "lead by example." Therefore, I keep this in mind when I am performing both tasks that I am assigned by God to do. This is why when one is given the great task of managing people, they must have a passion for what they are doing in order to do a worthy and notable job. Loving people is definitely a prerequisite.

The assignment of a servant is no different. It is that of an individual who understands that whatever God has equipped them with has already been ordained and approved by Him. When God calls you, the world usually does not and cannot understand the appointment that He has assigned for you to do. It is not for them to understand because it is tailor made just for you. It does not matter who you are, there will always be individuals who will hate you because of the anointing you carry. *If you were of the world, the world would love its own* (John 15:19). But by the same token, there will always be those who see the anointing upon you and will support and keep you lifted up in prayer. These are the ones who will give you words of encouragement and convince you to continue fighting the good fight. God always has His angels sent to minister to us just when we need it. *Then the devil left him, and behold, angels came and ministered unto him* (Mathew 4:11). When an individual does work for the kingdom, God's accreditation far exceeds man's approval. This simply means that God promises that He will reward His servant openly and ...*prepare a table before you in the presence of your enemies,* which implies that there will be some enemies. My experience has been that many times the very people who you thought were there to support and help you reach the next level, will be the very ones who hinder your success by speaking negatively about you and diminishing your competence - both professionally and spiritually. But we must believe and affirm that *God has not given us a spirit of fear, but of love, power and a sound mind* (2 Timothy 1:7). Although it hurts, we must continue moving forward.

THROUGH THE STORMS

As ministers of the gospel of Jesus Christ, we must always be ready for spiritual attacks, but God would never put more on us than we can bear. The devil gets angry when we do not fall apart from his deceitful strategies and tactics. The enemy has an uncanny way of dressing up in sheep clothing to infiltrate God's sheep. He has designed an agenda to misrepresent God's sheep by tarnishing their names and attempting to destroy their future. For this reason, God encourages us through the scriptures that through tests and trials we stay humble. Paul recognized God's wisdom in keeping him grounded in 2nd Corinthians as he refers to an uncomfortable pain he had in his flesh from a thorn. This thorn was so discomforting for Paul that he prayed about it three times! ...*and lest I should be exalted above measure through the abundance of the revelations, there was given to me a thorn in the flesh, the messenger of Satan to buffet me, lest I should be exalted above measure. For this thing I besought the Lord thrice, that it might depart from me. And He said unto me, My grace is sufficient for thee: for my strength is made perfect in weakness. Most gladly therefore will I rather glory in my infirmities, that the power of Christ may rest upon me (II Corinthians 12:7-9).*

It is through the pitfalls of life that those who trust the Lord are able to press forward and continue praising and thanking Him even while going through the storms. Thorns will continue to sprout up in our lives. It is natural for a person to not want to go through tests, trials and struggles, but no one is exempt. We all must at some point experience the hurt of betrayal, the disappointments of failures, and the frustration of problems; but nothing comes to stay. Everything that comes to you, comes only to pass away and each test leaves a lesson to be learned. However, if we do not learn the lesson, we are destined to repeat the test, so why not pass your test the first time around? At times it seems as though because you are saved that Satan continues to harass and throw fiery darts at you. We would hope that eventually your persistence in obeying the voice and will of God would tire him out, but he never seems to ever get tired! Your hope is that he will eventually leave you alone. Instead of leaving you alone however, he appears to get more aggressive and strategic. Ultimately we began to acknowledge that the thorns that we are experiencing are only in our lives to make us stronger. Trials come that they may take us to the next level in God. Paul's final position and belief after realizing that God was not going to remove the thorn was that, *in my weakness I become stronger (2nd Corinthians 12:10).*

David declares in the 23rd Psalm the following as it pertains to those who desire to see your downfall: *He prepares a table before me in the presence of my enemies: thou anointest my head with oil my cup runneth over.* This simply implies that in our times of comfort, we cannot become complacent because even people who we admire and have invited into our inner circle can actually be an imposter friend. Unfortunately, you do not expect the very people who are connected to you to be double-tongued and backstabbing. According to King David, the enemy is invited to the feast also. Watch, wait and resist the devil and the Word of God says that he will flee from you. We must ask for discernment in order to be able to see the enemy's schemes. And we must have a prayer strategy. We have to always be one step ahead of him. Just as he is strategic, we must also be strategic. When we pray, fast, study the Word and keep our relationship with God open and active, He guides, leads, informs, and instructs us. He never lets us be ignorant to the enemy's devices for long. God brings all things to the light at some point.

STRIVING TO PLEASE THE MASTER
Trust in the Lord with all thine heart; and lean not unto thine own understanding. In all thy ways acknowledge him, and he shall direct thy paths (Proverbs 3:5).

As mentioned earlier, I did not desire nor plan to go into the ministry. But one thing I do know, and that is that I have a passion to preach the gospel and a love for people. We are designed to praise God and transform others through our examples and gifts as children of the Most High. In these trying times of financial hardship and economic upheavals, I have discovered that God is still in control of His creation. Therefore, God has provided His children with unique opportunities to recognize His greatness and supreme authority and call on His name for assistance. God owns everything. *All things were made by him; and without Him was not anything made that was made* (John 1:3).

The earth is the Lord's, and the fullness thereof; the world, and they that dwell therein. For he hath founded it upon the seas, and established it upon the floods (Psalms 24:1-2). In order to please God, we must understand that God created things of pleasure so that men could experience a piece of the abundance of Eden. His direct plan is for all to prosper. *Beloved, I wish above all things that thou mayest prosper and be in good health, even as thy soul prospers* (John 3:2). This is done as mankind cares for and about each another. He says in

His Word that, *we then that are strong ought to bear the infirmities of the weak, and not to please ourselves* (Romans 15:10). This pleases God. I believe that it aches the heart of God when His children only think of themselves while forgetting about their brothers and sisters in Christ who struggle day after day. God says for us to *love our neighbors as we love ourselves* (Mark 12:34). Many of us quickly forget this conversation of love that God had with the disciples. God wants His children to develop caring hearts and have compassion as Jesus has compassion on us. Matthew chapter 25 teaches us that our DNA in the spiritual realm is identified as sheep not goats. Sheep belong to God and we know the voice of our shepherd. Jesus instructs us that upon His second coming, He will place the sheep on the right and the goats on the left. What side will you be on? The sheep are those who feed the hungry, clothe the naked, help the poor, and assist the needy. *For I was hungry, and ye gave me meat: I was thirsty, and ye gave me drink: I was a stranger, and ye took me in: naked, and ye clothed me: I was sick, and ye visited me: I was in prison, and ye came unto me* (Matthew 25:35-36).

MISSIONARY WORK

Several churches have adopted a name that represents a "Missionary Baptist Church." However, they are not governed by the biblical doctrines and spiritual foundation of a church committed to mission. On a regular basis, an offering is given during the morning service earmarked for local and global mission. More often than not however, these finances are never utilized for mission work. Instead, the sole purpose is to ensure that the needs and arrearages of the church are taken care of. It is our duty as Christians to assist our brothers and sisters who are in need and that often means leaving the four walls of the church to evangelize to those outside of the church. As a pastor, I hold a monthly mission meeting. During these meetings, we discuss and identify ways in which the church could assist in helping the community. There is always room for improvement and I admit that we can certainly do more. The mission ministry at my church is connected to my vision as the pastor. There is a gospel song that has the lyrics, *I don't feel no ways tired.* I truly believe that God desires His children to help the needy and continue providing people with substance, but there appears to be a struggle. However, I try to always keep that in mind, which is why we have the Mission Ministry at my church. *Be not weary in well-doing, for in due season, you shall reap if you faint not.* (Galations 6:9).

SUSTAINING FAMILY
One that ruleth well his own house, having his children in subjection with all gravity; For if a man know not how to rule his own house, how shall he take care of the church of God?
(I Timothy 3:4-5)

It is my belief that as a pastor, family time is essential. On a regular basis, I make a concerted effort to *make* time for my family. I emphasize the word "make" because as a pastor, one's schedule is always busy and it is easy to just want to come home and relax after doing so much in a day. It is understandable to not want to be bothered. For this reason, a pastor must *make* the time to spend with his family. Many people often ask, *"How do you manage to make time as an Assistant Principal, pastor, father and husband."* I often express to them that it is not me, it is God in me. There is a song that confirms my conviction. *"A charge to keep I have, a God to glorify a never-dying soul to save, and fit it for the sky. To serve this present age, my calling to fulfill; O may it all my powers engage to do my Master's will!"*

I want to please Jesus. How can a person please Jesus and neglect his own family? I continue to investigate new and unique ways to enhance family connections with fun, flavor, and honest discussion. As an administrator, I usually work long hours. There are times that I don't get home until after 10:00p.m some nights. When this happens, I inform my wife that if she and the children are not too tired, we can go to Denny's or another late night eatery. My family looks forward to this fellowship. I am inclined to believe that they miss me as much as I miss them or we are just insanely desperate for family connections. Even though this appears a bit farfetched, we make it work. I have purposed in my heart that my family will never be neglected. This is an important aspect for pastors to remember because if they are not careful, they will spend the majority of their time with members of the church and their problems that they neglect their own home. Charity begins in the home. Only after your home is taken care of should you go out and help others. If your household is not in order and/or your marriage is not on good terms, how then can you counsel another married couple? How can you help to solve someone else's problem? These things must be thought about as pastors.

    It is not as difficult as it appears to maintain a family and keep the bond strong. It is actually simple when you have deep love and appreciation for the family that God has given you. You must first *want* to keep that closeness with your family. Once the desire is there, the way will be made. At an early age, I established a unique relationship with my children. We talk about everything, even things I do not particularly feel comfortable with. However, I am challenged to remain daddy instead of pastor. The pastor in me does come out in most of these children-to-daddy conversations, but for the most part, I think I play my daddy role well, but sometimes it is hard to put the "pastor" role aside when it is in you so deeply. I teach my children through my actions as my parents taught me by theirs. I do not do one thing and practice another. Leading by example is the most effective and impactful kind of teaching there is. If I leave home in the morning without seeing them and I arrive home and they are asleep, I go in their rooms just to look at them or kiss them good night. Unfortunately (or fortunately for me), it ends up waking them up and leads to a long conversation about their day or their personal concerns. Through these dialogues, they have acquired a desire to hold conversations with me regularly. It is common for them to even regress to their younger days by sitting on my lap, forcing my attention of them just for what I call "me time."

My children are a part of the ministry that God gave me. I do not force them into ministry, I simply just lead by example. It is my belief that if adults live in a manner that pleases God, their children will see the Christ in them and desire to emulate their commitment to kingdom building. The Bible in several instances instructs us to be cognizant of the way we behave in the presence of children. When we behave unseemly in their presence, it can easily hinder their Christian walk and affect them as adults. *But Jesus said, Suffer little children, and forbid them not, to come unto me: for of such is the kingdom of heaven* (Matthew 19:14). It is wise to model good Christian values before your family. Growing up, I would often hear adults say, *"You don't do as I do, you do as I say do."* Well guess what? Children will eventually end up doing what you do and not as you say. Many times the children in the church will imitate what they see the pastor's children doing. And if the pastor's children are out-of-control, then how can we expect the other children in the church to behave? All we can do as adults is teach them, impart into them and lead by example. We can only hope and pray that when they are not with us, they are holding on to their teachings and behaving accordingly. It is impossible to be everywhere with your children, so my wife and I constantly remind them to behave with Christ-like behavior wherever they go.

CHARITY BEGINS AT HOME

Along with creating a positive relationship with one's children and family, it is far more important to maintain the fire and commitment with one's spouse. *Whoso findeth a wife findeth a good thing, and obtaineth favor of the Lord* (Proverbs 18:22). I am proud to say that I found my "good thing" and I make sure that I constantly show her as well as tell her how much I appreciate her being my wife. Without a doubt, I married my soul mate. Many Christian couples sometimes find themselves struggling to maintain and keep their marriage together. It hurts my heart when I have to counsel couples that are having marital problems because this is what the enemy wants. His desire is to tear the family unit apart and he starts with the demise of the marriage. He then goes to destroy the children. We must recognize what he is doing and fight for our families. For scores and decades, we have always heard the old wise saying, *"A family that prays together stays together."* Praying together as a married couple is a basic foundational principle that will keep a hedge around the marriage, but sadly many married couples - even pastor's marriages do not pray together. Many wives whose husbands are pastors find themselves feeling neglected. Many feel second place to the church, the ministry, and sadly they feel second place to other people's problems that their husband attempts to solve while sadly ignoring his own problems at home. His problems at home get bigger while his wife's frustration and hurt increases. Pastors, please take care of home first! Women are mentally and psychologically strong, but they can only take so much. Preachers and pastors sometimes become trapped by Satan's call to lust, and the various temptations that come in so many shapes, sizes, circumstances and situations can be extremely strong. History shows that some pastors have abruptly abandoned their marital commitment to have congregants lose respect and admiration for them. I believe in the sanctity of marriage. My wife is a part of me. We have been married for over 22 years and our relationship is as passionate and full of the emotions that we shared from the day we met. *Therefore shall a man leave his father and his mother, and shall cleave unto his wife: and they shall be one flesh* (Genesis 2:24, Ephesians 5:31).

Notice that God stands firmly on the sanctity of marriage. He states this in the old as well as the New Testament. If you ask a blind man who once had sight if he could receive his sight back, he would gladly agree to have his sight restored. In like manner, why would a pastor fight so hard to win back a member who left the church, but will not fight as hard to keep his marriage? As I have counseled marital couples throughout the years, I came to the conclusion that they suffer from a lack of communication. God created the world by communicating to a void space. And through His communication, the world exists. It is because of clear communication that a marriage continues to be healthy. When a couple places God first in their lives, the struggle of keeping Satan out of their business becomes easier to bear. Satan always will attempt to destroy what God has joined together. *And they twain shall be one flesh: so then they are no more twain, but one flesh. What therefore God hath joined together, let not man put asunder* (Mark 10:8-9). Satan is on a mission to destroy Christian marriages. That is why I make a concerted effort to arrange date night with my wife often and regularly. Marriages must *make* time for each other. There is that word "make" again. You make time for what is important to you. *Where your treasure is, there will your heart be also* (Mathew 6:21). In speaking with marriages in trouble, I now realize that many couples lose their emotional connection to each other because they keep inside what actually is bothering them. Usually for the woman, this confirms her husband's lack of attention and for a man her lack of understanding him. My suggestion for couples battling marital problems is to put God back first in your relationship and make an obligated effort to recommit yourselves to each other. Go on mini excursions leaving the children home and enjoy each other's company and companionship again, take her out to dinner as a surprise, go see a movie, bring her home flowers and cards on a regular day and tell her you love her frequently.

    Never let outsiders influence you with negative opinions about your spouse or speak derogatory comments to you about them. Keep people out of your business. This is basic marital maturity. *Give no place to the devil* (Ephesians 4:27). Never let people speak negatively of your spouse. When you reveal your marital problems to another, you have allowed room for the enemy to come in and wreak greater havoc in your marriage. You tell one person, they tell another, and so on. When everyone knows about your marital problems, you become the heated topic of gossip and your marriage becomes a public spectacle. And not many will come back to you and tell you that your marriage is the topic of conversation in every church click and in every member's household. Non members even get wind of it and your business is all in the community. Less than 5% of what is being said will come back to you and you are ignorant to the magnitude of it all. In the meantime, people are no longer listening to the Word of God coming from you speaking from the pulpit. They are looking at you and thinking about your bad marriage that more than likely has been made out to be worse than what it probably is. In an effort to ensure that this does not happen, couples must stop inviting the opinions of others into their marital affairs. When you tell outsiders about the struggles of your relationship without your spouse being there, the conversation is usually one sided and outsiders begin to take sides. We must fight for the very existence of marriage. There is an attack on the church, on Christian values, and on marriages.

In retrospect, the fight that lingers within me continues to be the driving force that pushes me to success in every aspect of my life. Many people find it hard to understand how I am able to persist and persevere in spite of things that I go through at times. It is because of the fight within. While in college, fellow classmates would advise me not to take so many courses at a time. I would take up to 21 credit hours a semester, which is equivalent to seven classes. Their advice was that I was going to burn myself out. Disregarding their advice, I stayed the course and completed my Bachelors Degree a year earlier than expected. This taught me a valuable lesson that people cannot control what God has ordained. Most of our struggles are in pleasing people rather than pleasing God. I will close with this wonderful scripture that I hope will bless your heart and encourage you to be strong in your faith in God. *Trust in the Lord with all your heart; and lean not unto thine own understanding. In all thy ways acknowledge him, and he shall direct thy paths (Proverbs 3:5-6).*

ABOUT THE AUTHOR

Miles T. Fitzpatrick, Associate Pastor is a graduate of Western Michigan University with a Bachelors of Science Degree in Communications and a minor in Psychology. Miles served as Pastor and Founder of Zion Christian Assembly for over 16 years and currently serves as an Associate Pastor at Christian Life Center in Kalamazoo Michigan with over 3,000 members. While the majority of his work has included pastoral ministry, in most recent years, Reverend Miles has served as an itinerate minister preaching in churches both large and small alike. Miles has served the Lord in Gospel ministry for over 25 years.

In 2000, Miles began his writing ministry with, "The Power of Divine Focus" which was widely distributed in Kenya, E. Africa, Northern Ireland, U.K., as well as the United States. In 1988, Miles and his wife Dianna launched Fitzpatrick Enterprises, which serves as an advertising firm for hundreds of businesses throughout Michigan, Indiana, and Florida. He and his beautiful wife Dianna have been married for 29 years and have four beautiful children Chris, 23; Brianna, 19; Gabriel (aka GiGi) 17; and Brandon, 17 (twins).

Miles has a vision of preaching the Gospel on every continent of the earth by providing humanitarian aid and relief where needed as well as preaching crusades and winning souls to the Kingdom of God. Miles also sees an Apostolic calling upon his life which will rise up those with a "Daniel Anointing". He can be reached for bookings at mtfitzpatrick@msn.com or by writing: Miles Fitzpatrick Ministries Int'l. P.O. Box 4057 Battle Creek, MI 49015-4057

Christian Life Center
1225 W. Paterson Street
Kalamazoo, MI 49007
Rev. Miles Fitzpatrick,
Associate Pastor

Chapter 16

Tested Faith

Written by Reverend Miles Fitzpatrick

And as Jesus passed by, he saw a man which was blind from his birth. And his disciples asked him, saying, Master, who did sin, this man, or his parents, that he was born blind? Jesus answered, Neither hath this man sinned, nor his parents: but that the works of God should be made manifest in him.

(John 9:1-3)

Over a 16 year period of serving as a Senior Pastor, I can personally recall great times of personal joy and fulfillment. Perhaps one of the greatest memories I have is when one of the special needs children from the church graduated from High School with perfect attendance and straight A's! This is no "small feet" for anyone to achieve - much less a child who suffers with severe Autism. James always impressed me even as a little child with his ability to recall scripture references and quotations perfectly without hesitation. He was also able to memorize lengthy passages of the Word of God! Not only was he able to recall these passages as he desired, but he also had a working knowledge of these passages and soon the entire Word of God! Eventually the time came that I felt the Lord's unction upon me to have James preach his first sermon. I never felt so much pride as I did that day. James also went on to deliver the commencement address at his High School graduation.

Every Pastor has to feel a great sense of gratitude when they see their church members roll up their sleeves and assist in feeding the less fortunate within the community. So it was with me as I witnessed our volunteer staff work tirelessly year after year in a program we called YOUTH W.A.V.E. Youth With a Vision for Evangelism. Our goal was to publicize an annual event that would have the whole community buzzing with excitement. We would rent carnival games, attractions, and of course all the hotdogs and hamburgers that one could consume free of charge. I remember asking one family if they had ever received Jesus Christ as Lord and Savior. They said, *"No Habla Ingles."* I then asked Lord to help me as I drew upon my rusty two years of High School and college Spanish and proceeded to lead that family to Christ. Yes, those were good times! Perhaps one of the most challenging times was when I was asked to officiate at a funeral of a young person who was a gang member with many fellow affiliate members that came up from Detroit to "represent." As soon as I took the pulpit, I began to witness about the love of Jesus Christ, His grace and forgiveness that is available to all. One by one they began to walk out and congregate in the foyer. It was right then and there that I decided that whether they liked it or not, they would here the Gospel of Jesus Christ that day. When you've been washed in the Blood of Jesus, nobody's "colors" can intimidate you. Recently, I received word that one of my members had passed away suddenly. He had served faithfully in many capacities for over a decade and I considered him to be a friend. When his wife told me of their financial situation, I knew that the Holy Spirit would see to it that this man would be honored and properly memorialized. I said to his widow, *"Don't worry. The Lord will provide."* and He did. A church building suitable for our needs was acquired at no charge and, perhaps the biggest miracle was that many of the old members of my church pitched in to help out with the program. It was a show of love and solidarity to a brother in "our family." You can't help but to feel that the Lord was pleased. At the end of my eulogy, I made an altar call and between 15 to 20 adults responded and received Jesus Christ as Lord and Savior. Now, that's a good day in ministry.

A WIDOW WOMAN TO REMEMBER

While in full-time ministry, I have had the opportunity to travel out of the country oversees on numerous occasions. A time that still overwhelms me is the time that a widow woman in a remote village in Kenya had fallen upon hard times. She had a mud-brick hut/home that was being destroyed by the rain which came through her tattered roof. It seemed as if she would never have a breakthrough in her bleak situation. She had no means of support and was already obtaining assistance from the other villagers. Excitedly, I returned home with a mission upon my heart. "Raise The Roof." Our project was simple, clear, and concise. Raise enough money quickly to get the contractors started and completed before the rainy season came. After that, the work would be virtually impossible and serious damage would be sustained. We worked tirelessly in various projects to raise money for Kenya. One that I am particularly fond of is "Cakes for Kenya" initiated by my mother. She had the idea of baking pound cakes and then sell them for donations. It worked. God anointed those cakes and they flew out of Mom's kitchen quicker than she could make them. In no time flat we had the money necessary to fund the project for the roof.

BLIND TO THE VISION

As the Lord began to move upon my heart with relief work and aid for Kenya, I was unaware of the dissention that was rising up from within our church. Slowly but surely, a murmuring began to arise that went something like this: *"Pastor, why should we be sending our money to Africa when we have got starving children in the inner city of Battle Creek?"* What was I to say? The claim was true. The need was and is real but should I shut up my compassion until such time that our home town is completely cared for? The answer was a resounding, "no." Luke 6:38 was no unfamiliar text in our church. For years, I had taught that as you give, it will be given unto you, *good measure, pressed down, shaken together, and running over...*" I was operating from the standpoint of "El Shaddai - The God of more than enough" I believe that the Lord knows no limit. He can multiply five loaves of bread and two fish and can feed multiplied thousands if we simply believe. This, however, was not the feeling of many families in the church and sadly many left.

Perhaps one of my most memorable moments in ministry came in the fall of 1997. I was traveling with my Pastor for the first time to Belfast, Northern Ireland. I was told repetitively that this was not going to be a vacation or holiday as they say. So, I was prepared to embrace whatever was to come my way. I remember very plainly that what those in Northern Ireland called "The troubles" was in full swing at the time. A lasting peace accord between the Irish Republican Army (IRA) and British Loyalist had not been reached as of yet and the bloodshed continued sporadically. I was certain that because I was "on assignment" from the Lord, that His protection would surely follow. It was a cool dark night and my pastor and another traveling companion from Michigan were navigating a winding country road just south of the border into the Republic of Ireland. All of a sudden a jeep flashed it's headlights at us from the side of the road. Two soldiers brandishing fully automatic machine guns emerged from the bushes. They motioned for us all to exit the vehicle. I began to pray in the Spirit. They demanded that we produce our passports and reason for our travels. It was then that great boldness rose up within me and I said, *"We're holding Gospel Crusades in neighboring hamlets!"* They asked to see what was in boot or trunk of the car. As we opened the trunk and revealed gospel literature and fliers, I said, *"Are you soldiers saved?"* I knew right then and there that I was at risk of not returning home but I was fearless. To my surprise and delight, they answered, "yes!" and wanted to know where the events were being held. I breathed a sigh of relief. God spared us from possible abduction or worse. This taught me as a young pastor that the Gospel of Jesus Christ works anywhere on the planet *if* the ambassadors carrying the message were fearless and unashamed.

THE PHONE CALL

It was the fall of 2003 that my life as a pastor, a father, and a husband would never be the same. I have been a man of faith from the beginning of my new birth experience with the Lord which started in March of 1980. I was thrilled to know that as a college student, God heard and answered prayers. I knew that He was real because He had proven Himself to me on many occasions prior to this. This day, I would be tested beyond that which I had previously known. Why, I wondered, would my doctor call me on the Wednesday before Thanksgiving? It did not seem logical. Couldn't whatever was on his mind certainly wait until after Thanksgiving? Thanksgiving is a day to spend with family members, carve the turkey, enjoy a big dinner, and watch football. Well, that was what everyone else was doing, but I was really wondering why my doctor insisted on seeing me and furthermore, why he wanted to bring my wife into the office with me. I was 42 years old and have never needed to have anyone go into the doctor with me before. As a pastor, I had been to Kenya on foreign missions a couple of times and needed special vaccinations to protect against Typhoid fever, Hepatitis B, and assorted indigenous diseases to the continent of Africa. So, I had been blessed to not contract any of those dreaded diseases during my travels, but what did my specialist want to talk to me *and* my wife about on the Friday after Thanksgiving?

I remember being prompt for our appointment. I don't remember any other patients being in the office and yet I do remember the receptionist and supportive staff being "extra conciliatory." I wanted to ask them, *"Do you guys know something that I don't know?" "The Doctor will be in to see you momentarily."* That was the longest moment in my life. The doctor came in and said, *"Your biopsy came back from both the University of Michigan and Regional Medical Laboratory. Both came back with the same results."* My heart seemed to begin to beat slower and slower. He then said the words that would change my life. *"You have a rare form of Cancer known as Cutaneous T-Cell Lymphoma."* He went onto explain that he would begin an aggressive regimen of Chemotherapy and Radiation after the holidays. I remember sitting there in near shock. I said to myself, *"How could this happen to me? I'm a Faith-Man. I'm a Word-Man. I'm Superman."* I listened to what the doctor told me and I sat there in disbelief. How could a man who had successfully prayed for the sick and seen God work miracles in other people's lives be afflicted with cancer? I could not believe it. I wouldn't believe it. I was respectful but I told the doctor that my faith was stronger than cancer. He set up a follow up appointment with the world renown medical staff at the University of Michigan. The doctors poked and prodded me. They drew blood and examined me thoroughly. The results came back same as before. I was in disbelief. I went on a Word saturation campaign and just meditated in God's Word day and night. I told the Lord, *"I believe that I receive right now as I pray in Jesus' Name!"* The days passed and the holidays were now behind me. I was convinced that before it was time for my first radiation and chemotherapy dose that all the cancer would supernaturally disappear. However, the first week of January was upon me and yet the cancer had not relented. I rebuked the devil with all that was within me and I kept ministering at my church with the same preaching schedule that I had previously. After much prayer and fasting, I came to the conclusion that I needed to bring the church family into this battle with me. After all, we were family, weren't we? I called a "special medical briefing" with my elders and asked them to pray. To my surprise, instead of support and love, I found that my faith was on trial by religious zealots that were more concerned with what door I had allowed to be opened to empower the devil to afflict me with cancer than helping me to close the door. It was at this point that I knew that I had a more serious problem on my hands than I had realized. I had cancer in my church! The cells (members of my church of 16 years) had begun to turn on themselves and their pastor. Just like cancer in a human body eats away at the healthy cells, the cancer (strife) within my church was slowly destroying the bond between members who had previously demonstrated unswerving faithfulness. I told the Lord that I was more concerned with my health than the health of the church and discerned that the enemy was using well meaning Christians to "divide and conquer." Nevertheless, I would fight on. I had members come up to me and say, *"If you're healed by the stripes of Jesus, then why are you still taking the chemo and radiation treatments?"* Statements like those were like a hot knife stabbing at my soul. It was as if, I was on trial for being sick. I thought to myself, *"Where else other than church do you see soldiers shooting their wounded?"* I recalled the text in the Gospels where someone asked Jesus, *"Who sinned, this man or his parents that he should be born blind?"* I cannot read that passage without feeling angry. Why? Well, it implies that if anything ever goes wrong in your life, it must be someone's fault. Such theology is judgmental, faulty, and leads to erroneous doctrinal conclusions. Jesus said, *"Neither, but that the glory of God should be manifested."*

WILL YOU STAND ON YOUR FAITH?

What is it that you are going through right now? What is the one area that seems to have a stronghold on you even as you read these words? I am here to tell you that it is not always about "how" or "why" you find yourself in this set of circumstances. If a thief breaks into your house and you discover him in your living room helping himself to your possessions, what is the first thing you do? If he's unarmed and if you are anything like me, I'm reaching for my Louisville slugger and I'm swinging with great accuracy. We must keep the main thing the main thing! In this example, the "main thing" is getting the thief out of my home as soon as possible. That is not the time to ask the question, "Who left the door open?" That is the time to get the enemy out first - then find out who left the door open.

THE RHEMA

I'm here to tell you that there is life after cancer. Cancer does not have to have the last word. If you will use your faith and refuse to waiver, you will see the salvation of God! *Man shall not live by bread alone but by every word (Rhema) that proceeds out of the mouth of God* (Mathew 4:4). The Greek word for "word" used in this passage means the "spoken word." It differs from the Greek word LOGOS which means "the entire sum of God's utterance." Faith comes by hearing and hearing by the Rhema/Word of God. Good messages delivered by the inspiration of the Holy Spirit are great. They can teach and inspire us to action which causes us to grow, but it is only the Rhema Word or the Word that the Holy Spirit speaks to our spirits concerning God's Word which causes faith to arise. Throughout my entire medical episode, I was praying, fasting, and listening to the Lord as to what He had to say about my situation. I was determined to hear from God. I remember it so clearly as if it was yesterday. God said, *"You will go through this and come out without the smell of smoke! Not one hair of your hair will be singed."* I remembered the three Hebrew boys in the fiery furnace. I remembered the fourth man in the furnace and the fact that they were not delivered from going into the fiery furnace. However, they were delivered from the effects of the furnace. Then I recalled the words of the beloved 23rd Psalm. Verse four reads: *Yea though I walk through the valley of the shadow of death I will fear no evil...* Notice that the Psalmist said that you will have to walk through some things. I think that too many times we think that just because we are Christians we will be immune from the test, trials, valleys, and tribulations of this world. The Bible tells us in Peter 4:12: *Beloved, think it not strange concerning the fiery trial which is to try you, as though some strange thing happened unto you.* Yet, all too often, we do exactly what this verse tells us not to do. We "think it strange" and ask questions that do not bring us to greater faith in Christ Jesus. I pray that the Body of Christ will begin to grow up and move forward in victory as we seek wisdom and receive the rhema/Word of God concerning our tests and trials. Temptations will come, but as the Word says, *There hath no temptation taken you but such as is common to man: but God is faithful, who will not suffer you to be tempted above that ye are able; but will with the temptation also make a way to escape, that ye may be able to bear it* (1st Corinthians 10:13).

THINK IT NOT STRANGE

So my friend, think it not strange when tests and trials come upon you. The Word tells you that those things that you must endure are "common to man". As a Christian, your faith will be tested and tried. Will you stand? Many say they have faith all day long - that is, until they have to use it and exercise it in their lives during the seemingly worst of times. Life is about how we respond to things. Will you stand on the Word? Will you trust that God will bring you out? Or will you crumble in the face of your hardships and trials? Although hard to do, the Word tells us that we are to, ...*glory in tribulations also: knowing that tribulation works patience; and patience, experience; and experience, hope: And hope makes us not ashamed; because the love of God is shed abroad in our hearts by the Holy Ghost which is given unto us.* (Romans 5:3-5) The Word tells us to glory in these things. I know it seems paradoxical to glory when you are hurt, frustrated, sad, sick, discouraged or brokenhearted, but can you praise Him? Can you find the strength to lift up your arms and praise Him?

I am still receiving radiation and chemotherapy treatments every Thursday, but I am still holding on to my faith. Faith without works is dead, so I am praying as though it all depends on God and doing my part as though it all depends on me. I have learned that you cannot force a healing to come; you can only believe and refuse to doubt. I have seen folks step on their glasses in an attempt to force the Hand of God to move. Such behavior is childish and immature. I have decided that *"The Just shall LIVE by faith."* So, I must LIVE first.

As I close, I want to remind you that you are more than a conqueror through Him that loves you. Please know a great indication as to how big your blessing is going to be once you overcome your tests and trials is the size of your test and trials. The greater the test, the greater the blessing. There is no **test**imony without a **test** and there is definitely no glory without a story.

ABOUT THE AUTHOR

Reverend Michael Anderson is the Senior Pastor of the New Jerusalem First Baptist Church, affectionately known throughout the Southern Region and caribbean as "The Church Unusual". Reverend Anderson has a holistic approach to ministering to the lives of people from communities all over. Under his leadership, the church has grown significantly by reaching out to the large, the least, the lost, and the left out.

As pastor, he has served his city as Police Chaplain and he has sat on the Master Planning Board and Victim's Advocate's Committee. He was recently named Broward County's Victim's Advocate of the Year. Pastor Anderson is a proven innovator and his program initiatives are often duplicated by other community churches and organizations for their ability to transcend barriers.

Michael's joy is people and seeing them made free in every aspect of their lives. To accomplish this, he has lectured on Interfaith Issues at Barry University and Nova Southeastern University. He has traveled as far as Canada to conduct and facilitate Marriage Enrichment Conferences, and has also held corporate training sessions in Argentina for Insurance Executives.

Reverend Anderson is a prolific pastor, preacher, and teacher and God has and is continuing to use him mightily to build up the kingdom of God.

He is the husband of the beautiful Sharon Anderson and they have been married for 28 years. They are the proud parents of two sons, Christopher Jordan and Cameron Marcell.

New Jerusalem Missionary Baptist Church
2254 Douglas Street
Hollywood, Florida 33020
Rev. Michael Anderson, Senior Pastor

Chapter 17

Trusted With Trouble
Written by Pastor Michael Anderson

When the enemy shall come in like a flood, the Spirit of the LORD shall lift up a standard against him.
(Isaiah 59:19)

I Dream of Destiny Station:

I remember the vivid dream as though it were yesterday. I stepped out of my building to hail a cab on the noise-filled streets of the city. To my surprise, today's jaunt came with little discomfort. Just as I was about to lift my hand and hope for mercy, the black and yellow anticipated my need and pulled the car up, coming to a well orchestrated stop handsomely close to the curb. I extended my hand toward the rear door handle, but it became instantly clear that the car was already occupied. There, in the back seat were two passengers with baggage between them, already nestled in. With no room in the back seat for me and anxious to make my destination on time, I simply hopped into the front seat, buckled in, and squawked to the cab driver my destination. *"Destiny Station"* I said. *"That, I know"* said the cabbie. The cabbie signaled and pulled away from the curb, seeming to be a very careful driver indeed. He assured me that he would get me there, on time, and in one piece. So...I should not mind the route too much. He further assured me that I would arrive at the lowest cost possible and not to worry. His voice seemed convincing enough, so I just settled in, more than ready to trust my travel in his competence and care.

Thoughts clear, no worry. *"How are you today Mr. Anderson?"* said one of the voices from the rear seat. *"You know me?" "We both do."* said the other. Startled, I turned to look again into the faces of my co-passengers, though this time served me no better than the first. These two were of no acquaintance to me. Sirs, may you introduce yourselves to me, seeing that you both seem to know me, while I know nothing of either of you. *"I am Trust."* said one of the passengers. *"I am Trouble."* said the other. *"One of us intrudes, while the other only rides when invited." "This the day of promotion"* said our cabbie. *The Prophet Job is busy reconstructing his life in Uz and is unavailable for today's sorted activities. So, you have been selected and trusted with his type of trouble."* Still buckled in, and now traveling a fairly swift speed, I pondered those words in my mind. *"...like the Prophet Job, who is busy reconstructing his life in Uz, you have been selected to be trusted, with his brand of trouble?"* I thought, *"Of all the things that I could be trusted with on this, the day of my promotion, why would trouble have to be one of them?"* The cabbie slipped me a scrap of paper signed by a one-named lyricist whose name was David entitled 'Song 113'. *"Try not to lose it, in case you are about to lose it."* Surely there was something more in what he was saying than just what he was saying, but I read it over, tucked it away, and turned to continue my examination of passengers that were sharing the ride with me.

As I began to navigate my turn, I noticed a signage right above my Cabbie's head. It was arduously written in Greek, Hebrew, and Latin, two of which I speak fluently, "TRUST AND TROUBLE; TROUBLE AND TRUST: NO GREAT TRAVELER IS EVER COMPLETE WITHOUT THEM BOTH". Just then, I also noticed our cabbie's identification card. His face was a little blurred from wear I supposed, but clearly I could see that he hailed from a little town near Bethlehem Judea, called Nazareth. Today, I have been "Trusted with Trouble." An odd compilation of words. Exactly, what does that mean? *"Three stops"* Said Cabbie. *"Three and you're free."* Maybe it will all make a little more sense to you after then. I seriously doubted that. But what could a strapped in candidate for promotion with a confident driver and two strange passengers traveling at incredible speeds do?

STATION ONE: THE TROUBLE WITH CHRISTIANS WITH TROUBLE

Our vast mishandling of "trouble" just may be the harshest self inflicted wound of all. -mka J.K. Rowlings, in her widely successful literary work created a reluctant spectacled teen-aged student hero by the name of Harry Potter. Harry is special. Harry, surviving the merciless attack of his generation's most ruthless offender lends to Harry's fame and notoriety. What killed others, including his beloved parents, Harry survived. The offender had become so feared among those that knew certainly of his existence sought to avoid all contact or remembrance, vowing never to speak the offender's name, fearing that to mention him, would run the risk of resurrecting him - a rhapsody of which far too many Christians have scored. Our offender is Trouble. We know that he exists; he is the insistent intruder that travels with us to some degree wherever it is we go. But we are maniacally motivated by misguided ministry manifestos never to admit its presence, lest we be thought far less blessed than others. We miss a massive ministry here. We give the false illusion that traveling with God means little or no trouble at all. With this flawed argument so prevalent in growing Christian circles, we rob God of His opportunities to be shown faithful, even amidst the most dire circumstances.

Trouble is trouble. No one can argue against that. But trouble is more than that. Trouble is also our trainer, our ordered and uncomfortable experience and experiment that we have been entrusted with. God, well aware of it all, grants us the strength, grace, and promise to pass each troublesome test with feet somehow yet standing, and faith intact. The best Christian sprinter cannot outrun trouble. The most gifted

Christian orator cannot debate it down. Trouble will have its day, but with faith in tact, trust fully engaged, trouble, even in its day will not have its win. Trouble, no matter how skillfully ignored, unearned, or unwanted, is maniacally committed to tag along for the ride!

STATION TWO: DAVID

David, I know him - secretly anointed as king, yet not publicly acknowledged as such, took the battlefield and fight that all others had a chance to accept, but took pains to avoid. Nobody, including King Saul, his best warriors, or David's three brothers that were present on the battlefield assayed. Nobody wanted the task of tangling with the Philistine Giant of Gath called Goliath, now, a name synonymous for big, gigantic, overwhelming. (Trouble should not be allowed to make his name on us!) When the call to fight came, all of Israel ran. David ran too.

And all the men of Israel, when they saw the man, fled from him, and were sore afraid (1 Samuel 17:24).

While the troops were panting, David asked the question of what would be given to the man that faced this looming threat against Israel's freedoms. The answer was the best that any man could offer. Money, freedom for the man's father's house, and a permanent place in the King's court by marrying his daughter. Now, I like to say, either the King and Israel were secretly broke and everyone knew that the monarchy could not make good on its promise of wealth or the anemic man on the battlefield had no love or aspiration for a better life for his tribe and family, or the King's daughter was so unattractive or abrasive that no man in his right mind or eyes desired anything to do with her. If this was not the case, then the only deduction left to be made is that these uniformed men of Israel were simply afraid! Scared! When the best that man could offer was offered, no man stood forth to take up the offer. David interrupted to speak. *"Fear of facing what was presently bigger than them rendered the best and bravest of Israel's army heartless."* They had been mighty in every battle before this one. But this one was different wasn't it? This one had a main character that was bigger, meaner, more intimidating than any enemy this army had seen to date. This was Trouble at a size and magnitude that we, the armies of Israel had never witnessed before. If I were to die today, it would be on my face, not my feet. Running was my working resolve. Fleeing was my learned formula. So, with the great teachers of Saul's elite army I ran! That is, until I heard the whole of the enemy's army laughing heartily with its champion, Goliath. The God of Moses' Red Sea crossing required defending today. Before now, this unwanted conflict with Trouble far larger than myself was going to be had whether I personally participated or not. Goliath has no intention of going away. Every moment I wasted trying to avoid him, only made him stronger. With each passing moment of commiseration, Goliath grew taller, meaner, and seemingly more invincible than the moment before.

A royal offer was made to the man that would face this behemoth on behalf of the kingdom, as you well know. It was the best that man could offer, but in facing Trouble of this magnitude, the best that man could offer, on this day, as all others, would not be enough. But there, I found David. In the company of the fight-depleted army, this young shepherd warrior entertained a holier, and higher equation. Beliefs in David, trumped bravado. And I, David, decided that this battle had more to do with the validity of this man's faith rather than the volume of this man's financial status. Today, I believe David reasoned, *"If today is the day that God is going to die, will it be then, on His feet, or on His face?"* Dagon died on his face, but not God. A God that dies on His face is no God at all. David's fight was not about palaces but principle. How dare this uncircumcised Philistine stand (on his feet) against the army of the Living God? The *Living* God! Unless God is already dead, this is not the way this happens. Unless God has died, and the memo of his tragic passing got hung up in the plains of Ono or the Valley of Chizzayon, that proverbial valley of vision, or someone shot down the trusted raven assigned to carry the message to the masses and it missed me on my way to the battlefield, what I am seeing is *not* to be seen among the people of God, now or forever, regardless of the impending circumstances that may tempt us to think otherwise. If God is still God and if the God that is still God is still alive, then Goliath must be faced, on our feet, even if it proves to be fatal. In the words of the captured Queen Esther, who stood rather on her feet than let God die on His face... *"If I perish, I perish!"* if this is my last day of life on earth as a lover of God, then so be it. I may die, but on my watch, my God will not. No casket will fit Him. No death song will suit Him. No eulogy shall ever be spoken in regard to His name. Again, I may die, but my God will not. So, the upstart David took his place, on his feet, gathered what was available, and simply "went" in the name of His God! His God was not dead, nor was He going to be allowed to die today.

David, without the King's armor, though keenly dressed in the Lord's anointing, had, with those words just joined, what he termed, the army of the *Living* God. The young warrior David chose feet instead of face. He gathered his goods and took steps squarely toward the battle with the larger, stronger, more experience, giant of a problem called Goliath. And please note: Goliath had become no smaller no less mighty, no less mean. No less willing to kill any child or "champion" Israel would dare put forth. No less willing to kill what he and the uncircumcised Philistine nation had come to conquer. One must not waste time asking problems to become smaller and nicer before they are dealt with. Goliath, the giant, a man of war from his youth, would offer no handicap due to size. *"I fight babies"* I think I heard him say. Goliath stood in the Valley of Elah poised to be a problem to anything smaller than him. Posturing today as all days before this day was this king-sized Trouble named Goliath. This mammoth menace felt no shame in conflicting with smaller things. But today would be the day that David would place words into the mouth of the trouble that came to trouble him and the people of his God. David won that day, you know.

That was the day that David proved that the best way to deal with trouble that is bigger than you is to face it with all the faith and available tools you have at your disposal. For all giants are shorter when they have been forced and laid on their backs! David helps us to recognize that there is some trouble that we may not have planned for, but find that we are adequately, unbeknownst to even us, prepared for. In his penned Song 13, David begins afraid, but finishes faithful. Hooray for King David!

How long wilt thou forget me, O LORD? for ever? how long wilt thou hide thy face from me? How long shall I take counsel in my soul, having sorrow in my heart daily? How long shall mine enemy be exalted over me? Consider and hear me, O LORD my God: lighten mine eyes, lest I sleep the sleep of death; Lest mine enemy say, I have prevailed against him; and those that trouble me rejoice when I am moved. But I have trusted in thy mercy; my heart shall rejoice in thy salvation. I will sing unto the LORD, because he hath dealt bountifully with me. (Psalms 131; 1-6:)

From "How long", to "How loved". Trust has triumphed over my troubles. Trouble, and any of its vast variations are always the invisible eight ton elephant in the room. Amid our bellowing choirs, the lofty monthly church themes with the matching bumper stickers, our streaming faith sermons, and the shepherd's well deserved reserved parking space, there is a secret place in which all saints dwell but few ever dare admit. It is the dungeon of despair. It is the modern Christian valimort. It is that place, that point of being that often maligns us while all too often, mis-defines us. It is the tyrant called

Trouble. Heaven, (not Harry) help us. What is trouble and how can I successfully avoid it? The first proposition will be much easier to answer than the last. The Hebrew word that defines the myriad of maladies we are often force to face is.... Trouble is everywhere. Your Apostle Paul declares that it destined to surface on "*every side*". (2 Cor. 4:8-10) There is an instance of some sort of trouble, challenge or discomfort in every book, if not every chapter of every book of the Bible. Why is this? And what if anything does it seem to convey? Is the entire volume of the Holy writ set to tell us that Job was right? That man *is* of a few days and full of trouble? Trouble seems to be born with us, in us, and dwells comfortably around us. Even when one can masterfully identify trouble in any one of its many disguises, does not guarantee that we will be successful at avoiding the very trouble we have successfully identified. The thing is, even when we, like Job, love God and eshewed or attempt to avoid sitting with trouble, Trouble may still decide to sit with us. Uninvited, Trouble may simply decide to pull up a chair and share a mocha-latte with us. Trouble is liable to crash our parties, though his name cannot be found on the guest list; Trouble may invade the wedding chapel, the honeymoon suite, and the birthing room. Trouble is a rude intruder. Trouble never minds its manners. Trouble behaves as if the world is exclusively its own. But why not? Who in your life have you ever found strong enough to stop or prevent it? Even when we take wise steps to rightly avoid those Troubles we have decided we can do without, there is still a quarry filled with Trouble's cousins seeking the smallest opening in which to enter, cut, or clutter our lives, our day, our dreams. It is time, well invested when we do not schedule the type of Trouble that we have decided we are better without, but it is empty effort to waste any portion of our purpose-filled living paralyzed by a passion to exert energy in attempting to dodge trouble which will not allow itself to be avoided. Our present strategies do not work. Trouble is not to be discovered and then out run. Trouble, once discovered, is to be acknowledged and then out done. *The fiercest enemy I ever had to face was Trouble. And the fiercest enemy trouble ever had to face was me!*

Do not call it bravado, call it belief, a giant is met in a forest. His composure declares that he has postured himself as an enemy. He is bigger than me, stronger than me, faster than me. Twenty of my fastest strides are erased by a single step of his. How long is running going to be the answer? Even with my most skillful, hopefully life preserving, ducking and dodging, swerving, and hiding, he is no fool. He, as well as my feet know full well that fleeing incessantly is not, nor never can be the proper response. If dying is what I must do today, then a decision must be quickly, firmly, and matter-of-factly made. Die on your face or die on your feet? To flee the trouble leaves my back exposed. The great giant that pursues me, soon closes the gap, and presses his large sandals into my back, the force driving me to the ground, both face and future smashed, with nothing to show for it but the testimony of my fear. OR, if this is my last day as a father, a mother, a pastor, a preacher, a teacher or executive, a *whatever* I have posed to be; Christian and believer, if this is my final day, and this is the trouble designed to trouble me to the one earthly place, some will mark as my grave, then let me die on my feet! At least the puny giant that would have won this day's war against me, will have to include my faith and bravery in his testimony about the day's activities. He has, no doubt seen so many cowards before, but this day he faces a fool with enough fight to face him squarely, a sight, no doubt, he will ever forget. The Christian faith requires nothing less.

We have enough encouragement, do we not dear Christian, to fully trust God in those times in which God is trusting us with trouble? Have you forgotten your Grandfather's scripture, *Trust in the LORD with all thine heart; and lean not unto thine own understanding. In all thy ways acknowledge him, and he shall direct thy paths (Proverbs 3:5-6).*

And your grandmother's song, penned by Horatio G. Spafford during the three year span that saw him lose wealth, property, and his four beloved children to sickness and the sea, when trusted with such trouble held fast to his faith in God during the dredge of his calamity? What exactly did he pen?

When peace, like a river, attendeth my way,
When sorrows like sea billows roll;
Whatever my lot, Thou has taught me to say,
It is well, it is well, with my soul.

Though Satan should buffet, though trials should come,
Let this blest assurance control,
That Christ has regarded my helpless estate,
And hath shed His own blood for my soul.

For me, be it Christ, be it Christ hence to live:
If Jordan above me shall roll,
No pang shall be mine, for in death as in life
Thou wilt whisper Thy peace to my soul.

It is well, it is well, with my soul.

If Job, Mr. Spafford and David can endure it; If Gideon, Jehoshaphat, Moses, Paul, and Joshua can be trusted with it;

If, as we know, the same God that promised them, remained present with them, then how is it so difficult for us to expect from such a one so faithful anything less than the same?

5:20a.m, my alarm rang.
I woke up, still squarely in my Savior's hands. Exactly where I will always be when Trouble has been entrusted to intrude; and I, like all my brother and sister Christians before and after me, am simply entrusted to trust. Exhilarated by the prospect of a being in the Hands of a God so good, a God that honors

covenant, a God that has promised not to place any more on any of us than He knows we are able to bear. I hurriedly prepared myself for the exciting day ahead of me, grabbed my lunch and brief and rush out the front door. The door of my brownstone swings open, and in a few steps I am at the curb of my beautiful city. I lift my hand to beckon a cab, and to my surprise, a black and yellow pulls up to the curb as to have anticipated my call. I extend my hand toward the rear door, and to my surprise find that it is already occupied by two already nestled in passengers. Once in, I thought to myself, I will ask their names. I look at the Cabbie and bark *"Destiny Station"*. Felt in my coat pocket, and found a folded slip of paper bearing the words 'Song 113'. I looked at the two passengers, looked up in the direction of my Throne Seated Sovereign God and Keeper, smiled, and wondered if perchance already well aware of mine.

226

ABOUT THE AUTHOR

Pastor Reginald Daniels began his pastoral journey in 1997 after accepting the call into ministry. He commenced to spread the Word of God as pastor of a thriving church in Madison, Florida for over five years in conjunction to working as a Literary Facilitator for the Florida State Correctional Department, preparing inmates for their GED examinations. Later, he explored the evangelistic field and then accepted the commission to lead Hickory Hill Missionary Baptist Church in Monticello, Florida.

He has been employed with the Texas-based *Marketplace Chaplains USA,* which provides on-call pastoral services to employees of many well known American companies. He is also a regular contributor to the Inspirational Broadcast Hour on WMAF 1230AM in Madison, Florida. In 2009, Pastor Daniels participated in the nationwide book tour *Authors With a Passion Book Tours.*

His first book is entitled *"Getting Along With You Know Who: A Practical Approach to Relationship Building."* The book explores the dynamics of all types of relationships. He defines "You Know Who" and provides techniques to building and improving communication skills in addition to relationships in general. Pastor Daniels published his second book in the spring of 2011. The book is entitled "Twenty-One: A Daily Devotion". The book takes the reader on a twenty-one day quest for a closer walk with Christ.

He enjoys conducting workshops, seminars, and meetings that are centered around family, marriage, and the community. He has been married to Lisa Daniels for 16 years and has two beautiful children: Relix, 14 and Jalisa, 9. In his spare time, he enjoys traveling and spending time with his family.

Hickory Hill Missionary Baptist Church
493 Bassett Dairy Rd.
Monticello, FL 32344
850-973-8165
Rev. Reginald Daniels, Senior Pastor

Chapter 18

Love Thy Neighbor as Thyself

Written by Pastor Reginald Daniels

Thou shalt love thy neighbour as thyself. There is none other commandment greater than these.
Mark 12:31

Many people think that a pastor's life is one of luxury, comfort, honor and perfection. Unfortunately, this is a myth that has permeated the minds of many people across the world. Yes, a pastor has a great deal of responsibility because they are called to be the earthly shepherds of the local church; but many do not realize nor understand that a pastor has to deal with an array of complicated issues, many of which affect him long after the benediction is over. It is important to understand that pastors are human and invest a great deal of time pouring themselves into the lives of others and the mission at hand all for the cause of building up the Kingdom of God. In order to effectively fulfill the call of God on our lives, love must be evident and in operation in and through pastors. There is no success in any endeavor without love. Jesus made it clear that if we loved Him, we would keep His commandments (John 14:15). We show our devotion and love to Him through our actions; for to love, is to fulfill the law. (Romans 13:8)

LOVING BY EXAMPLE

Every Christian is called to exhort one another daily. Pastors as well as everyday Christians must learn to look beyond our inner circles in order to extend ourselves to those who may not be in a position to stand strong on their own. It is true that not everyone wants to be helped, but we should at least have a heart for reaching out to them. We display selflessness when we look beyond ourselves and reach out to help others who may be lost or in an unfortunate position. This is why those who know the way should have a heart's desire to reach and to help out. That is the Christian way. Jesus, our great Teacher, taught by example the importance of displaying love to others. He practiced what He preached. He lived by example. Pastors must do the same thing. We must be following the same model that Jesus left for us to follow. It is one thing to profess the Word, but it is quite another to live the Word. The credibility of the pastor's Word has to be in their lives. The kingdom of heaven has no place for double-talking pastors. The Pharisees in Jesus' era could not understand how a so-called "man of God" or "son of man" could hang out with sinners and thieves and even those who some would call "whores" but thank God, Jesus came for all. For this reason, He said, *I came not to call the righteous, but sinners to repentance* (Mathew 9:13). Often, people become so religious until they forget the mission at hand, which is winning souls for the Kingdom and doing God's will. That is what all of us, as Christians who desire to walk the Christian walk are commissioned to do. We must do our part in advancing the Kingdom of God. That includes reaching out to the lost and the downtrodden.

BEYOND THE FOUR WALLS

I can recall when I started my journey in ministry that my pastor at the time had a big heart for the lost. We would be riding along in his vehicle and he would literally stop and go witness to someone. There were other times when we would be in a restaurant and he would fire up a conversation with a total stranger and they would end up seemingly the best of friends. Those exposures taught me that our mission is not limited to our assigned congregations nor should our desire to save have any boundaries or limitations. To be kingdom-minded is to have a genuine concern and love for all. That is why we were sent here on earth - to help, bless, contribute, and serve. I can recall several years ago just days after I delivered my very first public message that I received a phone call from my pastor. He asked me if I was busy later that evening. Those types of calls usually led me going on a mission of some sort with him, and each mission was different from the one before it. He informed me that he wasn't going to be able to make his monthly prison ministry visit and he wanted me to fill in for him. Initially, I was little apprehensive and nervous about going but then I was reminded that we must not limit our message to just the members who come to the church only. Our message of love must go far beyond our local congregations, so considering that, I graciously accepted the call to fill in for him. Too many pastors impart the message, dissect the Word and bless powerfully the members in their congregation, but they disregard or neglect outreach. We must "reach out" to those in the highways and byways, in the bars, clubs, street corners and crack houses. We have to be kingdom-building minded! Let's take a look at what Jesus had to say about His purpose:

For the Son of Man did not come to be served, but to serve, and to give His life as a ransom for many. Even as the Son of man came not to be ministered unto but to minister, and to give his life a ransom for "many". (Mathew 20:28)

This passage of scripture explains the reason why he was drawn to eat with and spend time with publicans and sinners. They were and still are included in the "many". He said that He gave His life as a ransom for many. That includes everybody! *When the fullness of time was come, God sent forth*

His son into the world, born of a woman, made under the law, that He might redeem those who were under the law, that we might receive the adoption of sons. (Galatians 4:4-5). We have all been redeemed!

And as he passed by, he saw Levi the son of Alphaeus sitting at the receipt of custom, and said unto him, Follow me. And he arose and followed him. And it came to pass, that as Jesus sat at meat in his house, many publicans and sinners sat also together with Jesus and his disciples: for there were many, and they followed him. And when the scribes and Pharisees saw him eat with publicans and sinners, they said unto his disciples, how is it that he eateth and drinketh with publicans and sinners? When Jesus heard it, he saith unto them. They that are whole have no need of the physician, but they that are sick: I came not to call the righteous, but sinners to repentance. (Mark 2:14-17)

It is clear that Jesus wanted to send a clear message then and the message is the same today: The most effective way to reach the lost is to make an asserted effort to show love for them *by example*. One of my favorite passages of scripture is John 13:35: *By this shall all men know that you are my disciples, if you have love one to another.*

A LOVE FOR OTHERS

And when he hath found it, he layeth it on his shoulders, rejoicing. And when he cometh home, he calleth together his friends and neighbours, saying unto them, Rejoice with me; for I have found my sheep which was lost. I say unto you, that likewise joy shall be in heaven over one sinner that repenteth, more than over ninety and nine just persons, which need no repentance. (Luke 15:7)

There is rejoicing in heaven when just one comes to accept Christ as their personal Lord and savior. However, there is usually something missing down here on earth. We do not rejoice the way we should when someone gives his or her life to Christ. The attitude seems to be one of, *"Oh well that's a good move you made"*. We as Christians who are members of the body of Christ, should have a genuine concern and love for each other. Every Christian has a "reasonable duty" of demonstrating love for people through their actions, but a pastor is called to walk a higher level of responsibility and accountability. If no one else does it, a pastor's love has to be displayed for others through his actions. A love for the people of God is a must. There is no compromising there and without this basic Christian principal operating, the spiritual demise of the leader is eminent. As pastors, we can seem to be pulled in so many different directions. Everyone wants the pastor's time. They want to speak with the pastor personally. There are some who are never happy and others who sow seeds of discord in the church; some who only want "the pastor" to pray for them; many who want "the pastor" to counsel them and all of these things can be very taxing on the man of God; but in spite of it all, we must still show genuine love and patience for God's people. After all, they each want and need healing and comfort for their soul and a pastor's job is to try and give that to them through the Word.

It is important to understand that just as you are not always in the spirit, pastors are not always in the spirit either. The flesh takes over often. We get tired and weary. There are times when we simply do not "feel" like studying the bible or we don't "feel" like going out to counsel someone, or we don't "feel" like even going to church. Sometimes the flesh wants to stay in the bed all day to watch the game and eat, but Pastors are called to carry a greater mantle. We must walk a higher standard. Therefore we must continuously press our way and it is not easy. It spite of it all, we must continue to show love for the people of God!

Walk in the spirit and you shall not fulfill the lust of the flesh, for the flesh lusteth against the spirit and the spirit against the flesh and these two are contrary the one to the other so that you would not do what you would. But if you are led of the spirit, you are not under the law (Galatians 5:18).

Pastors must realize that they were commissioned by the great Commissioner and they are not to seek glory from anything done for the advancement of the kingdom. The pastor needs to constantly remind himself of the following: *"It's not about me."* The Lord rewards the servant's efforts, but the efforts should not be done in a self-centered way. Our power, abilities, and resources are limited. John 15:5 declares that, *without Him we are nothing!* As children who now have peace with God through Jesus Christ, we have access to His power. His power is on the inside of us already. Everything we need to accomplish our mission here on earth is on the inside of us. We do not have to go searching for what we need through external things. We only need to raise our conscious level. It all starts from within. Whatever is on the inside, will show up on the outside. This is why Jesus was sitting and eating with the publican and sinners. He had a love for them internally and it showed outwardly everywhere He went. *Let this mind be in you which was also in Christ Jesus* (Philippians 2:5).

Then Jesus called his disciples unto him, and said, I have compassion on the multitude, because they continue with me now three days, and have nothing to eat: and I will not send them away fasting, lest they faint in the way. And his disciples say unto him, Whence should we have so much bread in the wilderness, as to fill so great a multitude? And Jesus said unto them, How many loaves have ye? And they said, seven, and a few little fishes. And He commanded the multitude to sit down on the ground. And He took the seven loaves and the fishes, and gave thanks, and brake them, and gave to His disciples, and the disciples to the multitude. And they did all eat, and were filled: and they took up of the broken meat that was left seven baskets full. And they that did eat were four thousand men, beside women and children (Matthew 15:32-38).

When the pastor displays compassion, it is a sign of maturity in Christ. Notice the portion in the passage where Jesus indicates that He has *compassion on the multitude*. I think this is where many pastors miss the mark. If there is any compassion at all, it is in the wrong place sometimes. Compassion is not only an important attribute, but it is also an action word. Jesus is our ultimate example of compassion. He loved helping people as they helped themselves. Note: He will not override our wills, but He will do many things for us as we reach out to Him. This is a valuable benefit of having a relationship with the Lord. One can be certain that the same Lord who saved you and loves you is the same Lord who will keep, preserve, and console you. These foundational principles should be displayed through church leaders at all times. There are many vivid times in my life where I wanted an excuse to hate as a result of things that happened pertaining to church affairs, but through prayer and meditation of the scriptures the Holy Spirit helped me to maintain my love for God's people and to try and think and forgive with the "mind of Christ". I had to come to the realization that it is impossible to succeed as a spiritual leader without love. Jesus reveals to His disciples that He has compassion for His followers:

Then Jesus called his disciples unto Him and said, I have compassion on the multitude, because they continue with me now three days, and have nothing to eat: and I will not send them away fasting, lest they faint in the way (Matthew 15:32).

The pastor must have this same Christ-like mindset. When a pastor observes the faithful remaining faithful, that faithfulness should be rewarded and appreciation should be shown for it. Notice the first few words that Jesus said in that verse. Again, He said *I have compassion on the multitude*. This is crucial because we sometimes, as we go through trials and challenges, view the Lord as being "distant" from us. However, He is actually closer than we think. We must learn to delve inwardly for our help. *The Kingdom of heaven is within you.* (1 John 4:4) We must therefore, know His promises and stand firm on them. It is written in the Bible that heaven and earth shall pass, but His word will never fail. Keyword here: Never! It would benefit you greatly to realize that the Lord will see you through any of life's obstacles, trials, and tribulations. Notice again that the Lord said, *I have compassion on the multitude.* Why did He say He had compassion on the multitude? In His own words, He said *"because they continue with me now for three days and have nothing to eat"* (v. 32). Notice the benefit the multitude had coming their way as a result of following the Lord for three days. They were going to have their needs met. In this case, their need was food. To the natural eye, they did not have enough food to eat although they had been given spiritual food - the bread of life. It is always convenient to give up and throw in the towel when things do not look good from the natural standpoint; but the victory may already be won in the spirit realm and on its way to manifest in the natural, but when we give up, we abort the manifestation because it is the faith that arrested the heart of God to send the blessing in the first place; but when faith diminishes, the blessing does too. For this reason, s pastor must constantly provide hope and compassion even in challenging conditions.

According Matthew 15:32-38, we find that the multitude had a very serious need - a need to eat! We all know what that feels like. The bible says that God will supply our needs according to his riches in glory by Christ Jesus (Philippians 4:19). In verse 32, Jesus assesses the need, and later in verse 35, He activated the plan that has *already* been ordained by the Father:

And His disciples say unto him, Whence should we have so much bread in the wilderness, as to fill so great a multitude?

And Jesus said unto them, How many loaves have ye? They said, seven, and a few little fishes. And He commanded the multitude to sit down on the ground.

The pastor has to understand that there is order with the Lord. He always has specific instructions to get you where you need to be. The only thing is that we have to learn "how" to listen and obey the instructions He delivers to us. We must get those instructions from the Lord Himself through prayer and not create them on our own. As previously mentioned, the multitude was faithfully following Jesus and they were rewarded for doing so. *And He took the seven loaves and the fishes, and gave thanks, and break them, and gave to his disciples, and the disciples to the multitude.* This was their reward. This may not be a big deal to some, but for a hungry person in the middle of a wilderness, this is very big!

And they did all eat, and were filled: and they took up of the broken meat that was left seven baskets full.

And they that did eat were four thousand men, beside women and children.

We serve a Savior like that. This is the evidence of compassion. This stems back to the Words Jesus spoke in the text that He had compassion on the multitude. Pastors must display this same kind of compassion as well. Everyone who comes in contact with us should experiences the compassion in us. Others should see the Christ in us as we exhibit love and compassion towards others.

GO AND DO LIKEWISE

It is imperative that we follow the example that Christ left for us. He cared for the multitude. He took it even a step further on Calvary's Cross. He *gave* His life for "whosoever" so that they would have an opportunity to be saved. In short, this is why John 3:16 is so popular and important because it reveals the love of God and Christ: *For God so loved the world, that he gave his only begotten Son, that whosoever believeth in him should not perish, but have everlasting life.* Pastors must, at the very least follow the model that Jesus left for us in the very familiar parable of the Good Samaritan.

But He, wanting to justify himself, said to Jesus, "And who is my neighbor?" Then Jesus answered and said: "A certain man went down from Jerusalem to Jericho, and fell among thieves, who stripped him of his clothing, wounded him, and departed, leaving him half dead. Now by chance, a certain priest came down that road. And when he saw him, he passed by on the other side. Likewise a Levite, when he arrived at the place, came and looked, and passed by on the other side; but a certain Samaritan, as he journeyed, came where he was. And when he saw him, he had compassion. So he went to him and bandaged his wounds, pouring on oil and wine; and he set him on his own animal, brought him to an inn, and took care of him. On the next day, when he departed, he took out two denarii, gave them to the innkeeper, and said to him, "Take care of him; and whatever more you spend, when I come again, I will repay you." So which of these three do you think was neighbor to him who fell among the thieves?" And he said, "He who showed mercy on him." Then Jesus said to him, "Go and do likewise." John 10:29-37.

As you can see, love is designed to go above and beyond. It is designed to go the extra mile. It is always good when we are able to display love even in the midst of turmoil. Notice in the parable how each individual had an opportunity to make a difference in the life of the wounded man. The priest was expected to help if no one else would, but unfortunately, he passed by, probably trying to make it to church. The priest could not see that the "church" was the wounded man that lay on the side of the road. A person was in need of help. The passage indicates that he was half dead and the priest (man of God) passed right by him and left him there to die. Where was the compassion there? The Levite was only partially expected to help considering the relationship of Levites and Jews during that era. So there was a fifty-fifty chance the Levite would help. He passed right on by him as well. Then the Samaritan, who was the least expected to help stopped and provided the man with the love and care that was needed. Out of all three individuals, the one who was least expected to help was the one who provided the assistance; and so it is today. The ones we least expect to make it in the kingdom will be the very ones to enter in first and who will be sitting high next to the judgment seat of Christ. We are expected to go above and beyond to help others. So often the leaders of our churches follow the path of the priest in this parable. They pass by wounded individuals in pursuit of "getting to the church". The question was asked, *"Who was the neighbor of them all?"* and the response was, the Samaritan. He was the one who put compassion and action to work. He looked beyond himself and made a difference in the life of someone else. It is therefore imperative that pastors today adopt this same mentality. We have to raise our awareness in terms of displaying love for others.

We often do not recognize opportunities when we see them because there is no sign that says, "THIS IS YOUR TEST FOR TODAY" or "THIS IS A GREAT OPPORTUNITY FOR YOU TODAY. In the book of 1st Corinthians 13, the word charity is used to describe love. This familiar and favored chapter provides a measuring stick to see if we are on the right track when it comes to love. We have to understand the real reason we were placed here. We are here because of love. *For God so loved, that He gave his life,* and we are called to love others the same way. We were placed here to glorify God! One way of glorifying Him is by displaying love for others. You may ask, *"Do I have to compromise my convictions and beliefs in order to get others to love me?"* We should never give up the right for the wrong as some believe. The bible simply commands us to love. Is everyone loveable in return? (No) Does everyone treat you the way you want to be treated? (No) Are you always going to receive the honor and respect you feel you deserve? (No) If anyone should have a clear understanding of this truth, it should be the pastor.

    The Word of God is clear. We are called to love even when things are not going our way. The pastor is called to lead by example. We are ministers and to minister is to serve. Jesus' final Words of instruction in the parable were to *go and do likewise.* In other words, He was saying that talking it is not enough. Preaching love alone is not enough. The pastor should live his sermons. We are expected to display love to our neighbors, but we do not always pass this very important test. Just as the Samaritan passed the love test, it is important that pastors embrace the Lord's instruction by going and doing likewise. As I close, I leave you with this final scripture that sums up the love that we should have for our neighbors:

A new commandment I give unto you, that ye love one another; as I have loved you, that ye also love one another. By this shall all men know that ye are my disciples, if ye have love one to another (John 13:34-35).

ABOUT THE AUTHOR

Bishop Fred Marshall is the Pastor of Souls Harvest Christian Center Ministries in both Broward and Dade County, Florida. He is married to Pastor and Prophetess Carolyn Marshall, who is the President of the 'Women of Integrity' Ministries within Souls Harvest.

Bishop Marshall served in ministry under the late Superintendent, E.J Anderson as an armor-bearer and associate Elder at New Mount Zion COGIC in Ft. Lauderdale, FL for twenty-one years. He has traveled throughout the United States and internationally evangelizing and preaching a life-changing and uncompromising gospel for over thirty-five years.

Bishop Marshall has been pastoring Souls Harvest Christian Center Ministries, a nondenominational, multi-cultural, five-fold ministry for over 15 years and through the prophetic anointing that God has placed on his life, thousands of souls have been blessed, saved, healed and delivered. He is also the founder and president of the Men's Ministry, 'Men of Distinction' at Souls Harvest Christian Center. He attended the Moody Bible Institute in Chicago, IL.

Bishop Fred Marshall and his wife reside in the city of Ft. Lauderdale, Florida and together they have seven children and sixteen grandchildren.

Souls Harvest Christian Center
972 Hallandale Beach Blvd,
Hallandale, FL 33009
954-559-3284
Bishop Fred Marshall, Senior Pastor

Chapter 19

The Power of the Prophetic Ministry

Written by Bishop Fred Marshall

Before I formed thee in the belly I knew thee; and before thou camest forth out of the womb I sanctified thee, and I ordained thee a prophet unto the nations.
Jeremiah 1:5

The scripture above are the very words that I heard in my spirit the day that God changed my ministry. When it comes to the gift of prophecy, everyone wants that anointing, but not everyone understands nor realizes the great responsibility that comes with being God's mouthpiece in the earth realm. There are many days of frustration, discouragement, rejection and even feelings of loneliness and depression that tries to come upon the man or woman of God as they speak the Word of truth. Walking with a prophetic mantel is a great, yet awesome responsibility. As we observe the times, seasons, and unprecedented events that have and are taking place the last several years, we can clearly see that we are living in the last days. As we continue to take note of the times, we see that there has been a great outpouring of God's spirit in the earth. The prophet Joel prophesied about these times in chapter two, when he said, *And it shall come to pass afterward that I will pour out of my spirit upon all flesh; and your sons and your daughters shall prophesy, your old men shall dream dreams, your young men shall see visions. And also upon the servants and upon the handmaids in those days will I pour out my spirit.* Beyond a shadow of a doubt, God has poured out His spirit upon the people of God in these last days. We must observe the times and act accordingly. It is written in Ephesians 4:11-12, *And he gave some, apostles; and some, prophets; and some, evangelists; and some, pastors and teachers. For the perfecting of the saints, for the work of the ministry, for the edifying of the body of Christ.* God has a special purpose for all of us in this great big plan of His. Let me take you on a journey that started a hunger for God in my life.

I grew up in a city in the panhandle called Pensacola, Florida. Being raised in a family that was respectable but not religious, I was a Baptist boy. Nothing in my life that happened, pointed me to the supernatural; so when I passed by churches where they were praising God and dancing in the "spirit", I became judgmental. Out of ignorance I would say, *"God is going to punish those people because they do not know how to act in church."* On the contrary, it was me that did not understand the moving of God. I loved God, but my revelation of Him was very limited because I was like most Christians, I didn't read my bible faithfully and I did not pray regularly. That leads to a self-absorbed life of whatever I wanted instead of what *He* wanted. After a while, my going to church slacked off until I was not going at all anymore. However, if one were to ask me at that time if I were a Christian, my response would be an emphatic "yes!"

My family and I eventually moved to South Florida in 1973 not knowing what God had in store for me. After going through some tests and struggles, God began His divine calling in my life. Many of us do not always understand what exactly is happening as God's voice speaks to us. I was invited to dinner, not knowing that this dinner was divinely set up by God just for me. My life was not where it should have been at that time and I thought it was just a simple social gathering. After I arrived however, I noticed that everyone was dressed up in suits and church clothes. But the boyfriend of the lady that invited me to the function and myself were dressed in regular street clothes. I quickly realized that many of the people there were very spiritual church people. At the end of the dinner, a man came to the table at the front and began to make an altar call. I didn't move. My friend who invited me to the dinner began to say to me, *"Marshall go up for prayer."* But I would not move. Her boyfriend began to say to me, *"Man you believe that stuff?"* Don't go up there; then she said to me, *"If you don't do it for you, do it for your kids."* So I got up and went for prayer. That started the cycle. While going through the process with God in that same year, I began going to church with my great aunt. I had no plans of giving my life to God, but when I got there to the church, it was not the Baptist church that I was used to. The music was loud and they beat on the drums like it was no tomorrow. I became offended and my head was pounding with the most terrible headache as a result of that loud music. When we got home that day, I said to myself, *"I am not going back to that church!"* I felt as though their music was way too loud and those people were acting crazy - dancing all around the church, falling out and speaking some kind of words that I did not understand. As I was thinking these thoughts, I heard a voice say to me, *"You did not say that last night when you were at the club and the music was just as loud."* The noise at the club was loud and the live band played, but I didn't complain about it until I went to church. I began to feel convicted, so I repented and told my aunt I would go back with her. When I did return, I sat all the way in the back like many sinners do. My great aunt went up to the front and sat with the mothers of the church. The spirit of the Lord was very strong in the church that day and the pastor made an altar call. I walked toward the front. While there, they placed me on the alter and told me to begin calling on the name of Jesus. To the Pentecostal church world, this is called tarrying. I cannot remember now how long I was on the altar, but I was getting tired and my arms became like lead. I began to pray *"Jesus will you please come and touch me like they said you would because I am about to faint from tiredness."* I heard people to my left screaming and falling onto the floor and then it happened! I saw a vision of Jesus sitting on a cloud with a sickle in his hand. I later learned that in the book of Revelations chapter 14:14, it says: *and I looked, and behold a white cloud, and upon the cloud one sat like unto the son of man, having on his head a golden crown, and in his hand a sharp sickle.* This was the beginning of my journey in this beautiful life called Christianity. We, the church and as the body of Christ need everything that we can get from God.

This is why the five-fold ministry is so important. The body of Christ simply cannot be effective without it. All of these ministry gifts are powerful tools in God's Hand. In the book of 1 Corinthians 12:12-14, it is written, *For as the body is one, and hath many members, and all the members of the one body, being many, are one body: So also is Christ. For by one spirit are we all baptized into one body, whether we are bound or free; and have been all made to drink into one spirit. For the body is not one member, but many.* The church is not a denomination or a doctrine, it is a living viable organization that is a part of Christ. Colossians 1:15-20 states, *Who is the image of the invisible God, the firstborn of every creature. For by Him were all things created that are in heaven and that are in earth, visible and invisible, whether they be thrones, or dominions or principalities or powers: All things were created by Him, and for Him. And he is before all things, and by him all things consist. And he is the head of the body, the church: Who is the beginning, the firstborn from the dead; that in all things, he might have the preeminence. For it pleases the father that in him should all fullness dwell. And having made peace through the blood of his cross, by him to reconcile all things unto himself; by him I say, whether they be things in earth, or things in Heaven.*

When the Lord saved me that Sunday morning, I saw Jesus in a vision sitting on that cloud and when He stuck the sickle into the earth, I was His harvest. The Holy Spirit picked me up off of the altar and I began to dance all over that church, under the wonderful power known to us as the third person in the Godhead called the Holy Ghost. This was very new to me. After I stopped dancing, one of the mothers came over to me after service and said to me, *"Um, um, He is good, isn't He baby?"* and I said *"yes ma'am."* And then she said this to me: *"That's not all yet."* Now in my mind, I was saying, *"What is she talking about?"* Well, I found out that God did save, but I had not yet been baptized in the Holy Ghost.

The day that it happened to me is a day that I will never forget. It was a Thursday night and I had just gotten home from work. At the time, I was renting a room from the same aunt that I had begun going to church with. Because of what I had been experiencing, I came home hungry for God and His power. After getting home from work, I asked my aunt to pray with me. When I went down on my knees to pray, my hands began to tremble uncontrollably, then I heard a voice speak in my ears, *"He is in your hands."* Suddenly, the power of God overwhelmed me and knocked me to the floor. My entire body began trembling under the power of God and I began speaking in tongues and in other languages uncontrollably. As I reflect on this most precious memory in my life, I am led to the book of Acts, 2:2-4, which states, *And suddenly there came a sound from Heaven as of a rushing mighty wind and it filled all the house where they were sitting. And there appeared unto them cloven tongues like as of fire, and it sat upon each of them. And they were all filled with the Holy Ghost, and began to speak with other tongues as the spirit gave them utterance.*

As a new Christian, there is that newness that all babies have to its environment. My pastor had a prayer meeting that lasted for months. This did something to and in me. When I received the Baptism of the Holy Spirit by speaking in tongues, God supernaturally opened my eyes. I saw the room that I was in filled with smoke, white, glowing and sparkling. It was awesome, to say the least. My prayer life grew rapidly and powerfully. I was taught how to study the Word, but while studying, the Holy Spirit directed my attention on the men and women characters in the Bible and some of their. Later, I began to read books by A.A. Alen and men like Franklin Hall. A.A. Alen talked about fasting and how he sought God's face to get his supernatural power. There is a price to pay for the Power of God and the price is high, but the return is worth it. It takes self-discipline, much prayer, seeking the face of God and much study and time in the Word. Don't let anyone fool you, the power and anointing of God is not cheap. It cost commitment and time.

THE PROPHET'S MANTLE

Many people are hurt, confused, discouraged and are looking for guidance. They are desperately seeking a Word from the Lord. For this reason, people flock to prophets, but as with all things, wherever there is a genuine reality, there will be counterfeits. There are many false prophets walking around in sheep's clothing and deceiving the people, but inwardly, they are ravening wolves. Psychics, witches, and tarot card readers are all false prophets who have taken their gifts and used them for the dark side. It is imperative to be able to discern the false from the real. *And you shall know them by their fruit* (Mathew 7:16). Just as Moses' God-given power greatly exceeded the power of Pharaoh's magicians, the power of God's true prophets will greatly exceed those of the false. If a false word is given to someone who is already in despair and losing hope, the false word may utterly destroy their hope for a better day. There is a warning for the false prophet who causes this to happen: *With lies you have made the heart of the righteous sad, whom I have not made sad* (Ezekial 13:22). God has a warning for the false prophets speaking in his name: *Therefore thus said the Lord, concerning the prophets that prophesy in my name, and I sent them not, yet they say, sword and famine shall not be in this land; by sword and famine shall those prophets be consumed. (Jeremiah 14:15).* God's Word, spoken through the prophet always has redemption, hope and love in it. Even His warnings of judgment always have an outlet of turning around and receiving His grace, mercy and forgiveness. God's Word always embodies love, hope, and faith. The Lord is fully aware of those who are going out and giving false prophesies and there is a punishment that goes with such blatant disregard for God's approval.

The Lord wants us to desire spiritual gifts, which are the most precious and valuable gifts because spiritual gifts do not tarnish. They are eternal because they are given from the ultimate Giver. However, it is written in 1 Corinthians 14:5 the following about desiring to prophesy: *I would that ye all spake with tongues but rather that ye prophesied: for greater is he that prophesieth than he that speaketh with tongues, except he interpret, that the church may receive edifying.* God wants us to desire the gift of prophecy so that the church may receive edifying and encouragement. God does not want His children frustrated and confused, but rather He wants them to trust Him and His Word. He wants to give you a direct message from Him spoken through His mouthpiece, the Prophet. However, many want the gift of prophecy for the wrong reasons. They want the gift so that they may be praised, honored, highly respected and viewed as preeminent above the people of God in the world. They want the prophetic gifts for the wrong reasons. We must be more concerned with doing God's will and walking in His grace than receiving recognition and honor for walking with a prophetic mantel. Those who deeply understand the magnitude that goes with true spiritual authority always seek the lowest places and always points the honor and glory to Jesus Christ, not themselves. They understand that, *No flesh should glory in His sight* (1 Corinthians 1:29).

There are some people who want the prophetic mantle so bad that rather than pray and wait for God to give them the anointing of the gift, they have self-proclaimed themselves as prophets and have begun giving false words to the people under the pretext of, "thus saith the Lord". There is a major price to pay for doing such things. The five fold ministry is revealed in the New Testament in the book of Ephesians Chapter 4:11: *And he gave some apostles, prophets, some evangelists, some pastors and teachers.* In the Old Testament, there was the priest, the prophet, the king. But Moses operated in the office of a prophet. The prophet speaks by revelation as a mouthpiece for God. He or she walks in an authority unlike the other offices. All have special authority from God and all are extremely important. God equipped Moses with a rod and power with his words that brought great judgment upon Egypt, Pharaoh, and all that opposed the righteousness of God. Moses carried a prophet's mantle and God put His words in Moses' mouth.

THE LIFE OF A PROPHET

The life of a prophet is not easy. It hurts when what is given to you by God to speak is rejected and people do not receive you. If you are not careful, bitterness can set in and you begin prophesying out of your hurt and adding to what God says, rather than speaking specifically what God is telling you to speak. True faith is characterized by courage. You will never be able to deliver a pure Word from the Lord until you are delivered from the fear of man and the desire for acceptance and recognition. Prophets who are more concerned about what people think of them will never fully walk in their calling and can quickly become false prophets. You must not allow rejection and bitterness to set in your spirit. Let's take a look at some of the prophets and what they went through:

Jeremiah

Jeremiah is known as the weeping prophet because God had shown him the final judgment that would come upon the children of Israel if they did not turn from their evil ways. Therefore, he prophesied often for people to turn from their ways and their doings, to repent, and to obey the voice of the Lord. However, he became depressed and discouraged often and he even cursed the day he was born out of discouragement.

There was a time when Pash'ur who was chief governor had been receiving prophesies of success, prosperity, and good health from the many false prophets that were in Israel, but Jeremiah, the true prophet was prophesying judgment that would come upon the people if they did not turn from their evil ways. Pash'ur heard about Jeremiah's prophesies, became angry, hit Jeremiah, then locked him up. When Pash'ur came to get Jeremiah in the morning, God spoke through Jeremiah and gave Pash'ur a very hard prophetic Word of judgment against him, his friends, and his false prophets:

And it came to pass that Pash'ur brought forth Jeremiah out of the stocks. Then said Jeremiah unto him, the Lord has not called they name Pash'ur, but Magormissabib (meaning terror). For thus saith the Lord. Behold I will make the a terror to thyself and to all they friends: and they shall fall by the sword of their enemies.
(Jeremiah 20:3-4)

After Jeremiah spoke these things to Pash'ur while in the spirit, his flesh took over and he became fearful, utterly discouraged and frustrated. He felt that the Lord had deceived him and that his prophesies would not come to pass. After all this trouble he felt that he had gotten himself into, he purposed in his heart that he would not prophesy anymore and that he would keep his mouth shut, but then look at what happened:

Then I said, I will not make mention of him, nor speak anymore in his name. But his Word was in my heart as a burning fire shut up in my bones, and I was weary with forbearing.
(Jeremiah 20:9)

When God gives you something to speak, you have to say it or it will be as fire shut up in your bones that will remain until you open your mouth and speak what God tells you to speak! Jeremiah thought that he would keep his mouth shut because opening his mouth *seemed* to have gotten him in trouble, but God will always vindicate his chosen vessel. However, the point that I am trying to convey by telling this story is that a prophet's life is not easy.

Elijah:

Elijah the Tishbite was sent to give a warning to the people of Israel and their leader King Ahab the husband of Jezebel, about worshipping the false God Ba'al. His question to the people was strong and straightforward: *How long have you been of two opinions? If the Lord be God, follow him: but if Ba'al then follow him. And the people answered him not a word* (1 Kings 18:21). Ultimately, God proved Himself through burning down fire on and consuming the burnt sacrifice that was to be offered to the false God Ba'al. Jezebel, the queen and wife of Ahab became consumed with anger and sent a message to Elijah saying: *So let the gods do to me, and more also, if I make not thy life as the life of one of them by tomorrow about his time.* (1 Kings 1:2). After receiving that message, Elijah ran away and became depressed. He sat under a juniper tree and asked the Lord to take his life. Of course, God took care of Elijah and eventually restored His peace and the joy of his salvation, but the point once again here is that a prophet's life is not easy!

Hosea

The Lord sent Hosea the prophet to go and speak a Word concerning the whoredom that was running rampant in the land. God even told Hosea to marry a whore as a sign to the children of Israel. Hosea had to speak some hard words to the people. He even called them a heifer: *For Israel slideth back as a backsliding Heifer. ...they have committed whoredom continually.* Hosea spoke Words from God such as:

> *Hear the Word of the Lord, ye children of Israel: for the Lord has a controversy with the inhabitants of the land,*

because there is no truth, nor mercy, nor knowledge of God in the land. (Hosea 4:1).

The spirit of whoredoms has caused them to err, and they have gone a whoring from under their God. (Hosea 4:12)

...your daughters shall commit whoredom and your spouses shall commit adultery. (Hosea 4:13)

The spirit of whoredom is in the midst of them and they have not known the Lord. (Hosea 5:4)

Israel is defiled (Hosea 6:10)

You have to know that calling out people in their sin will not be received well; and they will not immediately receive you or God's Word spoken through you. As a prophet, we are rejected, despised and targeted, but a true prophet of God will always be vindicated because God's true Word spoken through His chosen vessel will always come to pass.

In the New Testament age the gifts are described as these.

There are three power gifts:

      1. The gift of faith
      2. The gift of healing
      3. The working of miracles.

There are three vocal gifts:
      1. Prophecy
      2. Diverse kinds of tongues
      3. Interpretation of Tongues

There are three knowledge gifts:

1. The Word of wisdom
2. The Word of knowledge
3. The discerning of spirits.

All of these gifts are for the body of Christ. Edifying these gifts through the Holy Spirit keeps the church in the "know" about what God is saying and doing.

Through these power gifts, I have seen many miracles manifested. I can vividly recall a time that a nine year old little girl came into a service that I was conducting in Fort Lauderdale, Florida. As the pulpit was full of seasoned apostles and prophets, I was a young prophet in my twenties. The spirit of intimidation tried to come upon me when I asked the little girl what she wanted God to do for her. Her mother said, *"She is deaf in one ear."* A fearful voice spoke to my mind and said, *"Call for the apostle in the church or one of the seasoned prophets to come and help you."* But something stood up inside of me and said, *"You pray for her."* It was with boldness and power that I heard these words. I laid my hands on the little girl's ear and I began to pray. As I was praying, I heard the Word of the Lord speak these words in my ear, *"She can hear."* All of a sudden I looked up into the face of this little girl and all her teeth were showing with excitement. I asked her, *"Can you hear me?"* I put my finger in her good ear and spoke in the ear that had been closed. She was able to hear! The whole church witnessed this and people began shouting all over the building. That week was the most powerful week we had in that church. That was the beginning of all types of healing, miracles and deliverance.

Although there are days of discouragement and frustration walking with the prophetic mantel, there are also days of great rejoicing and happiness because of the awesome miracles that God does in the midst of His people. So I want to encourage you to stand strong in whatever gifts that God has placed inside you because there is a great reward for doing what He has called you to do for His glory!

ABOUT THE AUTHOR

Pastor Robert E. Ward is Founder and Senior Pastor of 'In Spirit and In Truth Family Worship Center, C.O.G.I.C.', a subsidiary of 'In Spirit and In Truth Ministries International, Inc.' where he is President and CEO.

A native of Florida, born and raised in the Ft. Lauderdale area, Pastor Ward graduated from South Plantation High School in 1981 then attended Bethune Cookman College in Daytona Beach, Fl. studying Business Administration. In his early days of ministry, Pastor Ward met his wife and First Lady, Jerilyn Ward, who worked alongside him before and after they were married. They both served as Youth Pastors.

In 2004 while in the hospital with Pneumonia, God gave Pastor Robert the vision for "In Spirit and In Truth Ministries". He and his wife Jerilyn have a mandate on their lives to preach the Gospel of Jesus Christ, as II Timothy 4:2 states so clearly;

"Preach the word! Be ready in season and out of season. Convince, Rebuke, Exhort, with all longsuffering and teaching."

To this union were born three children; Nicholas, Brea and Jessica Ward who have played a significant role within the ministry.

Pastor Robert Ward
In Spirit and In Truth Ministries
1102 SE 3rd Street
Suite 12
Deerfield Beach, FL 33441

Chapter 20

This Sickness is not Unto Death
Written by Pastor Robert Ward

> ... *this sickness is not unto death, but for the glory of God, that the Son of God might be glorified thereby.*
> *(John 11:4)*

Too often, we look at people, what they have obtained in this world or what they may be going through and judge them according to our humanistic rationale. We sometimes see affliction and disease that others may be suffering from and immediately say that God's judgment has come upon them by way of that disease, affliction or tragedy; but it is very dangerous to judge before the time. *Judge nothing before the time, before the Lord does come, who will bring to light the hidden things of darkness and will manifest the counsel of the hearts. (1stCorinthians 4:5)*

King David, a man after God's own heart sinned against God by taking for himself Bathsheba, the wife of Uriah. David knew that Bathsheba was a married woman, but he didn't care. After getting her pregnant, he tried to cover up his deed by ordering Uriah to return from war and go home to his wife. But instead, Uriah slept at the door of the king with the rest of the servants. Therefore David had to come up with another plan. He sent Uriah back to war and ordered that he be put on the front line of the battle, which predisposed him to getting hit the hardest and being killed; and that's exactly what happened. Uriah was killed. Even after all of that, David still did not acknowledge nor confess his sin, but rather married Bathsheba and brought her into his home. It took Nathan, the Prophet of God, to get David to see the evil of his deeds, which finally brought him to his knees in repentance before the God he served.

> *"Now therefore the sword shall never depart from thine house; because thou hast despised me, and hast taken the wife of Uriah the Hittite to be thy wife".*
> (2 Samuel 12:10)

We must understand that although God is a loving and forgiving God, there is still a price to be paid for sin. David, a man who sincerely and genuinely loved God had to pay for his sins, and so did every other biblical character in the bible who sinned; and the same applies to each of us. For persecuting and killing Christians, Paul paid the price by getting beheaded, but He died with the love of Christ in his heart and was accepted into the kingdom of heaven. Although God loves the sinner, He hates the sin, and although He loves and forgives us, He does not intervene with the law of cause and effect that He created to keep fairness and equity in this world. We are all subject to this law; but although we have to pay the cost for the sins we commit, God is merciful as we reap what we sow. The good news is that Jesus has already paid the ULTIMATE cost for all of our sins! In the end, we do not get damnation and hell as we deserve. But I must reiterate that there is no sin that we commit that does not have a penalty attached to it - even with God's forgiveness and love. WE MUST STILL SUFFER THE CONSEQUENCES OF OUR SINS!

Even though I am a pastor who loves my wife and family, I am now living with the consequences of my sins and the effects that years of unconfessed sins are having on me. Looking back over my life, there were and still are times when I say to the Lord, *"Who am I that you should bestow to me the honor and privilege of preaching Your Word and leading Your people as a pastor?* I am damaged goods!"

VIOLATED

I was raised the son of a preacher, an Evangelist at that. I am the middle son of four males, the tallest and the biggest of them all. As a boy, our family traveled every summer to New Jersey, Virginia, and Georgia because for years my father and his twin brother were labor contractors who supervised hundreds of people for seasonal agricultural work to harvest crops. Each summer we would travel to different cities within different states collecting workers to bring in the harvest for particular farm owners. We lived and spent our time in the camps. There were two rows of wooden houses that sat up off the ground on bricks with tin roofs. None of the houses had inside bathrooms or showers, so when we, as children took baths, momma would boil water on the stove and pour it into a large tin wash tub that sat in the middle of the small living room floor, and that is where we would bathe. The bathrooms (or outhouses as they were called) were outside in the back behind the camp, as well as the showers. The outhouse was large and double-sided with one side for the boys and the other side for the girls. Both had a long bench to sit on with about 6 to 8 individual holes on top and lids to do your business. One day while in the outhouse with one of my brothers, a teenage boy from one of the camps came in to use the bathroom. My older brother went out before I was finished and left me in there alone. That's when the teenager came over to me and began to fondle me. He put his hand on my private area and then put my hand on his private area. I am not sure how long this went on or what would have happened if someone would not have knocked on the door, which made him stop. He then pulled his pants up and walked out. I was only seven years old at the time. To this day, my father knows nothing about this nor did my mother who is now deceased. I was told years later when I was in my 20's that the then teenager who molested me in that bathroom died of AIDS in the 1980's. How was I to know that that incident would affect the rest of my life? I was later introduced to pornography by my oldest brother who kept magazines under his mattress. At ten years old, I found the magazines and it snow-balled from there. That perverted demon attached itself to me at that time and grew stronger as the years passed.

THE FOUNDATION WAS LAID

My mother, who was the nurturer and instructor in our home taught us how a woman should be treated. She tried to teach me from both sides of the coin, the female point of view and the male point of view, which I know was difficult for her being on only one side of the coin. She would tell me that all women were not the same, and not to be so eager to give gifts while dating, but to get to know a young lady first without getting all the "benefits" right away. It seems to be commonly accepted in today's world to have "friends with benefits" and despite my mother's teachings, when I became of age, that is all I wanted and unfortunately, at one point, it was what I pursued. Momma taught her four boys the best way that she could because daddy wasn't around very much during those impressionable years when we needed him the most. He was a Longshoreman, and his job took him away from the family for days and weeks, and sometimes we wouldn't see him for months at a time. Coming up, my mother would always tell us that our daddy was working, but the truth is that we never saw him. He would be gone for months and it took a toll on my mother as well as me and my brothers. My father had a good job, but the money he made never came into our household. My mother never saw that money and had to struggle to feed, clothe, and take care of her sons the best way she could. Looking back now, I can see that he was out living his life. He would stop by our every blue moon, I guess to see if everyone was still alive. It is clear to me now that my father had another life and probably another family. Even when he went into full time ministry as an Evangelist, it was the same thing - we would barely see him. The bottom line is that Poppa was a rolling stone. I was in my early twenties when I realized that that song was actually talking about *my* father. As I reflect, I believe that my mother tried to instill the right way to treat women in us because of what she was experiencing. I don't think she wanted us to treat any woman the way she had been treated. It impacted her severely.

My mother imparted within me wise nuggets that should have guided, warned, and prevented me from the pitfalls that life sometimes brings. We were warned, and the effective teachings were planted inside of me. But in all of mama's teachings and the goals and dreams I had as a boy growing up, I never saw myself or even imagined the turn that my life would take. My mother's teachings were my warnings and since I did not heed to those warnings, I was in for a rude awakening!

LIFE'S TURNING POINT

It was May of 1989, five months after the death of my mother that I decided to move back to Daytona Beach, where I had attended school at Bethune Cookman College and had afterwards called my home. I decided that once I left Ft. Lauderdale, Florida, I would never go back because there was nothing there that meant anything to me anymore since mom was gone. The most important person in my life, my mother and best friend had left me alone without anyone else to turn to. I packed up her little red Hyundai and hit the road headed back to Daytona. While there, I reconnected with some old college friends who invited me to go to church with them. I promised that I would go just as soon as I could get the chance. Keeping that promise, I finally went on a Wednesday night after work. As I walked up to the church facility and rounded the corner, I could see the area where they had the children's ministry. Through the window, I could see children inside a classroom with a young lady teaching and singing to them. She was responsible for taking care of the children while the adults were in church service in the other part of the building. There was something innocent and pure about this woman and I was compelled to her spirit. I asked my friends who she was. I was told her name and that she was 20 years old. Her entire family attended that church and was very active. We were married a year and a half later, but I had some secrets and I was still "damaged goods".

I never dreamt in a million years that I would end up cheating on my wife. That was never part of my dream. My God! I had become an adulterer. Considering everything I saw in my household growing up, everything my mother had instilled in me, and looking at the things that I despised the most and held with such contempt, I would never have thought that I would fall prey to the same temptations. The things I saw so-called "men of God" do as I was being raised, caused me to detest them and what they stood for. I vowed to never be that kind of man. However, the things I feared and hated the most manifested into my life. That's what happens when there is no deliverance. *For the thing which I greatly feared is come upon me, and that which I was afraid of is come unto me.* (Job 3:25)

DAMAGED GOODS

It wasn't even a week after I got married that while my new wife was at work, I went to a local adult store and rented pornographic videos. I slid them under the couch in the living room so that she wouldn't find them. However, when I arrived home that evening, the videos were out and on the couch. My new wife was sitting on the bed in the bedroom. When I entered the room, she confronted me about the videos. It was at that moment that I told her my story of being molested as a young boy, the introduction to porn at age ten, and the addiction that I had become slave to. Before that, I had not told anyone these things. I promised her that I would talk to our pastor and get some help. Unfortunately, it didn't stop there.

In 1995, after our third child was born, our relationship had drastically changed from how it had been in the beginning. We had begun arguing a lot and love-making became few and far between. I worked as late as I could for dread of going home and I would then take my time getting there. I started hanging out with friends, and eventually began picking up women off the street late at night before going home. This continued for about year. The shocking thing about all this is that I was involved heavily in ministry at the time these things were going on in my life. I was the praise and worship leader *and* an assistant to the pastor. I had helped to build the ministry from the ground up and knew the Word of God amazingly. The Lord would give me prophetic songs to write and we would sing them in the services. As a result, the anointing would fall. *The gifts and calling of God is without repentance* (Romans 11:29). People would be healed and set free as a result of the anointed praise songs. I made sure to do everything I knew to do in church in order to bring down the anointing, but I was still "damaged goods" - a powerful man of God with deep dark secrets.

There came a time that the guilt and shame of what I had been doing with those women was weighing me down. I could not bear the weight of the secret any longer. I called my pastor/friend and told him what I had been doing and that I was planning on telling my wife about it. I wanted help. I wanted to put it all out there and get delivered, but to my surprise, he said, *"No, don't tell her anything - she can't handle that right now"*. I thought that he was going to at least counsel me first and then bring her in to counsel us together, but it never happened. Nothing happened. I was never counseled and there was no intervention and no help for me. I eventually went right back to doing what I had been doing - picking up strange women after work before going home. I later discovered that this same pastor/friend that I had gone to for help was doing the same thing I was doing, but with some of the women in his church. His ministry is no longer in operation and the scandal that followed him was so bad that he and his family had to leave the state.

But where did that leave me? I felt that I needed a change in environment so in the year 2001, I moved my family to Orlando, Florida to begin a new life for us, thinking that I was putting everything behind me. My wife and I could start all over and work on our marriage. I could leave the past behind me and start fresh in a new place and a new environment where no one knew me or knew of my evil deeds - or so I thought... I soon discovered that you cannot run away from your deeds because they do catch up with you. When confession is made, the magnitude of the penalty diminishes and God's grace begins to cover you and His mercy manifests as you suffer the penalty, but without ever confessing, your sins will catch up with you and find you out! At this point, I had not confessed to anything.

"But if ye will not do so, behold, ye have sinned against the LORD: and be sure your sin will find you out".
(Numbers 32:23)

YOUR SINS WILL FIND YOU OUT

Both my wife and I were blessed to find good jobs in Orlando. The kids were in good schools and we were regularly attending a spirit-filled ministry where we both were actively involved. Everything was going well, and then disaster struck! It was a Sunday evening in January of 2002. I remember going in and out of the bathroom, trying not to wake my sleeping wife. I was vomiting and had a bad case of diarrhea. This went on for hours. I was sick and miserable. The last time I went into the bathroom was around 2:00a.m. on a Monday. I remember sitting there and repeating to myself; *"I have nothing left"* over and over. The next thing I remember was waking up in the hospital Wednesday morning. I found out later from my wife that I had had a seizure. When she realized what was happening, she called the ambulance. I regained consciousness two days after the seizure on a Wednesday morning. Looking around the room to see where I was, I felt around the bed, touched the cold railings, the gown I had on and the lights that were shinning from the x-ray panel on the wall. I was laying there on my right side with my hand hanging over the bed rail looking at the bright x-ray light on the wall when I heard a voice that was so loud I thought that someone was in the room with me. I am not the type of person to go around saying that I heard the "voice of God" tell me this or that because I have seen the damage that has caused by those who have claimed to hear from God as a way of bringing people into bondage and servitude; but I know beyond a shadow of a doubt that I heard this: *"This sickness is not unto death!"* No more no less, that is exactly what I heard. After I heard the voice, my wife entered the room and asked me how I was feeling. I asked her what was going on with me. She explained that I had contracted Bacterial Meningitis and had had a seizure because my temperature was over 104 degrees. She told me how the doctor had said that if I hadn't had the seizure, we would not have known that I was as severely ill as I was and I would have died within the next 12 hours, so the seizure turned out to be a blessing in disguise.

 I spent almost three weeks in the hospital being poked and prodded and having temperature spikes as my body would convulse and shake uncontrollably because of the fevers. I would have to be cooled down with bags of ice all over my body just to keep my temperature down. It was crazy. The temperature spikes continued to occur until the last day that I was discharged. The doctors could not figure out what was causing the temperature spikes, so they ordered one more blood test. He asked my permission to test me for HIV so that they could rule out certain things. I agreed because having HIV was the least of my worries. After taking my blood work, they released me to go home and the doctor said that they would see me in a week for the test results.

The meningitis and the medications were taking their toll on my thinking process and emotions. I was still trying to make sense of what had happened to me and trying to understand why it all was happening. A week after being released, I went back for my follow-up visit. After entering the room and giving the proper greetings, the doctor asked if he could talk to me alone. My wife left the room. I was very confused and asked him what the problem was. He began asking me questions such as if I had ever had sex with a man. Then he asked if I had ever been with any woman besides my wife while married. My responses made him take a step back because they were so convictionally loud with a resounding "No!" to each, although I knew I was lying. I asked, *"Why would you ask me something like that?"* He then informed me that my HIV test results came back positive for the virus. I began yelling and telling him, *"Your tests are wrong! There is no way that could be true!"* He asked if I wanted him to bring my wife in with us and I agreed. When she came back into the room, I asked the doctor to repeat to her what he had just told me. I kept saying to my wife and the doctor that I had never cheated and that I wanted to be re-tested. He turned and asked my wife if she wanted to be tested and she agreed. We made the appointment and left.

That same night about 1:30a.m, I sat up in the bed with tears in my eyes. Fear was dominating my heart and I was getting ready to pack my bags and leave. At that point, my wife woke up. She came around the bed and sat next to me. She said to me, *"What's wrong?"* How do I face the mother of my children, the woman that I stood up and vowed before God and many others that I would love and honor until "death do us part" when I have contracted HIV as a result of committing adultery? Time seemed to have stood still at that moment. I then began to confess to my wife everything I had done that brought us to this crossroad in our relationship. I began packing my clothes preparing to leave. I knew that she would have all the support she needed from her family and friends and that they would make sure that she and the kids were okay. I begged for her forgiveness and was talking when she cut me off and said something that even to this very day helps me to understand the grace of God: *"Robert I understand. We will work this out. We are married and we said for better or for worse. You do not have to leave."* Two weeks later, the tests confirmed that my wife was also HIV positive.

January 2012 will be 10 years since we were first diagnosed. We eventually told our children. All three were in elementary school at the time, 4th 5th and 6th grade. I do not think they understood the magnitude of it all back then. My wife had them tested just to be sure. They all tested negative. My wife and I did not tell anyone else until two years later when I contracted PCP Pneumonia and the doctors thought that it was the end for me. The HIV had turned into full blown AIDS. That's when my wife finally told my brother's wife and she told the rest of the family. The PCP Pneumonia is a virus that was brought on by AIDS. Everyone in the family was called to the hospital to come see me before I passed on. My father and brothers were there and I later found out that my father said this to my brothers regarding me and my illness: *"The wages of sin is death. Now we just have to wait to let God do what He has to do."* Needless to say, I was beyond hurt by his statement. Doctors, nurses, medical professionals and everyone involved in my situation didn't expect me to make it through the next two days as my "CD 4" count was less than 20 and my viral load was through the roof. At that point, they began to heavily medicate me so that I could go easily, ...but God had other plans.

THE VISION

While lying in that hospital bed with PCP Pneumonia, about 2:00 in the morning I prayed and said, *"Lord, is this it? Is this the end of my life? What about the dreams and the prophecies? Will they not come to pass? I thought you told me that this sickness was not unto death? Is this how I'm going to die?* I then looked up at the hospital ceiling and it was as though someone put up a movie projector and began to play a movie. A big screen opened on the ceiling and I saw myself preaching. Green flowers were all around the church and the carpet was red and I saw pews. I looked out into the congregation and on my right I saw my wife sitting on the front row. I was in a black suit. I was preaching on the subject of people with HIV who hide behind masks. After sharing my vision with my wife, she brought me a pad and pencil in the hospital as I was getting better and I began writing the vision and the sermons that God was giving me while there.

That was in 2004 and the fact that I am writing to tell you about it is a testament to the fact that God is still moving mightily in my life! Through all of that, I knew that the Lord still had me on His mind. He had not left nor forsaken me. He began giving me the vision for the ministry He had placed in my hands even with me having AIDS. When the season came, we launched 'In Spirit and In Truth Family Worship Center, C.O.G.I.C. a subsidiary of 'In Spirit and In Truth Ministries International, Inc'. I am Senior Pastor with my wife and children by my side. The doors that the Lord has opened for us have left us in awe of His Grace and Mercy. My wife and I are devoted to helping people living with this disease know and understand that their lives are not over as long as they are in Christ. We want people to understand that God has a purpose for their lives and that in spite of HIV/AIDS, their life is worth living.

"Being confident of this very thing, that he which hath begun a good work in you will perform it until the day of Jesus Christ:"
(Philippians 1:6)

IT IS MARVELOUS

When I was first diagnosed with HIV, I thought my life was over, but I realize that it was only the beginning. God's desire was to save me from myself and He did just that. He has blessed me with a humble, God-fearing, spirit-filled wife who loves me unconditionally and treats me with love, respect and adoration that I don't deserve. For years after the diagnosis, I found myself constantly apologizing to my wife over and over for what I had brought upon our family, but she holds no grudges. I feel blessed in many ways. I am now delivered from sexual demons and desires and I live my life to serve, praise and give glory to God. He has given me a ministry that helps people who are too scared, ashamed and hurt to tell people that they have AIDS, including other pastors. I speak life into their wounded spirits! My prayer is that if this is you, then as you read these words, it will bring you to the point of decision. And that decision is to fully give God your life and let Him bring the healing and deliverance needed so that you can live out your God given purpose.

God's design for my life was to preach. However it went, I was going to eventually arrive at that destination. I had a choice. I could have gotten there through the direct route (the straight gate) or through the scenic route (the wide gate). My decisions caused me to take the scenic route. It delayed me and caused some pitfalls, dangers, disappointments, obstacles and accidents, but eventually I made it and I am now in the will of God and it is marvelous in my eyes!

Epilogue

Many are called but few are chosen. This book has been an eye-opening, transparent, and very up close and personal snapshot of some of the things that spiritual leaders, specifically pastors endure as they lead God's people. Many times as pastors are serving as a source of strength and spiritual guidance to the congregants within their church, they are also simultaneously trying to deal with many of their own inner struggles. Pastors are called to a higher level of responsibility and accountability and sometimes it can be taxing, frustrating, and even discouraging for them, but as they continue seeking the direction and will of God for their lives and the lives of the people, God will always make provision for the vision. He will give an increase and a double portion of strength and wisdom that is needed to lead the sheep of God with excellence. It is my prayer and the prayer of every pastor/author in this book that you were blessed by their stories and that the heart of your understanding has been enlightened. May God bless you and keep you.

Dr. Mia Y. Merritt
M&M Consulting
1-866-560-7652

Church Directory

Christian Life Center
1225 W. Paterson Street
Kalamazoo, MI 49007
Rev. Miles Fitzpatrick,
Associate Pastor

Faith Community Baptist Church
10401 NW 8th Avenue
Miami, FL 33150-1010
305 691-3200
Rev. Richard Dunn,
Senior Pastor

Friendship Missionary Baptist Church
740 NW 58th Street Miami,
Florida, 33127
Rev. Dr. Gaston E. Smith,
Senior Pastor

Glendale Baptist Church of Brownsville
4501 NW 22 Avenue
Miami Florida 33142
305 - 638 - 0857
Pastorrick1964@comcast.net
Rev. Ricardo Peters,
Senior Pastor

Greater Love Full Gospel Baptist Church
18200 NW 22 Avenue
Miami Gardens, FL 33056
Rev. Dwayne Richardson,
Senior Pastor

Hickory Hill Missionary Baptist Church
493 Bassett Dairy Rd.
Monticello, FL 32344
850-973-8165
Rev. Reginald Daniels,
Senior Pastor

Jesus Christ is Lord Miracle Deliverance Center
6306 Pembroke Road
Miramar, FL 33023
 (Temporary address)
bishopisaiah@realworld.com
Bishop Isaiah Musgrove,
Senior Pastor

In Spirit and In Truth Ministries
1102 SE 3rd Street
Suite 12
Deerfield Beach, FL 33441
Rev. Robert Ward,
Senior Pastor

Koinonia Worship Center & Village
4900 W. Hallandale Beach Blvd.
Pembroke Park, FL 33023
Rev. Eric Jones,
Senior Pastor

Mount Sinai Missionary Baptist Church
698 NW 47 Terrace
Miami, FL 33054
305-751-5846
Rev. Johnny Barber,
Senior Pastor

New Generation Missionary Baptist Church
940 Caliph Street
Opa Locka, FL 33054
305-389-3308
Rev. Ranzer A. Thomas,
Senior Pastor

Peace Missionary Baptist Church
11700 NW 17th Avenue
Miami, FL
305-681-4681
Rev. Dr. Tracy L. McCloud,
Senior Pastor

Souls Harvest Christian Center Ministries
972 W Hallandale Beach Blvd
Hallandale Beach, FL. 33009
954-457-1955
Bishop Fred Marshall,
Senior Pastor

St. John Primitive Baptist Church
615 SW 1st Street
Delray Beach, FL 33444
561-278-2084
Elder Kenneth Duke, II,
Senior Pastor

The Fountain of New Life
4601 NW 167 Street
Miami Gardens, FL 33055
Rev. Wayne Lomax,
Senior Pastor

The Fountain of New Life
21113 Johnson Street
Pembroke Pines, Fl 33029
Rev. Wayne Lomax,
Senior Pastor

New Jerusalem Missionary Baptist Church
2254 Douglas Street
Hollywood, Florida 33020
Rev. Michael Anderson,
Senior Pastor

True Love Praise and Worship Church
15600 NW 42 Avenue
Miami Gardens, FL 33055
Rev. Fred Cromity, Senior Pastor
786-285-2924

True Praise Family Worship Center
1524 NE 147 Street
Miami, FL 33161
305-957-0031
Rev. Kevin Williams,
Senior Pastor

United Christian Praise & Worship Center
7626 NW 7th Ave
Miami, FL 33150
Rev. Dr. Dennis M. Jackson
Senior Pastor

www.ingramcontent.com/pod-product-compliance
Lightning Source LLC
Chambersburg PA
CBHW060113170426
43198CB00010B/875